Rage and Creativity:
How Feminism Sparked
Psychoanalysis

Rage and Creativity:
How Feminism Sparked Psychoanalysis

EDITOR

Lucille Spira, Ph.D.

International Psychoanalytic Books (IPBooks)
New York • www.IPBooks.net

International Psychoanalytic Books (IPBooks), Queens, NY

Online at: www.IPBooks.net

Cover and interior book design by Kathy Kovacic, Blackthorn Studio

ISBN: 978-1-949093-73-5

TABLE OF CONTENTS

" . . . And so what I believe is that having a daughter does not make a man decent. Having a wife does not make a decent man. Treating people with dignity and respect makes a decent man, and when a decent man messes up as we are all bound to do, he tries his best and does apologize. Not to save face, not to win a vote, he apologizes genuinely to repair and acknowledge the harm done so that we can all move on."

Alexandria Ocasio-Cortez, U.S. Representative 14th District of New York
(July 23, 2020—Issue: Vol. 166, No. 130 — Daily Edition 116th Congress (2019–2020)—2nd Session)

ACKNOWLEDGMENTS

There are many to thank for *Rage and Creativity*: How *Feminism Sparked Psychoanalysis*. First, I thank Dr. Arlene Kramer Richards for all that she contributed to this project, to women's psychology and to me. It's been an honor to share in this "collective" sparked by her. The generosity of all the discussants and authors, many of whom have seriously contributed to advancing our understanding of the psychology of women and psychoanalysis, is noteworthy. You have my appreciation and admiration for your scholarly and creative work.

Arnold Richards, publisher (IPBooks) and the *Journal of International Controversial Discussions,* where this volume began, deserves recognition for his years of commitment to making psychoanalysis and its literature more inclusive.

My appreciation to Sandra Buechler, Ph.D. for her generous back-cover comments and also to Bracha, and the Bracha L. Ettinger Studio for their contribution. I thank Dr. Julián Daniel Gutiérrez-Albilla for acquainting me with Prof. Ettinger's work on trauma.

Thanks to Tamar and Larry Schwartz at IPBooks for all their work and support; also to Kathy Kovacic of Blackthorn Studio for all of her work on this volume and *IJCD (Series 3) and Matthew Bach* for his work on that volume.

I thank my women patients who shared about their joy, struggles and victories of moving from girl to woman. On a personal note, I thank my ever supportive women friends and colleagues: Carol Munter, Lynne Herbst, Merle Molofsky, Lillian Berman, Barbara Rauch, Patsy Turrini, Laura Melano Flanagan, Carolyn Benbow Ross, Dotty Attie, Rochelle Slovin, Carol Thea and the NYSPP membership, and also the NYSPP Psychoanalytic Literary Group (Ellen Henschel, Sandra Parness, Barbara Hertzberg, Barbara Lewis, Roberta Espie, Nancy Cromer Grayson and Vicki Finkel). And my thanks to Bill Spira, who is with me during the challenges.

Lucille Spira, Editor

ABOUT THE CONTRIBUTORS: SECTION I

Rosemary Balsam, M.R.C.P. (Edinburgh),
F.R.C.Psych. (London). Psychoanalyst. Yale
School of Medicine, Psychiatry; Training
and Supervising Analyst, Western New England Institute for Psychoanalysis; Presenter
on topics of interest to psychoanalysts at numerous conferences; Author of various publications including *Women's
Bodies in Psychoanalysis.* Mary Sigourney Award recipient
(2018).

Sandra E. Cohen, Ph.D.; Training and Su-
pervising Analyst at the Psychoanalytic
Center of California in Los Angeles; Private
practice in Beverly Hills. She has recently
published a chapter on the film Broken Embraces (2009) entitled: "Voyeurs. Vampires
and Going Blind: Trying to Survive Oedipal Exclusion and
Loss" in *Pedro Almodóvar: A Cinema of Desire, Passion, and
Compulsion* edited by Arlene Kramer Richards and Lucille
Spira with Merle Molofsky. Dr. Cohen writes a blog about the
real human struggles of characters in contemporary and classic films at <u>www.charactersonthecouch.com</u>.

Paula Ellman, Ph.D., ABPP.; Training, faculty and supervising analyst in the Contemporary Freudian Society and the Washington Baltimore Center for Psychoanalysis; Overall Chair of the IPA Committee on Women and Psychoanalysis; Editorial Board of the IJP and Board Member  of the North America Psychoanalytic Confederation; Assistant Professor of psychology at the George Washington University Center for Professional Psychology; Visiting Professor at the Sino-American Continuing Training Project for Wuhan Hospital for Psychotherapy, China. Writes and presents on femininity and female psychology, unconscious fantasy, sadomasochism, trauma and enactment. Co-Editor and Contributor: *The Courage to Fight Violence against Women: Psychoanalytic and Multidisciplinary Perspectives* (with N. Goodman 2017).

Alison Feit, Ph.D., Faculty St. Louis Psychoanalytic Institute and the China American Psychoanalytic Alliance. Editor and Associate Editor of the journal *Contemporary Psychoanalysis* and  a member of the Artist Group, the Sexual Abuse Service and the LGBTQ Service at the William Alanson White Institute in New York. Her most recent work appears in R. Gartner's *Trauma and Countertrauma, Resilience and Counterresilience : Insights from Psychoanalysts and Trauma Experts* (2016) and R. C. Curtis' *Psychoanalytic Case Studies from an Interpersonal-Relational Perspective* (2018). Recently co-edited (with A. Slomowitz) *Homosexuality, Transsexuality, Psychoanalysis and Traditional Judaism* (2019). Although her physical offices are in NYC and Atlanta, she can most easily be found at freudina.com, where her online self hosts a podcast, runs workshops and generally promotes psychoanalytic ideas and self-knowledge.

William Fried, Ph.D., FIPA, Member IPTAR. Clinical psychologist, psychoanalyst, author, editor, teacher, and supervisor. He is also a photographer and poet. The office in which he conducts his practice is in Manhattan, close to Lincoln Center. Published on various topics including: *Critical Flicker Fusion* (Karnac, 2017),a study of film  from a psychoanalytic perspective; *Frida:* Portrait of a self. *Journal of Clinical Psychology*: In Session, *76*, 8 (In press). Seiden, H.M., Lin, P. & Fried, W. (2020). *"Ox Herding" and the art of psychoanalytic psychotherapy. DIVISION Review.* 20, Winter Edition. 36-44.

Nancy Goodman, Ph.D., Training and supervising analyst with the Contemporary Freudian Society, Washington DC, and the IPA. Served as Chair of all Institute Committees and is now faculty in the Wuhan, China Training Program. Her many publications reflect her interest in trauma and  symbolizing processes as well as female development and enactments. Publications include the following edited volumes: Finding Unconscious Fantasy in Narrative, Trauma, and Body Pain: A Clinical Guide (2017) (with Paula Ellman); The Courage to Fight Violence against Women (2017) (with Paula Ellman); Battling the Life and Death Forces of Sadomasochism: Clinical Perspectives (2013) (with Basseches & Ellman); and The Power of Witnessing: Reflections, Reverberations, and Traces of the Holocaust (2012) (with Marilyn Meyers). Founder and Director of the online Virtual Psychoanalytic Museum: www.virtualpsycho-analyticmuseum.org with IPBooks. She maintains a psycho-analytic practice in Bethesda, Maryland.

Cordelia Schmidt-Hellerau, Ph.D.: Train-ing and Supervising Analyst of the Boston Psychoanalytic Society and Institute and the Swiss Psychoanalytic Society. She has pub-lished numerous papers and three books on metapsychology, clinical issues and applied  psychoanalysis. Her 2018 publication of *Driven to Survive* at IPBooks was a finalist of the American Board & Academy of Psychoanalysis Book Prize. She has published her first novel, *Rousseaus Traum*, in German and will publish her second novel, *Memory's Eyes*, in 2020 at IPBooks. She works in pri-vate practice in Chestnut Hill by Boston.

Dorothy Evans Holmes, PhD, ABPP, FABP. Clinical Psychologist and Psychoanalyst in psychoanalysis and psychotherapy, Bluffton, SC.; Teaching, Training, and Supervising Psychoanalyst in the Psychoanalytic Center of the Carolinas; Professor and Program Director Emerita of the PsyD Professional  Psychology Program, The George Washington University; Teaching, Training, and Supervising Psychoanalyst Emerita of the Washington Baltimore Center for Psychoanalysis. Recent publication: Our country 'tis of we and them: psychoanalytic perspectives on our fractured American identity (2019) *American Imago*. Honored (2017) American Psychological Association's Division 39 Diversity Award; Honored Presenter (Jan. 2016) American Psychoanalytic Association Plenary Address; Served on the editorial boards of the *Journal of the American Psychoanalytic Association* and the *International Journal of Psychoanalysis*.

Lee Jenkins, Ph.D., Psychoanalyst and Training analyst NPAP and Harlem Family Institute, novelist, poet and Retired Professor of English. Presented at numerous psychoanalytic conferences and published extensively. Publications include: *Faulkner and Black-White Relations: A Psychoanalytic Approach* (Columbia University Press); *Persistence of Memory,* a volume of poems; Right of Passage, a novel published by Sphinxbooks.co.uk, 2018.

Kimberly Kleinman, LCSW, FIPA. Adult, Adolescent and Child training and supervising analyst, Contemporary Freudian Society. Visiting Professor at the Sino-American Continuing Training Project for Wuhan Hospital for Psychotherapy, Wuhan China. Published and presented on race, developmental theory, learning problems, gender and sexual object choice. Recent publications include: *From Cradle to Couch: Essays in Honor of the Psychoanalytic Developmental Psychology of Sylvia Brody,* Edited by B. Seitler and K. Kleinman, 2017 IPBooks; *The Plumsock Papers, Giving New Analysts a Voice,* Edited by P. Ellman and K. Kleinman, 2020 IPBooks.

Nancy Kulish, Ph.D.: Professor, Department of Psychiatry, Wayne State Medical School and Adjunct Professor of Psychology, University of Detroit/Mercy and a Training and Supervising Analyst at the Michigan Psychoanalytic Institute. Chosen as the National Woman Psychoanalytic Scholar for 2005 of the American Psychoanalytic Association. Currently on the Editorial Boards of the *Psychoanalytic Quarterly* and

the *International Journal of Psychoanalysis*. She has published and presented on topics ranging from female sexuality, gender, transference/countertransference, adolescence to termination. With Deanna Holtzman, she is the co-author of the 2008 book, *A Story of Her Own, The Female Oedipus Complex Reexamined and Renamed* and most recently, *The Clinical Problem of Masochism*.

Merle Molofsky: MFA (Columbia University School of the Arts; Psychoanalyst, fiction writer and poet, a produced playwright, and the recipient of the 2012 NAAP Gradiva Award for Poetry. She serves on the faculty of the Training Institute of NPAP, on the faculty and the Advisory Board of the Harlem Family Institute, and as a member of the Editorial Board of *The Psychoanalytic Review* and of the *International journal of Controversial Discussions*. She has published numerous psychoanalytic articles in various journals, chapters in psychoanalytic books, and a novel, *Streets 1970* and a collection of short fiction, *Necessary Voices*, both published by International Psychoanalytic Books.

Kerry Kelly Novick, Psychoanalyst Child, adolescent and adult Training and Supervising Analyst of the International Psychoanalytic Association. Serves on the faculties of numerous training centers in the United States. First trained with Anna Freud in London, England. Active in teaching, research, professional organizations and the community. Joined with other colleagues to found the award-winning non-profit Allen Creek Preschool in Ann Arbor, Michigan and the international Alliance For Psychoanalytic Schools. Served as

Chair of the Child and Adolescent Analysis Committee at the Michigan Psychoanalytic Institute; Instrumental in starting the first integrated child and adult training curriculum. Elected a Councilor-at-Large on the Board of the American Psychoanalytic Association; past President of the Association for Child Psychoanalysis, and is Chair of the Child and Adolescent Psychoanalysis Committee of the International Psychoanalytical Association. Written many book chapters and articles published in major professional journals. Recent Books: Emotional Muscle: Strong Parents, Strong Children (2010); With Novick, J., Barrett, D. & Barrett, T (2020). *Parent Work Casebook.* New York: IPBooks.

Jack Novick, Ph.D. Psychoanalyst Child, adolescent and adult Training and Supervising Analyst of the International Psychoanalytic Association. Serves on the faculties of numerous training centers in the United States. Trained with Anna Freud in London,  England. Active in teaching, research, professional organizations and the community. Joined with other colleagues to found the award-winning non-profit Allen Creek Preschool in Ann Arbor, Michigan and the international Alliance For Psychoanalytic Schools. Served as Chair of the Child and Adolescent Analysis Committee at the Michigan Psychoanalytic Institute; Instrumental in starting the first integrated child and adult training curriculum. Chair of the Child and Adolescent Psychoanalysis Committee of the International Psychoanalytical Association. Written many book chapters and articles published in major professional journals. With Kerry Kelly Novick: Fearful Symmetry : The Development and Treatment of Sadomasochism (1996); Emotional Muscle: Strong Parents, Strong Children (2010). Served two terms as North American Representative on the Board of the International Psychoanalytical Association, and is President-Elect of the Association for Child Psychoanalysis.

Arlene Kramer Richards, Ed.D., Psychoanalyst and a poet. Training and Supervising Analyst, Contemporary Freudian Society and the International Psychoanalytic Association; Fellow of IPTAR. Faculty at the CFS and Tongji Medical College of Huazhong University of Science and Technology at  Wuhan, China. Publishes on female development, perversion, loneliness, and the internal world of artists and poets. "The Skin I Live In" In A.K. Richards, L. Spira and A.A. Lynch (Eds.) *Encounters With Loneliness: Only the Lonely* (2013) and a book of her papers, *Psychoanalysis: Listening to Understand: Selected Papers of Arlene Kramer Richards* (IPBooks, 2012) *Myths of the Mighty Women* edited by Arlene Kramer Richards and Lucille Spira (Karnac, 2015), *Psychoanalysis in Fashion* edited by Arlene Kramer Richards and Anita Weinreb Katz (IPBooks, 2019); *Pedro Almodóvar: A Cinema of Desire, Passion and Compulsion* edited by Arlene Richards and Lucille Spira with Merle Molofsky (IPBooks, 2019). *The Laundryman's Granddaughter: Poems by Arlene Kramer Richards,* (IPBooks, 2011). Former representative from North America to the IPA.

Lucille Spira, Ph.D., LCSW: Psychoanalytic Psychotherapist, Member NYSPP, AAPCSW. Gradiva Award recipient (2014) with Arlene Kramer Richards and Arthur A. Lynch: *Encounters with Loneliness: Only the Lonely*  (IPBooks). Co-Chair APsaA Discussion Group on Loneliness and Aloneness; Published in various psychoanalytic journals and taught in numerous settings including NYSPP and AIP.

Facilitator NYSPP Literary Group. Recent publication: Co-Editor and Contributor, *Pedro Almodóvar: A Cinema of Desire, Passion and Compulsion* (2018, IPBooks).

Jeffrey Stern, Ph.D., Faculty, The Chicago Psychoanalytic Institute, past President The Chicago Psychoanalytic Society, Associate Editor for the *Annual of Psychoanalysis,* Visiting Professor at Wuhan University, China. Publications on self psychology,  Shakespeare, literature and film. Recent Publications: "Desperately Seeking Ivan or Healing the Vertical Split in Almodóvar's Women on the Verge of a Nervous Breakdown," in *Pedro Almodóvar: A Cinema of Desire, Passion and Compulsion,* edited by A.K. Richards, L. Spira with M. Molofsky (2018) IPBooks, and "The Pilgrim's Progress: A Therapist and Patient Journey to London" in *Psychoanalysis, Self and Context.*

FOREWORD

Jeffrey Stern, Ph.D.

Psychoanalysis and feminism have from the first been natural, albeit on occasion strange, bedfellows. This is because both psychoanalysis and feminism are about the return of the repressed: in psychoanalysis the patient's repressed desire and rage, in feminism the repressed subjectivity and the silenced voices of women. It is perhaps no accident that Bertha Pappenheim, a woman suffering from hysteria—a malady thought to be caused by a uterus that refused to know its place—named psychoanalysis *the talking cure*. There have of course been missteps along the way. *What woman wants* was for decades claimed by psychoanalysis to be the penis she was told she envied—she didn't—although she may indeed have wanted—when it pleased her. Fortunately the genius of Freudian psychoanalysis with its free associative method and privileging of the unconscious was that it offered feminists the means of deconstructing its phallocentric theories and replacing them with ideas more reflective of women's actual experience.

In 2012 I was invited to teach self psychology in Wuhan, China by Arnold and Arlene Richards who had established an experimental program there teaching psychoanalysis to Chinese psychiatrists, psychologists, and social workers. I thought I was going there once for eight days but have been part of this program for nine years along with Arlene and Arnie and a group of wonderful colleagues, some of whom are contributors to this volume of papers responding to Arlene's "Rage and Creativity: How Second Generation Feminist Thought Collective Influenced Psychoanalysis." To date we've been to Wuhan some fifteen times. Psychoanalysis didn't exist in China in 2012 but as a result of our program and others it has caught on like summer fire.

All of us have found the energy, intelligence and passion with which our Chinese students have responded to us transformative, but the impact Arlene Richards has had on these students, especially the women, is difficult to describe. In a culture where women have been horribly discriminated against for millennia, up through and including the years of the sexist *one child policy* (during which girls often learned that at their birth their fathers and grandparents left the hospital in disgust, female fetuses were routinely aborted, and female infants given up for adoption or even killed), Arlene Richards is a figure of profound reverence. At the celebration that concludes every "training" her students —men and women but women most ardently—dance around her, sing to her, shower her with gifts. Every woman wants a picture with her they can show their families and post online. Arlene represents wisdom, eminence, graciousness, and perhaps above all the power they have largely thought the exclusive province of divinity.

In America we have spent three and a half years in the death grip of a tyrant whose rapacious patriarchy has been supported by an army of largely but not entirely male apparatchiks wholly incapable of independent thought. They are engaged in a war on truth. Opposition is silenced, science mocked, and the free press reviled as *the enemy of the people.*

The project resulting in this volume represents an antidote. Each collaborator was invited to riff on "Rage and Creativity." Where they went was entirely up to them. The result is an expressionist tapestry figuring forth the sort of *thought collective* Arlene's essay celebrates. Everyone's hope is that the project will generate new writing, new subjects for conference panels, new professional relationships, new politics that will support the ongoing forward movement of feminist psychoanalysis. In addition to *the talking cure* Bertha Pappenheim called the work of psychoanalysis *chimney sweeping.* We don't sweep chimneys these days. But stirring up trouble is perhaps what feminism and psychoanalysis do best.

–**Jeffrey Stern,** Ph.D., Faculty, The Chicago Psychoanalytic Institute, past President The Chicago Psychoanalytic Society, Associate Editor of the Annual of Psychoanalysis, Visiting Professor at Wuhan University, China. Publications on self psychology, Shakespeare, literature and film. Recent Publications: "Desperately Seeking Ivan or Healing the Vertical Split in Almodóvar's Women on the Verge of a Nervous Breakdown," in Pedro Almodóvar: *A Cinema of Desire Passion and Compulsion,* edited by A.K. Richards, L. Spira with M. Molofsky (2018) IPBooks, and "The Pilgrim's Progress: A Therapist and Patient Journey to London" in Psychoanalysis, Self and Context.

INTRODUCTION

Lucille Spira, Editor

Rage and Creativity: How Feminism Sparked Psychoanalysis, through the voices of its contributors, expands the conversation that began in the *International Journal of Controversial Discussions, Series 3.* This anthology, as with Series 3, leads with an essay by Arlene Kramer Richards, "Rage and Creativity: How Second-Generation Feminist Thought Collective Influenced Psychoanalysis". The discussions that follow, in **Section I,** add body to femininity as the authors speak from a feminist psychoanalytic perspective.

By inviting the contributors to discuss Arlene Kramer Richards' thesis the discussants are awarded an opportunity to be part of a feminist collective. Each of the discussants focuses on some aspect of her work that resonated or did not resonate for them. They expand on concepts she introduces, raise questions about particular points she makes and offer their own perspective. A number of the essays describe and examine a facet of the authors' professional and/or personal developments, particularly in relation to feminism and the psychology of women.

Through these contributions, the reader can follow the authors' perspectives on how creativity, perseverance and scholarship modified psychoanalytic theory to better reflect the desires, inner conflicts, experiences and needs of women. Beyond, the accomplishments discussed here, the reader sees how, at a particular point-in-time, a feminist collective/s of psychoanalysts found and developed its/their voice.

As one follows the discussions one sees both a continuum and departure between the ideas of pioneer women psychoanalysts, formerly ignored by mainstream psychoanalysis, i.e. Karen Horney and Melanie Klein. How early contributions are built upon and integrated with more contemporary ideas. In other words, the dynamic aspect of psychoanalysis is highlighted. This is in line with Shapiro (2002), who focuses on the contribution and path of women psychoanalysts who early on departed from classical Freudian theory and thereby empowered others toward more independent thinking. One difference here is Richards' focus on the force of second wave feminism, as an important variable, that energized a feminist thought collective to achieve change from within.

Some of the discussants agree with Arlene Kramer Richards' thesis that second wave feminism sparked a thought collective within psychoanalysis that led to the debunking of early Freudian ideas, such as anatomy is destiny; leading to accepting that women were full human beings. Others are not so sure that the positive changes noted by Arlene Kramer Richards have yet led to more substantive changes within various organizations and within our psyches. They express concern that groups and interests of the less powerful are marginalized.

One person raises the question as to whether psychoanalysis has become women-dominated. Others question whether organizational psychoanalysis is up to the task of the changes necessary to widen its scope to welcome all forms of diversity. This speaks to how psychoanalysts are interested in conflicts that arise both internally and also are generated by societal beliefs, structures and strictures.

Arlene Kramer Richards' responses to each discussant illuminate her position *vis-á-vis* any controversy or disagreement raised here and advance the conversation. The breadth and depth of her responses highlight the multiple ideas, perspectives, and considerations in play when a thought collective "listens to understand". They serve as a model of non-confrontative response to difference. This bird's eye view of how feminism sparked psychoanalysis, consolidates the past, highlights the present and points to the future.

A brief vignette of Dr. Margaret Morgan Lawrence, the first African American psychoanalyst, illustrates how racism and sexism converge. She is an example of someone, who achieved her ambition, and the respect of her colleagues, despite negative pushback rooted in prejudice. A discussion by an African American male psychoanalyst elegantly illustrates, with passages from his novel, how the "liberation of white women and black men intersect".

Section II focuses on the interplay between feminism and psychoanalysis, and highlights the various ways these streams of thought and ways of being, impact the authors' work, relationships and/or individual psychology. These personal essays, all by psychoanalytic thinkers, some who are also psychoanalysts or artists, for me, reinforce the link between feminism, psychoanalysis and creative work—they are all paths to finding and empowering the true self. Thus, they are also implicit expressions of gratitude for what the individuals here received by engaging with these forces.

The **Appendix** begins with an original artwork and statement by Bracha L. Ettinger, an Israeli-born French painter, psychoanalyst, and theorist. Her evocative narrative and artwork allows us to consider her concept of the "matrixial gaze" and the "feminine" in art and life as important both for healing trauma and understanding aspects of the culture and our psyche.

A discussion, by Arlene Kramer Richards and Lucille Spira, of Marcel Proust's great novel from the perspective of what it might teach us about prejudice and social snobbery follows Bracha L. Ettinger's contribution. It serves as an historical illustration of how the psychological and the social intertwine in prejudice and social snobbery.

Also in the **Appendix** is a link to a Wikipedia review of second wave feminism and one to a passage from the Congressional Record where Representative Alexandria Ocasio-Cortez calls out a congressman for verbally abusing her. Ocasio-Cortez' response illustrates, among other things, how labeling a strong woman a "bitch" and suggesting she is "other" is the bully's attempt to keep a woman out of what he falsely sees as his space. She shows how one strong woman confronts a bullying gatekeeper. This real life event resonates with abusive actions by men towards women described by some of the contributors in this volume, reminding us that respect and equality for women is still a work in progress.

In conclusion, as I think about this project and the time in which it was created—during the COVID 19 pandemic—I recognize that we were all more isolated from our community activities and professional social engagements. Thus for me these contributions were a welcome source of stimulation and particularly relevant given the current movement toward social justice. As I read the essays from the contributors here,

I realized my good fortune in being a part of what I and many others also experienced, as a thought collective—an important subject discussed in this volume. On ending, I think about a New York Times column, "By the Book", where authors are interviewed about their work and literary interests. As part of the interview, they are asked what authors, living or dead, they would invite to a dinner party. All the authors who contributed here certainly would be on my list. I would also include Marcel Proust, Dorothy Parker and Pedro Almodóvar, fully realizing that they might be otherwise engaged, each for their creative voice and commitment to human rights.

References

Shapiro, S. (2002). "The History of Feminism and Interpersonal Psychoanalysis". *Contemporary Psychoanalysis*, 38, 213-256.

Essay and Discussions:
Rage and Creativity

CHAPTER 1

Rage and Creativity: How Second Generation Feminist Thought Collective Influenced Psychoanalysis

Arlene Kramer Richards

Women in science have been historically and cross-culturally few, isolated and undervalued. Interestingly, women have been prominent in the early days of several modern sciences (Hedy Lamar, Marie Curie, Ada Lovelace, Grace Hopper, etc.). Yet women have not been able to form a mutually supportive, mutually inspiring and enduring collective in any science but psychoanalysis, and later psychology and psychotherapy. How and why did this happen? Women were pioneers in psychoanalysis. But the women in psychoanalysis were not able to change analytic theory that positioned penis envy as the bedrock of femininity until a feminist collective strongly influenced mainly female analysts.

Fleck (1979) described the formation of what he called a "thought style," a kind of consensus achieved in a particular time and place that generates all the concepts capable of being thought. This style develops in a "thought collective," a group of people who have contact with one another. This contact can be through any medium, not just in person. It always results in a shift in thought. The knowledge gained in the thought collective is passed from an inner circle to a journal audience and to popular media. Communication in popular language involves increase in simplicity, certainty and vividness. This feeds back into the inner circle. I will show how this process has led to a change from second generation feminist thought to a profound change in psychoanalysis.

A major tenet of the second generation post World War II feminists was: The personal is political. This meant that politics impacts on personal life and that personal choices affect social arrangements.

First, the personal. Being brought up mainly by a grandfather I identified with work outside the home. Being part of a family supported by my mother's work outside the home I expected to be a breadwinner also. Being named for a paternal grandmother who supported her husband and fourteen children by her business as a flour miller, I aspired to be like her as well. So I became an equality of opportunity feminist.

Second wave feminists Betty Friedan, Simone de Beauvoir, Sherry Hite, Shulamith Firestone, and Ingrid Bengis, challenged the idea that women would be happiest being homemakers. They were reacting to a post-World War II American insistence that women belonged in the home and men in the workplace. Consequences of this were the decrease or elimination of equal opportunity for women, the devaluation of feminine "traits" and values, and lack of child-care options outside the home. American Freudian psychoanalysts "helped" their female patients adapt. But many educated and skilled women failed to thrive when deprived of intellectual and social stimulation and prevented from using their skills. The socially imposed aspects of femininity exacerbated what had always been a female dilemma: whether to spend one's energies on being a mother, a powerful person, or a sexually attractive woman (Hollander, N.). Women writers put it most eloquently. In a letter to her future husband, Jean Stafford wrote intensely, "I know this Cal, and the knowledge eats me like an inward animal: there is nothing worse for a woman than to be deprived of her womanliness" (Laskin, 2000, p. 110).

Betty Friedan's *The Feminine Mystique* (1963), embraced a demand for equality of opportunity, which was the feminist position that Freud himself maintained. But women who consulted the Freudians of their time had no idea of Freud's point of view. Indeed, some were counseled that they should look into the origins of their wishes to be treated more like men rather than act to satisfy these wishes. As a result, they thought that Freud was a patriarch since the Freudians they knew were busily promoting submission to the inequality of opportunity in their male dominated culture. What did feminists want?

A. Equality

Some second wave feminists worked toward women receiving equal treatment. This was a battle that had been won in the United States after the Civil War when so many young men were killed that many young women were not going to be able to find husbands and the rise of machines made it possible to run households with fewer servants. This led to the establishment of women's colleges: it also led to the institution of "women's professions": primary school teaching, social work, and nursing. But after World War 1 men returning from war could not find jobs. Veterans marched for jobs, eventually joblessness led to economic depression and socially women were seen as depriving men of their right to earn a living and support a family. For this reason, after World War II, women were persuaded or forced to retire from the paid workforce, marry and establish families in suburban settings while men commuted to work in the cities.

Betty Friedan was an educated woman who had become one of these suburban housewives. She found it a lonely and largely unfulfilling life. She wanted an end to the inequality of opportunity in the workplace and she wanted the support at home to use that opportunity. Her book addressed the problems of educated women who had been forced, seduced, or lured into suburban homes where they were alone or with young children all day. That those women were not happy with their homes, their household appliances, and their childrearing and household responsibilities was treated as their neurosis, not a social problem. Analysts tried to help them be content with what seemed to them to be very posh lives.

Sharing responsibility for housework and childcare is crucial to increasing job responsibility for women. In 1968, Alix Kates Shulman (1998) created a model plan for a marriage agreement to share household tasks that was reprinted in several major periodicals. Although her own marriage eventually fell apart, Shulman's attempt to make gender roles more equal had an effect on the ideals people espoused, though less impact on what they actually did in the home. Still, Shulman influenced the feminist movement and her ideas have changed the consensus of what women want.

Naomi Weisstein (Brownmiller, 2000) was a cognitive psychologist who could not get a job because she was a woman. She attacked analyst Erik Erikson for valorizing "inner space" in women and Bruno Bettelheim for asserting that a woman's primary satisfaction was in her becoming "the womanly companion" of a man.

Carolyn Heilbrun (1979), the first woman to be tenured in Columbia University's English department, resigned to write a book about her view of what the feminist agenda should be. For Heilbrun, equality must be thoroughgoing: there must be equality in household tasks, equality in educational opportunities, and equality in taking male ideals and male models of achievement and using them to establish a life of satisfying femaleness. She criticizes "psychoanalytic conservatism according to which any emotional attachment, genital or not, that women formed with other women was pathological" (p. 38).

Heilbrun uses Freud as the symbol of all that is anti-female in society when she says: "There is strong evidence, in short, that accomplished women in male-dominated professions are, as the phrase goes, male-identified. Freud and especially his followers have perhaps irremediably damaged that phrase, leaving one with the sense of a sexually disoriented woman, of someone with gender confusion. Nothing could be further from the truth. These women accept allegiance with the males of whose group they are a part, even while themselves wholly female in their sexuality and gender identity" (p. 46). Heilbrun criticizes the women who worked with Freud and those who have become analysts since for becoming apologists for female subservice. That this criticism is not true is clear from the work of Clara Thompson, Karen Horney, Melanie Klein, and countless others in South and North America and in Europe who have thought and written about the female experience in non-subservient ways.

Heilbrun was so determined to prove that Freudian thinking was anti-feminist that she ignored the opportunities that psychoanalysis offered to women who made careers as analysts. She failed to read their staunch defenses of feminist values. But even if they had supported the predominantly male-centered theoretical points of view that some male analysts propounded, they would only have been acting as Heilbrun herself advocated professional women should act: exactly like the men in their disciplines.

Germaine Greer's (1970) understanding of the "Freudian" developmental psychology of women is that it goes from penis envy to the passivity of the mature woman. From subject, she declines into a toy for men. She contends this is illustrated in the popular imagery of the missionary position and all the paraphernalia of pornography. In this sense she is similar to the Lacanian feminists who believe that female desire is valuable. Anselma Dell'Olio (1998) saw the dilemma in feminism as a clash between equality and difference: Are you an equality feminist or a difference feminist? That was the watershed question then, around 1969-1970, and, in many ways, it still is now ....

B. Difference

Other Second Wave feminists valorized the differences between men and women. A radical moment in feminism was the publication of Anne Koedt's (1971) paper "The Myth of the Vaginal Orgasm." Reprinted widely, it was the clearest challenge to the then accepted view among Freudian ego psychologists that the source of much unhappiness among women was failure to achieve "vaginal orgasm." Once the idea that vaginal orgasm was somehow more mature than, and preferable to, orgasm achieved in any other way was challenged, the way women were treated in psychoanalysis and psychotherapy had to change as well.

Some feminists devalued sex. Dana Densmore (1998) put it this way: "We thought that the ideology of sex as a need was a myth perpetrated by men for their own convenience. We took for granted and, indeed, would have insisted on our own sexual freedom. But we classed sex with other enjoyable but optional activities: fun at the beach, ice-cream sundaes, amusement park rides. We might choose to do any of these occasionally, but we would consider the price that was paid. If the price was too high, any could be passed up without regret" (p. 87).

Jo Freeman (1998) believed that the sex versus intimacy issue was paramount. For Roxanne Dunbar (1998) and other feminists in Cell16, the Boston feminist group, Freud was anathema for his belief that sex was a primary drive.

Meredith Tax (1998) asserted: "By psychology we didn't mean Freud, we meant the way it felt to be a woman" (p. 312). Difference feminists were first interested in what they did not want in sex. Abortion and rape were the two big issues. They recognized that pregnancy as the result of unwanted sexual encounters was something every woman feared from puberty to menopause. There were no consequences to the man for conceiving a child with a woman with whom he was not intimately involved. But the woman was faced with catastrophe. By 1968 there was increasing pressure for abortion law reform, which was increasingly tied to other health issues such as involuntary sterilization of poor women and the uninvestigated side effects of birth control pills (Wolfson, 1998).

Susan Brownmiller (2000) reported rape, prostitution, marriage, motherhood, and the sexual abuse of children as the issues that galvanized speak-outs in New York and formed the basis of consciousness raising groups in neighborhoods all over New York, Boston and other cities during the 1970s. These groups, based on the Freudian model of talking about fears and wishes rather than suppressing them, became the stepping stones to speaking aloud and powerfully the thoughts and feelings that women had been suppressing and suffering from. In this way, women's liberation led from silent suffering to something more closely approximating equality of opportunity to speak out publicly.

One sexual issue that became important as the women's liberation movement grew was the issue of lesbianism. Radical feminism encouraged this but was also torn apart by the argument that to be a true feminist, one had to hate men and love women. In the midst of this, the idea that rape was the terror that held women back from full participation in the world was articulated for the first time. Kate Millett's (1970) *Sexual Politics* was the origin and Brownmiller's (1975) *Against Our Will* was the fully developed statement that led to change in rape laws and practices that finally allowed women some measure of protection from the fear of rape. Combined with child and spousal abuse laws, these laws made women more equal by allaying the fear and shame that had attached to their victimhood. At least two modern Freudian woman psychoanalysts have since asserted that rape is the female fear equivalent to male castration fear (Bernstein, 1993; Richards, 1996).

While Freudian thinking about the importance of feelings and the usefulness of talking about feelings had an important influence on feminism, the effect of feminism on Freudian thinking has been to re-affirm Freud's championing of equality for women and to correct Freud's idea that difference is dangerous, because it can be used invidiously to justify lesser opportunities for women than for men. The revision of the theory of the superego to account for the moral integrity of women based on their concern for human values and people's feelings, and the concomitant increase in the respect accorded to difference has changed psychoanalysis profoundly.

The new appreciation of women's conflicts, fears, and pleasures has changed attitudes of analysts toward female analysands. Connectivity has been added to independence as a value. Concern for the welfare and feelings of others has been spotlighted in psychoanalytic theory. This led to a great focus on narcissistic pathology as a reflection of lack of empathy and to a new concept of the relationship between self involvement, self cohesion, self-esteem and the way people are treated in a social context. Crucially, Freud's idea that penis envy is the bedrock of femininity has dropped out of the analytic literature entirely.

A very important effect of feminist thinking has been in the area of understanding the importance, value, and potential of parenting, so that the old idea that only mothers can be caregivers has been deleted from Freudian thought. An important analytic response to the call for less sexist and more human child rearing was investigated by Lynne Rubin (1996) in a dissertation on fathers who take paternal leave to bond with and care for their infant children. Ernst Abelin's (1971, 1980) work on the importance of paternal care in early infancy is another analytic response to the feminist critique. Important work on analysis with gay and lesbian patients, a compendium on female psychology by Eleanor Schuker and Nadine Levinson (1991), the supplements on female psychology in the *Journal of the American Psychoanalytic Association*, the emergence of the journals *Gender and Psychoanalysis* and *Studies in Gender and Sexuality* are all responses to the feminist critiques. Feminism has a debt to psychoanalysis, but analysis is also indebted to feminism. Feminist rage fueled by injustice has been a spur to creativity in the analytic world.

Fleck marveled that it took psychoanalysis to recognize

child sexuality, even though the evidence was there in everyone's memory and observation. It took a group of people interested in the psychology of motivation to make the observation together and convert it into a scientific fact. The social reinforcement perpetuates the fact. "A thought collective exists wherever two or more persons are actually exchanging thoughts" (Fleck L. 1979, p. 102).

When such a collective extends in time it constrains thought. Patient and analyst constitute such a collective. Psychoanalysis as a field is such a collective. So is the IPA. And the second generation feminists constituted such a collective. Did that collective influence the psychoanalytic collective? One way it could have done so was through the feminist academic thought collectives.

In 1989 Chodorow answered that question this way: For the most part psychoanalysts do not seem to be aware of or to care much about the enormous exciting ferment in psychoanalytic feminist theory that is in the forefront of a number of academic disciplines (p. 179).

It took a long time, but the feminist thought collective affected the psychoanalytic thought collective so strongly that current day analysts take as a fact that female psychology does not either begin or end with penis envy. It took women psychoanalysts as a collective within the analytic field to see the scientific fact that women are constituted of our biology, our history, and the social circumstances in which we live.

Is all this purely history? No. A strongly moving example of the persistence of unfair treatment of women is presented in the 2019 film "One Child Nation." The film records the experiences of residents of one town in China during the years of the One Child Policy. Unlike birth control attempts in India, for example, there was no enforced sterilization of men. A man could have as many babies as he could persuade or force women to carry. A man who fathered multiple babies suffered no consequences. There is no mention in the film, just as there is no record in China, of men being forcibly sterilized. The policy was a war on women, women's bodies, and, in particular, against women's fertile bodies. It was a war against mothers and potential mothers. Psychologically, it was a war against all mothers. The individuals who thought it up and those who carried it out were expressing their own feelings as well as participating in the national plan. Psychologically, they were reversing their own position as helpless infants of all powerful mothers. The one child policy deprived China of a whole generation of workers, and many potential wives and mothers, and enough young people to care for the elderly. It was an economic mistake that unleashed deep psychological resentments.

I personally believe that it was a backlash against the newly empowered women of China. It came just after the rise of a generation of women who were the first to escape foot-binding, and to get educations, and become workers outside the home. They were the first-generation of professional women, political leaders, and women of power in their culture. Exemplified by Jiang Qing (Madame Mao), they were seen as usurping male power, and were universally hated for that. The one child policy expressed all that.

Within these broad categories of equality and difference there are many weights of many values. For example, a story in the New York Times of September 14, 2019, tells of how coal miners losing their jobs in Appalachia adapted to the loss of their roles as wage earners. Their wives went to school and became nurses, thus supporting their families. Neither the reporter of the story nor any of her sources considered the alternative of the men going back to school, becoming nurses, and continuing in their roles as bread winners. The men chose to stay at home and do housework.

To me, this illustrates the deep and early learned value of not doing girly things being much more important that the later in life imperative to support the family. The newspaper story emphasized the men's reliance on female family members to help them with the at home chores. Clearly the men were not unambivalent about doing child rearing, shopping, preparing food, cooking, cleaning, repairs and other chores. Yet their work at home was what their wives had been doing when they worked in the mines. The men required more help with the housework than their wives had. Presumably this was because they found it more difficult to do this work than their wives had. Ambivalence uses energy, they clearly were ambivalent about staying at home.

The economic change has led to a change in women's values. One woman who went to work said: "Women now, they got a little taste of freedom," Ms. Bowling said. "Men has been able to do whatever the hell they want for so long while women has had to sit in a chair and keep their legs closed and be nice and polite. Now they don't have to."

Men, on the other hand, find the change more difficult: "The way of life is changing so bad," Mr. Rose said. He grew quiet. "You'll get overwhelmed if you think about it too hard."

The change Mr. Rose finds so hard to think about involves changes in gender roles that modify and even contradict what little boys learn early and that they reinforce in themselves and each other throughout their later years. Boys do not do girly stuff. Real men are not nurses; real men work hard with their muscles and their hands. Real men carry guns, shoot, dig, build, excavate, produce hard objects. Men who do fashion, hairdressing, nursing, teaching nursery school and other soft jobs are not real men. They are sissies. They are as devalued as the women in their society have been.

Another hypothesis, suggested by Delia Battin, (2019) about why men do not become nurses in such a situation is that men want to be nursed, longing for the mothering they enjoyed in infancy. I believe that in this scenario men have pushed away the mothering that they shunned in favor of masculine self-sufficiency, therefore they still long for it but must abjure it in favor of macho independence.

In sum, while what women want is attuned to what men want women to want; what men want is to be lord of the manor, with a woman attuned to her man's every wish. And to the extent that this is true, patriarchy is entrenched while matriarchy, or even equality, is a hard sell.

Recent attempts to change have come from Third World feminists. Eltahawy (2019) posits anger, attention, profanity, ambition, power, violence, and lust as ways to fight against the power of patriarchy. She advocates socializing young girls to resist being influenced by patriarchy by fighting against it in all its forms. Her idea is not to win over the men who derive advantage from it, but to fight against them. Adichie (2017) advocates the same kind of social pressure with the mother as teacher for a girl from infancy onward. She emphasizes self-respect and self- actualization so that the mother is a model for the girl to identify with. She also suggests having the father be a full partner rather than a helper in raising the daughter. Refusing gender roles in girl's toys, interests and capabilities, accepting power in women, teaching daughters to read and question assumptions in language, not seeing marriage as an achievement, not seeing pleasing others as a goal, and accepting her own identity, physical body, and teaching her the words for her own sexuality. These ideas involve actively resisting sexism, but not in the angry key Eltahawy advocates.

So feminists now are advocating socializing girls as non-conforming with the larger society's patriarchal standards, thinking against the grain, being self-centered, abrasive, and strong. Will psychoanalysts accept such a stance? Are we ready to think of our patients as successful when they are rebellious? Are we able to see strong-willed, non-conformist women as our society's achievements rather than "ball busters"? Can we use the influence of these modern feminists to create a new vision of our own work? As one who has achieved a partial and limited success in doing this, I am hoping that we can.

References

Abelin, E. (1971). The role of the father in the separation-individuation process. In *Separation—Individuation: Essays in Honor of Margaret S. Mahler,* ed. J. McDevitt and C. Setdage, pp. 229-252. New York: International Universities Press.

——— (1980). Triangulation, the role of the father, and the origins of core gender identity during the rapprochement subphase. In *Rapprochement: The Critical Subphase of Separation-Individuation,* eds. R. Lax, S. Bach, and A. Burland, pp. 151-179. New York: Aronson.

Adiche C. (2017) *Dear Ijeawele, or A Feminist Manifesto in Fifteen Suggestions.* New York: Knopf.

Battin, D., (2019) Personal communication.

Angier, N. (1999). *1X0man: An Intimate Geography.* New York: Houghton Mifflin.

Baxandall, R. (1998). Catching the fire. In *The Feminist Memoir Project: Voices from Women's Liberation,* eds. R. Duplessis and A. Snitow, pp. 208-224. New York: Three Rivers Press.

Bern, S. (1992). *The Lenses of Gender: Transforming the Debate on Sexual inequality.* New Haven, CT: Yale University Press.

Benjamin,]. (1988). *The Bonds of Love: Psychoanalysis, Feminism, and the Problems of Domination.* New York: Pantheon.

Bernstein, D. (1983). The female superego. *International Journal of Psychoanalysis,* 64: 187-202.

——— (1993). *Female Identity Conflict in Clinical Practice.* Northvale, NJ: Jason Aronson.

Brownmiller, S. (1975). *Against Our Will: Men, Women, and Rape.* New York: Simon and Schuster.

——— (2000). *In Our Time: Memoir of a Revolution.* New York: Dial.

Chodorow, N. (1978). *The Reproduction of Mothering: Psychoanalysis and the Sociology of Gender.* Berkeley: University of California Press.

——— (1989). Feminism and Psychoanalytic Theory. New Haven: Yale

——— (1998). Psychoanalysis and women psychoanalysts. The role of women in the of psychoanalysis: Ideas, practice and institutions. Presentation at the International Psychoanalytic Association meeting, London, July 16-18.

Dell'Olio, A. (1998). Home In: *The Feminist Memoir Project: Voices of Women's Liberation,* eds. R. Duplessis and A. Snitow, pp. 149-170. New York: Three Rivers Press.

Densmore, D. (1998). A year of Jiving dangerously: 1968. *In The Feminist Memoir Project: Voices from Women's Liberation,* eds. R. Duplessis and A. Snitow, New York: Three Rivers Press.

Dunbar, R. (1998). Outlaw woman: Chapters from a feminist memoir-in-progress. In: *The Feminist Memoir Project: Voices from Women's Liberation,* eds. R. Duplessis and A. Snitow, pp. 90-114. New York: Three Rivers Press.

Eltahawy, M. (2019). *The Seven Necessary Sins for Women and Girls.* Boston: Beacon

Firestone, S. (1970). *The Dialectic of Sex: The Case for Feminist Revolution.* New York: Morrow.

Fleck, L. (1979). *Genesis and Development of a Scientific Fact.* Chicago: U. Chicago Press.

Fleigel, Z. (1973). Female sexual development in Freudian theory. *Psychoanalytic Quarterly,* 42: 385-409.

Freeman, J. (1998). On the origins of the women's liberation movement from a strictly personal point of view. In *The Feminist Memoir Project: Voices from Women's Liberation,* eds. R. Duplessis and A. Snitow, New York: Three Rivers Press.

Friedan, B. (1963). *The Feminine Mystique.* New York: W. W. Norton.

Gilligan, C. (1982). *In A Different Voice: Psychological Theory and Women's Development.* Cambridge, MA: Harvard University Press.

Greer, G. (1970). The politics of female sexuality. In *The Madwoman's Underclothes,* pp. 36-40. New York: Atlantic, 1986.

——— (1973). Seduction is a four-letter word. In *The Madwoman's Underclothes,* pp. 152-168. New York: Atlantic Monthly Press, 1986.

——— (1974). Review of Conundrum by Jan Morris. In *The Madwoman's Underclothes,* pp. 189-191. New York: Atlantic 1986.

——— (1986). *The Madwoman's Underclothes.* New York: Atlantic

Grossman, W, and Stewart, W (1976). Penis envy. *J. Amer Psy. Assn.* (Supp.), 24: 193-21.3.

Heilbrun, C. (1979). *Reinventing Womanhood.* New York: W. W. Norton.

Hite, S. (1976). *The Hite Report.* New York: Ddl.

Hrdy, S. (1999). *Mother Nature: A History of Mothers, infants, and Natural Selection.* New York: Pantheon.

Koedt, A. (1971). The myth of the vaginal orgasm. In *The Radical Therapist.* pp. 127-137. New York: Ballantine.

Laskin, D. (2000). *Partisans: Marriage. Politics, and Betrayal among the New York Intellectuals.* New York: Simon and Schuster.

Langer, M. (1992). *Motherhood and Sexuality.* Trans. N.C. Hollander. New York: Guilford.

Millet, K. (1970). *Sexual Politics.* New York: Avon-Doubleday.

Paskauskas, R. (cd.) (l9C)j). *The Complete Correspondence of Sigmund Freud and Ernest Jones 1908-1939.* Cambridge, MA: Harvard University Press.

Person, E. (1974). Some new observations on the origin of femininity. In *Women and Analysis: Dialogues on Psychoanalytic Views of Femininity,* ed.]. Strouse, pp. 250-261. New York: Grossman.

Person, E. (1982). Women working.].Amer Acad. Psa, 10: 67-84.

Poussaint, A. (1974). A threat to blacks. *New York Times.* May 6.

Richards, A. (I 996). Primary femininity and female genital anxiety. *J Amer Psa Ass.* (Supp.), 44:261-283.

——— (1999). Freud and feminism. *J Amer Psa. Assn,* 17: 1213-123.

Robertson, C. Sept. 14, 2019 In Coal Country, the Mines Shut Down, the Women Went to Work and the World Quietly Changed. In *The New York Times.*

Rubin, L. (1999). A study of employed men who have taken parental leave to be caregivers of their infants. Dissertation Abstracts. University Microfilms.

Shulman, A. (1998). A marriage disagreement, or marriage by other means. In *The Feminist Memoir Project: Voices from Women's Liberation,* eds. R. Duplessis and A. Snitow, pp.284-303. New York: Three Rivers Press.

Tax, M. (1998). Bread and roses! Bread and roses! In *The Feminist Memoir Project: Voices from Women's Liberation,* eds. R. Duplessis and A. Snitow, pp. 311-323. New York: Three Rivers Press.

Toulmin, S. (1966). Ludwik Fleck and the interpretation of science. In: Cognition and Fact: Boston Studies in the Philosophy of Sciences eds Cohen, R. & T. Schnellle. Boston: Reidel.

Wolfson, A. (1998). Clenched fist, open heart. In *The Feminist Memoir Project: Voices from Women's Liberation,* eds. R. Duplessis and A. Snitow, pp. 268-283. New York: Three Rivers Press.

Section I: *Essay and Discussions: Rage and Creativity*

DISCUSSIONS AND RESPONSES

CHAPTER 2

Women in psychoanalytic theory:
Two steps forward, still one step back:
Response to Arlene Kramer Richards'
"Rage and Creativity"

Rosemary H. Balsam

Arlene Richards has written a spirited, highly readable, and useful bird's eye view about (especially second wave) feminism in the United States, and how it has affected psychoanalysis and vice versa. She ends by talking of feminism in China and Third World countries, and wonders how much people could actually stand the result of those women scholars who advocate extreme behavioral rebellion against males and society, in order to try to re-socialize girls to refuse their submissive status quo. She raises (perhaps indirectly) the question of what has (or has not) been learned by women and the movement from about WWI onwards, including in the world of psychoanalysis; and what has been translated into psychosocial values that improve the present psychosocial position of women. Her central thesis is expressed on page 11: "Feminist rage fueled by injustice has been a spur to creativity in the analytic world." I agree with this, and add here my own sense of a continuity in this struggle, while recognizing improvements since the 1970 watershed.

Dr. Richards addresses the mobilization of women's creative abilities in the 1970s to form working groups. This was a substantial change. She identifies this as the process of a "thought collective," which seems a useful way of thinking. It helped individual women to emerge from their isolation, urged along by storied leaders and feminist writers (well-documented here) who became public figures. This created much stronger group voices with which to air complaints and support each other's life complexities—a positive alternative to suffering in the previously expected silence. Hopefulness was in the air, and fueled women's attempts to look for better solutions in their lives. Some of the problems back then were due to a lack of the opportunity to work outside the home—work once perceived as the bailiwick of men alone. WWII had necessitated that women join the work force, but once men were demobilized, the jobs had once more returned to them. Women, however, by then had had a taste of the pleasures of the work world. Education and the labor situation for females has definitely improved socially over the years, especially in the last 50, affirmed by a US Labor Department Blog in 2017: "The proportion of women with college degrees in the labor force has almost quadrupled since 1970. More than 40 percent of women in the labor force had college degrees in 2016, compared with 11 percent in 1970."

Arlene does not mention that it remains, however, that high-paying high-echelon jobs for women are still few (if increasing) in 2020, and that the glass ceiling, say, in the business world, is barely cracked. So even though there is a far greater acceptance of women's desire to work outside the home, the old "gender problems" abide in many sectors. Arlene interestingly describes at the end of her piece, a labor crisis in 2019 among miners in Appalachia, where men were forced out of their very "masculine" jobs as miners, and a need to re-tool was evident. But the old gender complications surfaced. The wives left the hearth and became nurses to support the families. But their husbands opted awkwardly to be "at-home" fathers rather than themselves becoming nurses or health care workers, rejecting the opportunity to stay in the work world. Arlene points out that these jobs were "too soft" for them. Apparently, in that modern society, not much changed about male attitudes about women – but the women's life situations, by their own report, were still improved by the opportunities they took advantage of to work outside the home.

Attitudes towards females, of course, are linked to their childbearing and child raising, which kept women homebound. Feminist writers attacked this arrangement in particular in the 1970s. I think that it is hard to review this literature as a batch, as Arlene does here, and as it relates to psychoanalysis, because some authors are more interested in completely conscious attitudes, whereas others pay more attention to the disavowed and unconscious attitudes that can shine through. Therefore, at times, based on conscious complaints, some feminists naively postulated that women could and would readily give up child-raising if only men were more eager to take it over. The latter position did not take into account the possibility of women's complicated conscious and unconscious ambivalence about giving the baby over to someone else—even the father—after having carried and given birth to a child; or struggles with the deep internalization of a woman's own mother that can be activated in pregnancy that will affect her attachment style. There is evidence, however, that these socially progressive suggestions as a whole bore some fruit, mostly in building women's collective confidence to step further into the work force, and also to feel freer to seek outside help in caring for their babies. Mothers were and are on the whole less condemned socially in the US for this practice than pre-1970. (Of course the Victorian era in Europe and females in the "upper classes" had yet another set of social disapprobations, where looking after babies was considered menial and thus 'the mother' in the household did not engage in much hands-on care. These culture and era shifts are complex enough to warrant closer inspection than is possible in this format.)

I would contend, however that there may be much less relative success in the more complex and deep psychological issues that result in the way many women see themselves, are seen, and are treated both in their being backward about assuming social equality (in the way that Arlene describes personally), and in their being able to recognize their valuable differences to men in very important ways. I see a continuing struggle in this regard, reflected in society, that is also an opportunity for psychoanalysts to help, given our own on-going work to become more enlightened in our theory-making.

The Struggle Continues in both Society and in Psychoanalysis.

Dr. Richards says enthusiastically that the feminist awakening "process has led to a change from second generation feminist thought to a profound change in psychoanalysis." I am rather less sanguine than Arlene is about the "profound" change in psychoanalysis. I do acknowledge some change in psychoanalysis—especially in the clinical arena. The "good news" here—and Arlene perhaps means this aspect—is a sea-change in daily psychoanalytic practice. No longer are women confronted by analysts (mostly male but also female analysts who used to follow party lines, as it were) telling them that their main troubles were (their "inevitable") "penis envy," and that the way to improve their lives was to become more positively involved with their husband's successes!

The "bad news" for me is that I am also very impressed with how groups (including psychoanalysts) regress too, unknowingly remain regressed due to unconscious and disavowed mentation, and how deeply inscribed are assumptions that elements derived from being embodied as female is a problem for society. Lay people as well as analysts from all schools, for example, still need to compare, contrast and thus evaluate as "better" or "worse," males vs. females, with the female portrayed as "lacking" in something. The equalities of "both/and" are often missing. Just read a few journal case reports randomly from this point of view as an experiment! This psychic evaluative situation I believe is regressive, but normalized since Freud affirmed it in 1908 and onwards. Incidentally, I do not agree with Arlene that Freud was so free of gender bias, just because he had favorite women like Helene Deutsch and many others who adored him, whom he encouraged professionally. He did not send his own daughters to Gymnasium, for example, indicating that their future would not be in the university. Freud was ambivalent. His bias was likely unconscious—he couldn't help himself. One cannot deny the negativity towards women in his writings that many of the mentioned feminists in Arlene's piece, noticed accurately! Nevertheless, it is also true, as Arlene notes, that his method, which he can be credited for inventing by being prepared to listen with great interest to women talking (a definite plus!), is and has been extraordinarily valuable to countless women's increased self-esteem.

One way that a contemporaneous unconscious fear of females can persist in psychoanalysis is in "gender blindness" in theory and in the conduct of therapy, rather than active "gender bias." It is as if we were all "alike" and sex and gender history can be ignored, say in an exclusive focus on here-and-now transference/countertransference dilemmas. It is as if Freud made "too much" of it all. These asexual attitudes can flourish also where there is a preferred focus on "the archaic," implying the everything important in psychic life is "presexual". "Out" with drive theory and biology: "In" with philosophy and a disembodied mind! Two very recent presentations about Bionian theory that I have attended bring up this theme. One is in a search for "the erotic" in "the container," and the other applies Bionian theory to an open question about where has sexual detail gone in current case reporting about adults. Another recent theme that I have been writing about myself is essentially my allergy to "the feminine" being used as a theoretic shorthand when thinking and theorizing about women. A close look at this term makes me want to recommend that it be put on the shelf to accumulate dust because of its obfuscations and assumed value judgments!

Regarding our analytic history of thinking about female psychology—with the exception of Horney's excellent beginnings, for which of course she got punished by the New York Psychoanalytic Association, like the proverbial whistleblower, in 1941, and a few others—I have actually feared the ineffectiveness of struggling to articulate a psychoanalytic psychology of women that openly and consistently rejects Freudian comparisons and replaces it with a focus on the female. An example might be Arlene's comments about equating women's rape fears to men's castration anxiety. Yes, each embodied sex has its own severe anxieties based on reactions to their own anatomical vulnerabilities. Many women analysts have written excellent but sometimes just single random papers correcting clearly this or that element of Freudian thinking, and rightly placing it as culture and era-bound. These can get lost as single items. Compendiums and journals can help in forming "thought collectives." Many single papers can be found in Shuker and Levinson's wonderful 1991 "Female Psychology: An Annotated Bibliography." At the time, this book was a bible of information. I, for one, greatly benefited by their research and commentaries. This was before our present digital era which opened the readier ability to search for oneself in the PEP archive that was just being conceived in 1991. Further "thought collective" help was provided in the US by both Harold Blum and Arnold Richards in their roles as chief editors of JAPA. They gathered together in 1976 and 1996 batches of significant papers on "female psychology." A new journal, "Studies in Gender and Sexuality" was initiated in 2000 by chief editors Virginia Goldner and Muriel Dimen. Bonnie Litowitz, as a JAPA chief editor in 2014, introduced a seminal paper of Julia Kristeva on maternal erotics to an American audience. Claudia Lament in 2015 collected papers on "The War against Women in Psychoanalytic Culture" in *The Psychoanalytic Study of the Child*; Jay Greenberg as the PQ chief editor had catalyzed many "conversations" from different points of view in his journal, some involving theory involving female development. Such publications and editors can be an enormous help in supporting "thought collectives" and bringing a topic alive to the general readership and to general analysts.

The founding of COWAP (Committee On Women) within the IPA in 1998, by the London social psychologist/psychoanalyst Joan Raphael-Leff, has also provided a crucial support system for further thinking about female development in psychoanalysis. But when I have looked at who contributes papers to these projects, I found that regrettably only a handful of male writers has actually been able to come out and declare Freud in error about women's "psychosexual phases." I think that this is significant for our field as a whole as a sign of lack of acceptance in our field—and perhaps even a very subtle dismissal of new critical work as "woman talk."

I thank Arlene Richards and Lucille Spira for their great energy and delight in this shared project that we all feel enthusiastic about, and their now opening this mode of keeping up a lively collegial interchange in this new way.

Response to Rosemary Balsam

Arlene Kramer Richards

I am so grateful to Rosemary for her full and interesting response and her view of the impact of feminism on psychoanalysis. What I value most about her response is that it recalled a memory of a crucial turn in my own life. As an adolescent I tried hard to maintain a link with my parents. Having been raised through my sixth year by my grandparents, I had a sense of them as parents rather than my own parents. So when it came time to differentiate or, as Erikson had it, to deidentify with my parents, I was simultaneously trying to get closer to them and to individuate as separate from them.

In this conflict, I chose to go to my father's business after school every day. I would go get coffee, do filing, sweep the floors. I loved the colors and textures of the fabrics lining the walls of his store and I loved sending out postcards with tiny samples to prospective buyers. I loved talking with the young designers who came in to buy small yardages for sample dresses, and with the custom shirt makers who needed the finest, silkiest, most expensive cottons.

One day, after several months of this, my father called me into his office to tell me that he had heard I loved the business but he wanted me to know that the best I could ever be in it was bookkeeper because this business was for his son. I never went there again. I went home crying. I told my mother. She said he would need to send me to college instead.

The result of this incident was that I became the first person in my family to go to college. And the corollary was that I was deeply touched by Freud's entrusting his family business to his daughter.

For me this made him a feminist hero. That he was willing to see her as a person with commitment, passion, and intellect was marvelous.

He never sent her to gymnasium. But in that time and place and in his financial condition that may have been unthinkable. He would have had to send her to gymnasium in 1909. At that time in Vienna there were very few gymnasia for girls, and there were no other pathways for higher education for children of the middle class (Friedenreich, 2002). Girls in aristocratic families could have tutors, but Freud was so poor then that he never even owned his house. He was supporting his six children, his parents, his wife, and his sister-in-law as well as a maid. His referrals were still few. He had alienated much of the medical community with his radical ideas.

What kept Freud from educating his daughters the way Rosemary and I would have liked him to was not his disrespect for their abilities; it was a result of his own inability to support his extended family in middle class comfort and of a society in which there was no provision for higher education for girls.

That Freud did not send Anna to a school that did not exist in that time and place cannot be used as evidence that he was not a feminist. In fact, his willingness to educate her through inviting her to his Wednesday evening seminars, in the face of a society that did not accept women's education, took courage and conviction.

As a feminist, he insisted that her mind was equal to that of his medical colleagues as well as the other university educated men in his circle. Psychoanalysis has been one of the few sciences open to and respectful of women ever since.

Freud's theories about female sexuality, on the other hand, have been objected to and corrected. He could not understand female sexuality, agreed that he did not understand it, tried to, and failed to, and finally left it up to the female psychoanalysts to finish that part of the work of understanding our women patients. It was that change in theory that was finally to reface his views that was accomplished by women empowered by second wave feminism.

References

Freudenreich H. (2002) Higher education in Central Europe, In: *The Encyclopedia of Jewish Women*. Brookline, MA: Jewish Women's Archive.

Section I: *Essay and Discussions: Rage and Creativity*

CHAPTER 3

The Trauma of Having No Voice
Response to Arlene Kramer Richards' Paper:
Rage and Creativity

Sandra E. Cohen

Being silenced is traumatic, whether by forces from without or within. Having no voice against abusers or repressors, no voice for anger, sadness, or for all of the things that have hurt. That is the most poisonous deterrent to creativity on all levels. And, of course, that creates rage. But what is the most potent weapon against those silencing forces? Being able to Speak out. Or, Yell. Yet some women can; some can't.

This is the psychoanalyst's job: to give voice to all that has been silenced; to free the imprisoned voice inside our patients; to be a "background object" (Grotstein, p. 369) for gaining the courage to rage. That is why Arlene Kramer Richards' paper with its title, *Rage and Creativity*, is necessary. The two are inveterate partners. They must be.

In *Rage and Creativity: How Second Generation Feminist Thought Collective Influenced Psychoanalysis*, Arlene takes us through the history of a feminist movement that arose out of women's rage. The history of women coming out of silence. The misunderstandings. The threat to the "powers" that both

35

were and are still looming. Along with the inevitable back-lash in attempts to re-impose silence and control. We see it now. And, we see the fighting back. Arlene has given us an important task:

"Feminists now are advocating socializing girls as non-conforming with the larger society's patriarchal stan-dards, thinking against the grain, being self-centered, abra-sive, and strong. *Will psychoanalysts accept such a stance* (italics mine)? Are we ready to think of our patients as suc-cessful when they are rebellious? Are we able to see strong willed, non-conformist women as our achievements rather than "ball-busters?" Can we use the influence of these mod-ern feminists to create a new vision of our own work? As one who has achieved a partial and limited success in doing this, I am hoping we can."

I think we can. As a thought collective here in the new *International Journal of Controversial Discussions Vol. 3*, we have the forum to do so. Thank you for this challenge, Arlene. More than ever, it is important to be creative in our current world-order of COVID-19, imposing new restrictions and frustrations. Yet, how can a woman be creative if not in touch with rage? If she can't use aggression to push boundaries of an old guard to move into something new (whatever that old guard might be within the outer world or in one's mind)—with a voice to do so. We must honor the angry voices.

The Power of Anger

Arlene gives us a thorough history of the power of anger. The power of Second Wave Feminism. Anger gets things done. Anger frees women (and men) from somatic disorders (Miller, 2004; Van Der Kolk, 2014), depression, panic, tor-ments of the soul (Ferro, 2015), the psychological symptoms of being silenced. Anger is necessary. Today the power of its necessity is witnessed in what seems to me a Third Wave of Feminism: the #Me Too movement. Yes, it is about sexual abuse and misconduct. And, it is also about not being seen or heard. About a history of being too afraid or ashamed to speak. Keeping sadness and rage locked into a numbing prison. Gone dead inside.

We've discovered the ways victimized women have been silenced. How powerful that silencing is. How it has sent women into hiding. And just how terrified they are to break down those walls of silence (Kantor & Twohey, 2019). Yet we've also seen women get angry. How #Me Too (a phrase of awareness created in 2006 by Tarana Burke) caught fire and became a Movement in 2017. We've seen how life-affirming anger can be.

#Me Too: The Start of a Third Wave of Feminism?

A movement that began as a counter-insurgency to the Trump presidency's war on women, might we call #Me Too the start of a Third Wave of Feminism? It certainly is a thought collective. One formed when Rose McGowan and other women came forward to speak out against the abuses of Hollywood Producer Harvey Weinstein. When Alyssa Milano called out for women who had also been assaulted to tweet "#Me Too" (Geisler, 2019). Giving many who have been silenced since childhood or early adulthood the courage to join in and speak up. Starting an unmistakable viral *roar* (Geisler, 2019). Yes, a collective does help.

In 1937, Patricia Douglas didn't have such a collective. A dancer, and only 20 years old at the time, Patricia was courageous enough to speak out about sexual abuse by Hollywood studio moguls at MGM. MGM didn't listen. She went to the Culver City police. MGM owned the police. She tried telling her story to the media. MGM owned the papers: "The power MGM had is unimaginable today. They owned everyone— the D.A., the L.A.P.D. They ran this place." (Shewfelt, P. 10). Patricia was silenced (Shewfelt, 2017). That was then. This is now. Women scream: "NO MORE."

These women refuse to be oppressed. Have the courage to speak out. Get elected. Get predators like Harvey Weinstein convicted. We are hearing women. Outspoken women like The Squad: Alexandria Ocasio-Cortez of New York, Ilhan Omar of Minnesota, Ayanna Pressley of Massachusetts, and Rashida Tlaib of Michigan. A Pressley tweet says: "We are more than four people ... our squad includes any person committed to creating a more equitable and just world."

Arlene calls for us to have that same commitment. We know how to listen. Freud taught us about that. But listening isn't enough. We must support the anger and aggression that needs to be spoken and lived. As Eltahawy (2019) says: "I believe all girls are born with that pilot light of anger (p. 15) ... angry women are free women (p. 35)." Anger is not "a sin."

We can't afford to be complacent; to let the old powers (of, shall we call it, the white male patriarchy?) pull us backwards. We can't allow women's voices to be taken from them in control over their bodies, reproductive rights, gender and racial equality, or in any repressive attempts to silence them. Even in the Kleinian world (much of which I agree with and respect), aggression and anger are at risk of being equated with destructiveness. We must say, "No" to that idea as well. To put it mildly—aggression and anger are good. They are part of the forces that work to give women (and all those who have been oppressed) their voices. The power to speak out.

Can we, this psychoanalytic thought collective, following Arlene's lead, be a part of a Third Wave of Feminism? One in which women are standing up and shouting: "Time's Up"—to the forces that try to shut them down. Our work can and must support them. Because rage is the only way to release creativity from its prison of silence.

Our Psychoanalytic Task

Arlene aptly writes in her 1999 paper, *Freud and Feminism: A Critical Appraisal*: "Sigmund Freud invented psychoanalysis as the art and science of listening. He was a listener who tried to hear and who worked hard at making sense of what he heard, and he listened to voices that in his day received very little attention, the voices of women ... he broke ranks even further with the men of his time by listening *especially* to women" (P. 1213). Even more importantly, in contrast to the later misunderstanding and misuse of Freud's ideas, Freud considered women —equal.

Yet, and Arlene makes this very clear in *Rage and Creativity*, equality isn't enough. Today, we as psychoanalysts are faced with an even bigger challenge than psychoanalytic and feminist misunderstandings of Freud. Arlene addresses this challenge clearly: allowing women their rage and aggression. Allowing each a voice.

Whether Freud was wrong about penis envy, the castration complex, the realities of child sexual abuse, or feminine sexuality, he did (as Arlene points out, p. 1232, 1999) foster and support women's creativity. It was important to him. He gave women voices; he published them; he cited their ideas; he was a champion of women. Sure, he made his mistakes. But he did teach us to *listen*. We can do better. Women do want and need to be heard. Yet just as equality is not enough, it's not enough to listen.

We are the first responders, the ones on the front line.

When rage is finally unleashed towards us in the transference, let's not shrink away or defend ourselves, even if our intentions are misunderstood. Let's take that anger in, embrace it, encourage it, explore those misunderstandings (real or imagined). Let's understand the rage—its roots. We are the testing ground. We can make anger safe. Justifiable. Rage isn't wrong. It's not a monster. In fact, anger can set our patients free. And even more, as psychoanalyst Paul Williams says about his own traumatic childhood in his deeply affecting and honest book, *The Sixth Principle*, "Anger will keep me alive."

Privileging anger, helping our patients see that it is necessary, normal, and not "ball-busting," is one of the important calls to action in Arlene's *Rage and Creativity* paper. But can we go further and, once again, ask ourselves: what *else* do women want?

What Do Women Want?

Freud's obscurely cited question: "What does a woman want?" is traced by Ernest Jones to a conversation with Marie Bonaparte. These are Freud's musings, tinged with (I would say) more than an ounce of humility: "The great question that has never been answered and which I have not yet been able to answer, despite my thirty years of research into the feminine soul, is '*What does a woman want?*'" (Jones, 1953, p. 421). Isn't this an important question for each of us to ask, if we are to help the frightened and silenced women in our consulting rooms come out of hiding?

Here are some things I've witnessed in my own work: For their feelings not to be too much. For their anger not to "destroy." Not to be put into the repressive boxes of theory, assumptions, or diagnoses. Help speaking truth to power, including the oppressive, shaming, voices in their own minds. To get free of obligation, of "shoulds," and self-hate. To be seen, known, and accepted. For exactly who they are. Including their differences.

Honoring A Feminism of Difference

It's true: women are both equal to and different than men. But, perhaps even more important, each woman is different. Different histories. Hurts and needs taking different forms. Each woman's own individual versions (*their* truths) must be seen and heard. This is the value of psychoanalytic work. To find *that* woman, *that* frightened little girl, the one who's been hiding deep inside… for a very long time. One who's been afraid to raise her head, her hand, to expose her anger, to be visible. We can offer this. To see her, not in the shame she fears, but in the realities (and richness) of who she really is. We can lend a voice. Reach out a hand.

In *Rage and Creativity*, Arlene tells us how feminism (and psychoanalysis too) must "correct Freud's idea that difference is dangerous because it can be used invidiously to justify lesser opportunities for women than for men" (P. 8). In fact, as we see in the different voices of Second Wave Feminism, of #Me Too, of all of us as respondents to Arlene's paper, in the different voices of psychoanalytic thinkers: difference, again, to put it mildly, is good. Difference offers complimentary perspectives. And, best of all, a dialogue that supports understanding and change.

Psychoanalysis is a thought collective. A patient and analyst are a thought collective too. Arlene highlights these facts. We exchange ideas. In doing so, we hear *that* patient's individual voice; filling out the picture of who she is. We find the silenced one inside. Help our patients speak that quieted voice, yell it out, fight for what they believe, use their aggression for change, and *rage* for their own creative thinking.

We can all say #Me Too—to taking out our microphones and speaking truth to the powers that try to suppress us and take us over. We can stand up to those shaming voices in our minds. We can help our patients do just that. This is what the Women's Movement started. This is what psychoanalysis, Freud's talking cure, is truly all about. Yes, we can all say to silence, "NO MORE."

References

Eltahawy, M. (2019). *The Seven Necessary Sins for Women and Girls.* Beacon Press: Boston.

Ferro, A. (2015). *Torments of the Soul.* Routledge: London.

Geisler, C. (2019). *The Voices Of #Me Too: From Grassroots Activism to A Viral Roar.* Roman & Littlefield: Maryland.

Grotstein, J.S. (1981). Who Is the Dreamer, Who Dreams the Dream?: A Study of Psychic Presences. In *Do I Dare Disturb the Universe?* Ed. by J.S. Grotstein. Routledge: New York.

Jones, E. (1953). *The Life and Work of Sigmund Freud, Volume 2.* Basic Books: New York.

Miller, A. (2006). *The Body Never Lies: The Lingering Effects of Hurtful Parenting.* W.W. Norton: London.

Richards, A.K. (1999). Freud and Feminism: A Critical Appraisal. *J. Amer. Psychoanal. Assn.,* 47(4):1213-1238.

Shewfelt, R. L. (2017). In *#Me Too: Essays About How and Why This Happened, What It Means, and How to Make Sure it Never Happens Again,* ed. By Lori Perkins, Riverdale Books: New York.

Van Der Kolk, B. (2014) *The Body Keeps the Score.* Penguin Books: New York.

Williams, P. (2010). *The Fifth Principle.* Karnac Books: London.

Response to Sandra Cohen

Arlene Kramer Richards

Thank you Sandra for hitting the nail on the head. Your response to what women want is right on target. Women want a voice. Just like men want a voice. We all want to be in control of our own lives. Living in a social world limits the extent to which we can do that. Other people's rights and wishes clash with our own. Other people's needs sometimes come first. No one can get it all. But we can all at least have the right to say what we want without being shamed for saying it. And we can all have the right to say what we are afraid of without having to feel shame about that. And we can all ask the questions about morality that guide our own actions and those of others. And we can all come to the resolutions of our own conflicts that make sense to us.

Insisting on our right to be heard may be abrasive to those whose interests lie in our willingness not to bother them in pursuing their own agendas and maintaining dominance. So we do need to be willing to be abrasive. And we need to be willing to be rebellious when we are being mistreated. We do need to push back. In this sense we can understand those women who say "I am not a feminist." They are the ones who want to keep the peace. They want to be liked. I believe that from a thought collective we can get the courage to be willing to be disliked by the oppressor. The answer to the fear of being disliked by the oppressors is in having a thought collective. If my sisters like me, I can tolerate being disliked by those who want to keep all of us down.

In this sense psychoanalysis does indeed have a potential for disrupting the social contract. The psychoanalytic ideal of speaking one's own truth, suppressing nothing, and respecting where one's own mind wanders, encourages analysands to speak out in other situations just as they do in the analytic space. And the analyst's respectful acceptance and response becomes what the analysand expects of other people. Expectation can evoke a complementary response. So the willingness to accept rejection and the expectation of acceptance become complementary forces in the push to be what we want to be, and have what we want to have. Thank you Sandra for your courageous and encouraging response in this discussion.

CHAPTER 4

Self-agency in the Woman, Acceptance of Difference: Discussion of Arlene Kramer Richards' paper, "Rage and Creativity"

Paula L. Ellman

Arlene Kramer Richards' paper "Rage and Creativity: how Second-Generation Feminist Thought Collective influenced Psychoanalysis" offers us an opportunity to examine the interplay between feminist development and the development of psychoanalytic theories of femininity. Richards offers us a review of the contributions of Second Wave feminist thinkers and the social context that gave rise to them. She also welcomes us to come to know some of her own personal narrative, both in terms of her family history and her professional development as a psychoanalyst, with regard to her own feminine identity formation, inviting a sense of intimacy as we read her contribution.

Richards poses the question "What did feminists want?" This is reminiscent for me of the recent COWAP (IPA Committee on Women and Psychoanalysis) Conference entitled "What Do Women Want Today?" in Washington D.C. on November 2019, organized by Margarita Cereijido and Nancy Goodman, North American COWAP members, at which Richards presented, along with a number of other leading female psychoanalytic thinkers from North and Latin America. Presenters offered ideas on themes such as "Liberating 'female' from 'femininity'" (Rosemary Balsam); "The feminine: plurality of desires" (Leticia Glocer Fiorini); "What women want and what is wanted of women" (Richards, herself); "What should a wife want?" (Janice Lieberman); and "Self-agency in the feminine: what females need today" (myself). The Conference offered opportunities to collaborate on these relevant topics that are very much alive, topics where societal context and psychoanalytic thought intersect. Richards' contribution emphasized the central place of equality for the woman, equality of opportunity, as she likewise emphasizes to us in this paper. For me, as I suggested in my conference presentation, crucial to having equal opportunity is the woman finding her self-agency, her voice, the only way she can have her grounding in her selfhood, direction, identity. Agency accompanies sexual and gender identity—not just accepting the assignment of gender identity, but choosing it. Also, agency encompasses aspects of unconscious fantasy that provide the scaffolding of the inner world and includes introjected cultural conceptions (Ellman & Goodman, 2017).

Issues of women's equality and self-agency continue to have a central presence in popular culture. With the fairly recent outbreak of Covid-19, many television series have been quite popular, and recently suggested to me was a 4-episode television series entitled "Unorthodox" that poignantly captures these principles of equality of opportunity and of self-agency. The series (based on the autobiographical memoire of its producer) depicts a young woman, Esty (for Esther) raised in a sect of Hasidic Jews in New York, and her flight from her community as she poignantly discovers her voice, once outside the restrictive confines of her prior highly ritualized life. Esty lived according to the strictures of her religious community, and was raised by a loving, religiously observant grandmother, as her mother had left the community when she was three years old; Esty was falsely told that her mother had abandoned her and was "dead," even though her mother fought as best she could to keep Esty, failing in the end in the midst of threats of legal proceedings. Esty had a secret with her grandmother—the secret was her exquisite singing voice. Because of Hasidic prohibitions against women performing in any way, Esty's voice was not permitted to be heard. Esty made the decision to leave her newly matched husband and community, seemingly because of the loveless marriage of which the only aim was to procreate in the most dispassionate mechanistic (and painful) way. Not only was sexual intercourse terribly unpleasant for Esty, but also her husband proclaimed to her that he wanted a divorce because "something was wrong with her," and her mother-in-law made frequent unannounced visits to lecture her on the need to make her son feel like a "king" in the bedroom. Upon discovering her pregnancy (her husband did not yet know) Esty took flight to Berlin using the German citizenship her German mother had left her with (offering her a way out of the imprisonment of the community). It was with her departure from her religious community, and from the tight hold of her grandmother (her grandmother died of a heart attack on the same day Esty auditioned at a music conservatory in Berlin, symbolically freeing her from her past) that Esty could take her own life path. Esty found her voice, found her agency, found what she longed for, thereby enabling her to pursue the equal opportunity to set her direction in her life. This series is a moving narrative of a woman finding equality, the freedom to choose. In keeping with concerns of feminine equality, also new to television is a series entitled "Mrs. America," an excellent depiction of the early 1970's Second Wave feminist movement at the time of the ratification of the Equal Rights Amendment which includes portrayals of Gloria Steinem, Shirley Chrisholm, Betty Friedan, Bella Abzug, and Phyllis Schlafly. There is no coincidence that the "Mrs. America" series, speaking to the critical importance of the woman having charge of her body, is of popular interest now when Roe v. Wade is under attack. Now is a time that calls for revisiting the minds and thinking of the Second Wave feminists.

Richards offers the crucial consideration that Freudian thinking is not necessarily anti-feminist as espoused by Carolyn Heilbrun, the first woman to be tenured at Columbia University. Richards gives careful thought to enumerating the female analysts, Clara Thompson, Karen Horney, Melanie Klein and many others in all global regions who "have thought and written about the female experience in non-subservient ways" (p. 5).

In her discussion of equality, Richards likewise recognizes the place of Difference, in her consideration of the "Difference feminist" whose first interest was in what they did not want in sex, and insisting on sexual freedom. Also, Richards calls our attention to the consciousness raising groups where speaking, expressing feelings, wishes and fears—having a voice— was greatly valued.

"While Freudian thinking about the importance of feelings and the usefulness of talking about feelings had an important influence on feminism, the effect of feminism on Freudian thinking has been to re-affirm Freud's championing of equality of women and to correct Freud's idea that difference is dangerous because it can used invidiously to justify lesser opportunities for women than for men" (p. 7-8). The right to equality, Richards reminds us, particularly with regard to equal protection, must address the problems of rape, involuntary sterilization of poor women, uninvestigated side effects of birth control pills and abortion rights, the rights over decisions about one's own body.

I had the privilege and good fortune of being a member of the first graduating class of the Contemporary Freudian Society, Washington DC (then the New York Freudian Society), and seven women from my cohort upon graduating formed a study group where our first project was to write about our analytic listening. We studied as a group what was on our minds the moment before we spoke to our patients, in our effort to trace the mind of the analyst in the process of forming their interventions. We seven, presented for our first time at the IPA Congress in Barcelona in 1993—seven young non-M.D. analyst women—assigned two prominent male analyst discussants: Michael Feldman and Jorge Canestri. We found comfort and strength in the femaleness of our group. Our next study group topic took us more closely into the area of femininity and women. In our ongoing case discussions we discovered a lag between our theories and our clinical practice, where we identified an emphasis in our clinical work on penis envy as bedrock. In spite of the many then current readings on feminine development and psychology, we found that we were all too rooted in an older classical view of Freud's. It was through our discussions that we created an expansion of space in our thinking to hear more possibilities of meanings of penis envy and female body concerns and we reported on the effect of our self-study in writing and publishing of "Hearing what cannot be seen: a psychoanalytic research group's inquiry into female sexuality" (1996). This work led us to follow up with examining the further development of our listening to our female patients. Our interest was to create an open way of listening that would serve to consolidate our patients' feminine identifications and provide a forum to mediate the work on gender difference. As a group we wrote, presented at an IPA Congress, and published "The Riddle of Femininity: The interplay of primary femininity and castration complex in analytic listening" (2001). I now reflect back on our work, our female analytic training cohort joining to study and develop our feminine analyst identities, a kind of analytic consciousness-raising group, which led not only to our productive work as a group, but also to our further differentiating our analytic identities beyond our studying and writing together as a group. We each developed out of the group in different ways. The group served the effective function of the female container for the development of our separate female analyst identities.

Richards' ideas on the thought collective are quite relevant, both its power to influence and open thinking and also, if too extensive, its potential to constrain thought. Feminist rage made for furthering policy and laws that were more adequately protective of women's rights. Richards ends her paper referencing the recent film "One Child Nation" that records the experiences of a town in China during the 'one child policy' and evidencing the policy as a war on women and their bodies. Richards offers her analysis of this policy and describes it as effecting the reversal of the helpless infant position in relation to the all-powerful mother, essentially "a backlash against the newly empowered women in China" (p.10). This phenomenon is emblematic of "the masculine protest" articulated by both Adler and Freud, the deep anxiety in men about their feminine identifications, based on the dread of the male rendered helpless in the hands of women. Resulting is the fear and repudiation of passivity and femininity, often presenting as both fear and hatred of women. The hypermasculinity we bear witness to, a kind of masculine masquerade, Richards describes as "the macho independence" (p. 12). Jessica Benjamin, in her recent keynote presentation at the COWAP conference in Mexico City, conducted virtually due to Covid-19, spoke to the repudiation of femininity constituting the definition of masculinity, along with denigration and projection of all vulnerability into a feminine object. There remains the enduring belief that the powerful mother can undo masculinity. The infant is dependent on the mother for regulation, and without being able to mitigate those early effects of helplessness, the construction of masculinity aims to solve that problem. Chodorow (2003) describes the psychic 'fault lines of masculinity' as based on a dual repudiation: a) of the mother identification and b) of the identification with the little boy as opposed to the adult man. In this sense masculinity is defined by negative identifications as 'not female' and not 'a boy.' Vulnerability is split off, projected and expunged, and the sadistic paternal ideal becomes an eroticized hard masculinized object. There remains a profound fear of fragmentation and loss of self-cohesion that comes to be combined with ideas of gender. The masculine armor becomes a solution as the helpless woman represents the needs of the baby-self (Benjamin, 2020).

When Richards speaks to "Difference" and the "difference feminists," I believe she is calling attention to the idea of the recognition of the other. The resolution of the oedipal complex, the movement into the depressive position, the possibility of the creation of the triangular space, the third, creates a place of equivalency, where the other is seen in like terms, where violence and subjugation are no longer necessary, where perspective shifts. Here, creative thought becomes possible, and vulnerability is not attacked. Carol Gilligan, in her keynote plenary at the 2020 American Psychoanalytic Association meetings in New York, offered a new rich, powerful read of the Old Testament story of Eve as a story of resistance to patriarchy. Eve's opposition to Adam is actually her being the "help-mate"—"the sustainer beside him" (which is what the Hebrew actually translates, "helper by opposing"); Adam needs Eve to help him with what he cannot do on his own, that is, to help him break out of patriarchy. The recognition of the difference of the other offers the opportunity to open a third space, not one of subjugation but one, according to Benjamin (2020), of creativity, affirmation of lawfulness, and sharing witness to the trauma of violence. Women, like the original icon of Eve, can become the feminine container where mutuality is possible if difference is allowed.

I thank Richards for her meaningful contribution that is evocative of continued thought for us all.

References

Basseches, H. et.al. (1996). Hearing what cannot be seen: a psychoanalytic research group's inquiry into female sexuality. *IJP,*40 (S):511-528.

Benjamin, J. (2020). Keynote speaker. IPA Committee on Women and Psychoanalysis Conference, Mexico City. April 24-25/2020.

Chodorow, N. (2003). Hate, humiliation and masculinity, in Varvin S. and Volkan V. (eds.) *Violence or Dialogue?* London: International Psychoanalytical Association.

Ellman, P. & Goodman, N. (2017). *Finding Unconscious Fantasy in Narrative, Trauma and Body Pain: A Clinical Guide.* London: Routledge.

Freud, S. (1919). A child is being beaten, *S.E.* XVII.

_____(1923a). A seventeenth century demonological neurosis, *S.E.* XIX.

Fritsch, E. et al. (2001). The Riddle of Femininity: The interplay of primary femininity ad castration complex in analytic listening. *IJP,* 82(6): 1171-1182.

Gilligan, C. (2020). Plenary speaker. American Psychoanalytic Association Meetings New York City. February 12-16/2020.

Response to Paula Ellman

Arlene Kramer Richards

Thank you Paula. In your excellent response I see an added dimension of the feminine collective power. You are giving us a way to see the extent of change in the analytic world by showing the prestigious presentations at the International Psychoanalytical Association (IPA) and its Committee on Women (COWAP) that really institutionalize newer understandings of female development. These changes include more attention to social and political factors impacting ego development, more attention to the overt expression of inner feelings and thoughts, and more willingness to focus on individual experience as it shapes development.

COWAP was, at the time when I was North American representative, the only committee of the IPA that actually made money for the parent organization. I believe that this is still true. The meetings all over the world have been attended by many analysts, some have also been open to therapists and some to the general public as well. This makes COWAP a forum for the presentation of psychoanalytic ideas in the larger community. It attracts potential analysts and analysands. It thus brings back to the larger public ideas from the psychoanalytic thought collective. It also opens psychoanalysts to the questions, objections and confirmatory thoughts of that larger public.

Even more permanent exposure of psychoanalytic thinking about women has been effected by the many publications of papers from those meetings. The publications make available the latest ideas on the subject and keep a record of the changes over time. Because they are from all of the regions of the IPA they also allow us to compare issues affecting women in different societies. This allows us to see the commonalities and the, often vast, differences between the experiences of women in the different countries of the world.

The institutions found common ground in the local component societies of the IPA so that the American Psychoanalytic Association has also honored speakers on the subject. All of this ensures that the battles fought and won will not easily be forgotten. It means that younger women analysts will be empowered to speak out. It also means that we do not need to be thinking of ourselves as only rebels against a patriarchy, but we also can see ourselves as builders of something better.

CHAPTER 5

A Letter to My Sons, July 2020: Response to Arlene Kramer Richards' "Rage and Creativity"

Alison Feit

To my sons,

Greetings and welcome to the year 2020. As I write this, Paris is burning, or at least the Notre Dame burned about a year ago and at present there are fires of rage and outrage outside our window as thousands (including your own parents) take to the streets to protest the violence perpetrated upon brown and black bodies for so many years. Perhaps we do so fruitlessly, as our family has a long legacy of civil rights activity that leads nowhere, but we are driven with the sense that, as the Talmud says, "It is not upon you to complete the work but neither are you free to refrain from it." You have spent the last 12 weeks of the pandemic cooking and cleaning and caring for one another as I work countless crazy hours, zooming with person upon person about death after death. We have just returned from Florida where your aunt wore a mask as she buried your uncle, who was denied the Jewish burial rites he facilitated for so many others for over 40 years. Death surrounds us and suffuses our home, but I am rooted and grounded by the banal normalities of everyday life: "Can

I dye my hair?" and "How do I share a Netflix password with more than 5 people in the house?" I sit here while the earth turns upon its axis and for a time reality as I know it seems impossible, so perhaps all things are equally possible. What is reality-testing anyway when I step out in a mask and wave to my parents through a window? So hard to know where reality begins and ends when you haven't really left the house in 12 weeks and you no longer need to change out of pajama bottoms.

So, I hope as you Back-to-the-Future it to this paper, you will note that I am living in this admixture of the morbid and the mundane as I write to you. I am reading Dr. Richards' paper in which she asks herself (and I ask myself) important questions: "What do I want for the next generation of women? Do I want them to be 'strong-willed and non-conformist'? 'Rebellious'?" I think about these questions but I really don't know the answer. I am not a mother to girls; I have not been blessed with the privilege to look at the female-identified face of the next generation and to ask myself, "What would I like her to be when she grows up and how shall I do my best in order to shape it, to actualize it for her?" I have never had the pleasure of going to a mother-daughter night or brushing out long, tangly hair, and I have never needed to control my urge to comment on potentially too-tight shorts and the message they send. Instead, my life has been full of the questions of a psychoanalyst raising four boys (all born within six years of one another). The questions of my motherhood have been, "Should he take hormone shots as the doctor recommends for fear he won't grow tall enough, and what does that even mean?" "Should I admit that pregnancy and nursing are among the greatest gifts of my life and that I am saddened that he will never have the possibility to have this – what I have had with him?" "Is it odd that I consider it normal that the boys cook and clean so that I can work upstairs finishing this psychoanalytic paper?" (I hope not, or I will never get this in.) In short, guys, Dr. Richards has asked what I want for the next generation of women and I have no idea whatsoever, but I do know quite a lot about what I want for the next generation of men—for you.

Sandra Buechler (2004) asks how a clinician can evoke a range of values in his or her patient—curiosity, hope, kindness, courage, a sense of purpose, emotional balance, the ability to bear loss, and integrity—and I have asked myself the same question in raising my children. In everything I do, these are the values I hold most dear. I want you to grow up to be men who are not combative, obnoxious or dissociative when your wives, professors or daughters demand multiple things that cannot be achieved at the same time. Men who are not tripping up women in their desire to become what gives them the most pleasure and satisfaction and joy in life, but facilitating it in all its complexity.

I hope to raise men who, irrespective of their sexual orientation, see the impossible needs of their partners as their own impossible needs as well. But I especially hope that my sons who choose women as their life partners will bring these sensitivities to their most important relationships. This way, whatever the women of this generation grapple with, so will my sons, with deliberation and thoughtfulness and with kindness. I expect and hope that they will choose women in their lives who in turn will treat my sons' problems as their own. As the Babylonian Talmud says, (Ketubot 48a) "Ishto k'gufo, ba'al k'ishto", one's wife is like his own body; a husband is as one with his wife. Jewish thought views a husband and wife as one unit. As any good Interpersonalist in the spirit of H.S. Sullivan, Frieda Fromm-Reichman, and Eric Fromm knows, there is no self per se but only a self in relation to others. So the Talmud was onto something when it told its male reader that his wife was like his own self; a marital unit, whether good or bad, is a unit—that is, singular. We exist in relation to one another, either in dyadic attunement or in negation. Such is our lot in life, to live as relational beings, and our success as happy and fulfilled *individuals* only goes as far as the spontaneity, mutuality and harmonious discourse we achieve with the people we engage with.

My thoughts as to who I wanted to be in the world, and the ability to think beyond the neighborhood and environment in which I was raised, were a direct result of the creative and empathic parenting of your grandparents and were facilitated by your Dad (who is editing this paper as I write it). Unlike the subjects of Betty Friedan's work, I did not feel seduced or pushed into a role in life which did not suit me. In *The Féminine Mystique* (1963), Friedan notes the dysphoria, the baseline unhappiness of many educated women who somehow, because of unseen cultural and interpersonal forces, found themselves in the company of only their young children and a shiny new washing machine. As Dr. Richards notes, their dissatisfaction was treated as a neurosis by the psychoanalysts of the time and not as a social problem. In this sense, the psychoanalysts were co-opted by the culture to help these women become content with what to the outsider looking in were very privileged lives.

I was more fortunate. My deep and meaningful supervision and friendship with Miltiades Zaphiropoulos (1914-2015) (who had personally known the "greats" in Interpersonal Psychoanalysis and truly understood their work) introduced me to Sullivan's (1956) concept of *selective inattention,* the process of how we unconsciously shift awareness away from anxiety-laden interpersonal situations in an attempt to place out of awareness things that can cause conflict. This enables a person to free up conscious awareness for new and useful information, but also precludes us from dealing with potentially difficult interpersonal patterns. This selective inattention limits our ability to perceive the obstacles that stand between us and a fulfilled life. The women in Friedan's book would have foreseen their own unhappiness had they been able to think with "evenly hovering attention" (Freud 1909) about the conflict between their career interests and society's expectations of how they would mother. But they unconsciously shifted their awareness away from this conflict until they were living a particular sort of life that did not suit all of their various selves.

This was not my lot. I was fortunate to find a career and a life that let me "unite my avocation and my vocation," in the words of Robert Frost (1934). Psychoanalysis and feminism were a wonderful counterpart to mothering. I was lucky in that both feminist and psychoanalytic voices spoke out loud the things I might not have attended to, that might have gone unseen and unnoticed, much like the case of the women in Friedan's book. Moreover, training as an Interpersonal Psychoanalyst at the William Alanson White Institute and undergoing training analysis with a deeply empathic, rigorous and extraordinarily kind and courageous analyst gave me more of an ability to make my unconscious conscious (Freud, 1905, 1915)—a life-experience for which I am eternally grateful. This exposure to the thoughts and feelings that might have gone unnoticed, but came unbidden (Stern,1990), gave me a chance to actualize my own way of being in the world and to meet with joy and pleasure the choices I would make if given my actual druthers. Not only did feminism and psychoanalysis allow me a clear-eyed view of what lay ahead— they continue to inform my philosophy of parenting and my relationship with my sons.

So please know, my sons whom I love so much, that the most important part of what I have done on this earth is to attempt the impossible. To facilitate your becoming empathic, psychologically-minded, and thoughtful—and maybe a little less cutthroat and Uber-competitive—without diminishing your alpha-male potential. You've competed on the basketball court and the soccer field with the best of them. But I also know that when one of you falls asleep on the couch, another will drape a blanket over him, and I have witnessed the odd staring of friends as they see the unbelievable: four teenage boys curled up together on the couch like puppies. We have encouraged you to become physicians or artists or teachers or religious figures. To contribute meaningfully to the world while at the same time earning a living and being able to stand on your own two feet. We have watched you succeed academically while at the same time turning down lucrative summer job opportunities in favor of just one more year of being a counselor in camp to the kids you have been watching year after year. Some might call these feminine traits, but it seems right and just to watch as you volunteer to deliver packages to elderly people stuck at home during this damned epidemic and how you continually place the needs of others ahead of your own. Have your parents succeeded in raising you? I have no idea. What I can say is that you embody the best of human ideals, not just of masculine ideals. That we knew no other gender in raising you, so we raised you as best as we could.

So if some day you are disappointed about missing out on a promotion, remember that moving up the ladder is a wonderful thing, but not the only thing. That you once were the children who cleaned the house and made the meals (chili every damned Tuesday) and took care of the dog so your mother could work. And that she tried to make the sacrifices of your childhood worthwhile by utilizing the time you freed up for her wisely. And that you were kind, and good, and nurturant, and supportive. You were masculine but you performed "men's work" and "women's work" and whatever your mother needed. That you are essentially just wonderful human beings that have allowed me to write this letter telling you how proud I am of you and that the woman in me would not have said it for fear of the narcissistic man you would become but that the masculine in me has to call a spade a spade so I am just being honest. Please read the rest of the papers that accompany this one in the journal so that you can see how the women of the past generations have tried their hardest to create a reality that was better for both you and the women you adore. And whether you choose male or female partners, or no partners at all, you are deeply loved, irrespective of gender identification or sexual preference. Forgive us where we went wrong and do better with your own kids, should you choose to have them. Ants on the shoulders of the feminists who preceded you—my four feminist sons.

dralisonfeit@gmail.com

freudina.com

References

Babylonian Talmud, Avot 2:16.

Babylonian Talmud, Ketubot 48a.

Buechler, S. (2004). *Clinical Values: Emotions that guide psychoanalytic treatment.* The Analytic Press, Freud, S. (1900). The interpretation of dreams. Standard Edition 4-5.

Freud, S. (1909). Analysis of a Phobia in a Five-year-old Boy. *Standard Edition* 10:5-147

Freud, S. (1915). The unconscious. *Standard Edition* 14: 159-204.

Friedan, B. (1963). *The Feminine Mystique.* New York: W. W. Norton.

Frost, R. (1934). Two Tramps in Mud Time. Saturday Review of Literature', October 6, 1934,

Stern, D.B. (1990). Courting surprise: Unbidden perceptions in clinical practice. *Contemporary Psychoanalysis* 26:452–478.

Sullivan, HS. *Clinical Studies in Psychiatry.* Norton, 1956.

Response to Alison Feit

Arlene Kramer Richards

Thank you Alison for bringing in the Interpersonal psycho-analytic tradition to our discussion of how psychoanalytic thought collectives were influenced by second wave feminism. Both the European immigrants who brought Freud's drive psychology and those who were immersed in ego psychology thought a lot and based their theories on the motivating effects of the body. But the mainly American Interpersonal tradition based its theory on the mind shaped by human interaction. This made the physical differences between the sexes more relevant and more critical to the drive theorists and the ego psychologists, while it was less prominent in the thinking of the inter-personalists. So there was less change needed in inter-personalist theory than in drive or ego psychology.

Indeed, I remember reading Harry Stack Sullivan's clinical vignette of a woman with postpartum depression whom he treated by recommending that she go back to work. As it happened, the case meant a lot to me at the time because my parents, my close extended family, my neighbors and my friends all thought I was either dumb or crazy to want to go to graduate school when I had a doctor for a husband and three lovely children to take care of. I was startled to find that my analyst thought the same way. It made for some great battles.

But my husband and my son supported me in pursuing my career. My daughters were still too young to weigh in on that. And they liked that we all went to school together on the Riverside Drive bus and had lunch together and went back on the bus together,

They were not so happy on the evenings when I went back to class, but their willingness to put up with all that meant a lot.

I had grown up in a family in which my mother supported herself and my father, and helped to support my grandparents and her three younger brothers. They were recent immigrants who got to the U.S. just in time for the depression. My mother had a marketable skill. She made hats. She worked until I was born and went back to work soon after. So when I asked where my mother was, it was always at work. I always wanted to go to work. My grandfather was a laundryman, so he could and did take me to work with him. As the family changed, my father got a job, and I went to live with my parents, my mother gave up working to stay home like an American lady and play mah jong. She seemed to me to be depressed from then on. She was a perfect example of the point Betty Friedan had made. My analyst eventually put up with this genetic explanation.

It seems to me that you knew a similar culture. In addition, as you experienced Jewish culture, women were regarded as different from and equal to men. Since both you and your husband saw things that way, there was no conflict. To the extent that you were a mother of boys there was no competition with you. So there was a sense that your boys could grow up to be men who would treat women with respect.

What about boys who grow up in less ideal circumstances? Would you expect the same for them? Do you expect that of your patients? Your supervisees? Your students? How would you react to men who do not respect women? What could be done to change their attitudes? Do you have a relationship that could be thought of as a thought community that deals with such issues? Can we be that thought community?

Section I: *Essay and Discussions: Rage and Creativity*

CHAPTER 6

Freud's Rib

William Fried

Dr. Richards' paper is a concise review of the cross fertilization between feminism and psychoanalysis over a period of approximately five decades. It covers many key developments in this sometimes uneasy rapprochement, but fails to mention a concomitant circumstance that is crucial to an understanding of the events she describes. I refer to the remarkable transformation of psychoanalysis itself, from what originally was a profession practiced almost exclusively by men, to one that has become, overwhelmingly, the province of women. This change occurred in approximately the identical five decades covered by Dr. Richards' survey, impelled by several conjunctures.

Among the first was the challenge to the hegemony of Freudian theory by Melanie Klein and her followers, whose reversal of the formulation that the function of the object is to gratify the drives was momentous and revolutionary. Here was a woman proposing that what is fundamental to the psyche is the relationship, with its origins in the link between mother and child, not the reduction of organ tensions that had long been an axiom of psychoanalytic theory. Moreover, she promulgated her theory in the teeth of the most powerful possible opposition, while blithely maintaining that she was simply adhering to the essentials of Freud's thinking. An indispensable corollary of her position was that the most elemental formative experience of personality occurs in earliest infancy during the time Freud had called the oral period, and that, therefore, the crucial influence in the life of a child is its relation to its mother, and not the oedipal struggle with the father to which Freud had assigned primary importance.

Melanie Klein's first analyst was Sandor Ferenzci, whose divergent views on the seduction theory and active therapeutic methods led to a rift with Freud. Her second analyst was Karl Abraham, another intimate of Freud's who, in disagreement with the master, emphasized the pregenital stages of development as predominant. By the time Klein emigrated to London in 1926, there were several influential female members of the British Psycho-Analytical Society, including Susan Isaacs, Paula Heimann, and Joan Riviere, who supported her in the struggle against Anna Freud, regarded as the heir apparent to her father's theoretical and organizational authority. Of course, there were other woman analysts who stood by Anna Freud: for example, Kate Friedlander, Dorothy Burlingham, and Barbara Lantos. Still others, among them Sylvia Payne, Ella Freeman Sharpe and Marjorie Brierley, attempted to reconcile the competing factions.

My point, here, is that significant female representation in the British Society, no matter their allegiance to Klein or Freud, provided a climate that was highly favorable to the emergence of new and profoundly influential strains of psychoanalytic thought that reflected a uniquely feminine cast of mind. The body of theory and practice thus formed was quickly carried to other parts of the world where it took root and flourished. The singularly stringent Kleinian version of object relations theory eventually spread northward from

Argentina and other Latin American enclaves to the United States, where, softened and liberalized, it constituted a major element in the foundation of what became the Relational Turn.

Another momentous occurrence that contributed to the feminization of the psychoanalytic profession took place in November 1988, when the law suit brought against the American Psychoanalytic Association by four psychologists, alleging restraint of trade, was settled without a trial. As part of the settlement, the American conceded to psychologists and other mental health professionals the right to obtain the training necessary for their becoming psychoanalysts with full certification and unencumbered by the waivers that formerly had prevented them from practicing. The gates were thus opened for the women who, already, comprised a large majority of the mental health professions, to apply for and be accepted for training in institutes approved by the American.

Even prior to that, however, the number of woman candidates in the many non-medical psychoanalytic institutes had increased exponentially. In New York City, for example, the Institute for Psychoanalytic Training and Research had been founded in 1958 by a group of women who were psychoanalytically experienced, accomplished, and sophisticated. They were called "the Founding Mothers," only somewhat facetiously, chiefly by the men who later joined the institute. Although the William Alanson White Institute had always been somewhat receptive to woman candidates, their numbers rose significantly during the four or five decades in question, especially beginning in the mid 1950's, when it discontinued the practice of denying non-MD graduates certification as psychoanalysts and, at the same time, admitted more psychologists for training. Likewise, the Postdoctoral

Program in Psychotherapy and Psychoanalysis at New York University, established in 1961, attracted progressively greater numbers of woman candidates whose responsibilities as wives and mothers were more easily interwoven with a scheduling of courses, supervision, and clinical work that was designed with greater flexibility than those of the older, free-standing, traditional institutes.

Postdoc was also the first training establishment to bestow formal acceptance on the Relational Turn in psychoanalysis, by creating a track under that rubric, alongside its extant Freudian, Interpersonal-Humanistic, and Independent tracks. This innovation resulted, in large part, from pressure exerted by the increasing numbers of female graduates and candidates who embraced relational theory and practice as far more congenial to their perception of themselves as women and healers. Relational perspectives were also seen as consistent to a significantly high degree with the evolving spectrum of feminist thought.

The influx of women and their innovative contributions to psychoanalytic theory and practice were a necessary and welcome corrective to the phallocentric culture that had become sclerotized under Hartmanian Ego Psychology. In this context, it must be recalled that the analysts who came to the United States as refugees from the European Holocaust of World War II, fell roughly into two groups according to their political inclinations: those who leaned to the left included Otto Fenichel, Sandor Rado, and Wilhelm Reich; those of a more liberal bent were represented by the Ego-Psychological troika of Hartman, Kris, and Lowenstein, and Heinz Kohut, the originator of Self-Psychology. No matter their ideologies, however, they shared both a susceptibility to dogmatism and a support for male preeminence in their profession.

Such qualities merged with the traditional, entrenchment of male privilege, power, and control in the United States medical profession to produce a rendition of psychoanalysis that was authoritarian and dominated by men. Another force that conduced to this near monopoly was economic: psychiatrists had far lower incomes than their colleagues in other medical specialties and therefore tended to be more jealous of their status, prestige, exclusiveness and other prerogatives. Be it recalled that psychoanalysis became the dominant paradigm of psychiatry at a time when the psychiatric formulary was pitifully meager and, when this condition was changed by the discovery and use of new and more various psychotropic medications, fewer and fewer psychiatrists opted for psychoanalytic training, a circumstance that cleared opportunities for entry into the profession of unprecedented numbers of non-medical mental health professionals, most of whom, as I have already mentioned, were women.

At this point, I should like to consider some of the consequences of the current psychoanalytic incumbency of women. First, as I have already mentioned, it supplanted the classical imperative of the oedipus complex with its own canonical mother/child; self/other; breast/mouth; reciprocal gaze formulations. Second, its culturalist bias provided a refutation of Freud's popular aphorism, "Anatomy is destiny," and at the same time, struck a blow against Freud's insistence on the coeternality and dialectical confrontation between eros and death. Henceforth, the belief in the inevitability of aggression and its sinister derivatives (sadism, hostility, ruthlessness, brutality, etc.) would be challenged with the assertion that these dark entities are attributable, ultimately, to corrupt societal institutions that are amenable to remediation. It was thus conceivable that malignant forms of aggression could be eradicated and humans might treat each other with kindness and respect. In addition, the culturalist perspective lent impetus to the necessity of social justice as a concept integral to psychoanalytic theory and practice. This, it may be noted, was a direct outgrowth of the restoration of Freud's seduction theory in the form of assumptions regarding the actual occurrence of myriad forms of child abuse and traumatization.

As feminized psychoanalysis evolved its own conventions, traditions, variations and value system, it also attained its own sclerosis in the form of political correctness, suppression of some salient forms of competitiveness and aggression, intolerance of certain types and contexts of dialogue, and a mammocentric hegemony to supplant that of the phallus. Symbols of erection and all but the most mild assertions of masculine identity were disapproved of as sexist, abusive, oppressive and persecutory.

If drives are deemed primary and relationships secondary, Feminists infer that men are motivated by their impulses and are, therefore, by their very nature, ruthless, abusive, exploitive, and egocentric. By contrast they posit that the elemental considerations for women are compassion, nurturance, support, and dependence and that this makes them, by their very nature, vulnerable, generous, empathic, and altruistic. The attention Dr. Richards calls to the revision of Freud's theory of the superego "…to account for the moral integrity of women based on their concerns for human values and people's feelings…" constitutes a singular irony: the widespread application of Kleinian and Relational views afforded feminist theorists an axis on which to reverse the belief that compared to men, women were deficient in moral integrity. If relatedness is the quintessence of the feminine, and the satisfaction of drives of the masculine, the superiority of the female over the male superego is unarguable. The irony consists of the uninvited reappearance in a new guise, of Freud's maligned aphorism, "Anatomy is destiny."

In the section of her paper titled "Equality," Dr. Richards refers to so-called "women's professions," citing primary school teaching, social work, and nursing, as examples. In another irony unanticipated either by Dr. Richards or the profusion of women in current practice, psychoanalysis has itself become a women's profession.

In a significant sense, the set of events I have tried to describe has amounted to nothing less than a revolution. Comparing the current order with the structure against which it set itself, one might justifiably conclude that there are now not one, but two psychoanalyses, the earlier male, and the later female; the earlier derived from the experiences, biases, and conceptualizations of men; the later from those of women. I would add that the foundational assumptions of each theory, together with the practices to which they give rise, are valid within their own frame of reference, and juxtaposing them in tandem and opposition would certainly conduce to the comprehensive enrichment and deepening of psychoanalytic understanding.

Section I: *Essay and Discussions: Rage and Creativity*

Reply to Bill Fried

Arlene Kramer Richards

Thank you Dr. Fried for giving us another perspective on the changes in psychoanalysis that enriches our understanding of what has happened in psychoanalysis in the United States in the past 70 years. It is a good corrective to our thinking. It substitutes an economic understanding for a more narrowly historical one. In essence, it says that we are now free of psychiatric dominance in American psychoanalysis and are free to understand our patients as the products of their relationships to their parents, early caretakers, and siblings rather than embodied selves wrestling with their desires, fears, moral prohibitions and attempts to defend themselves from conflicts and inhibitions. I agree completely with your suggestion that the two ways of understanding mental pain are complementary and that it increases our therapeutic armamentarium to use both in attempts to understand our patients.

I do not completely agree with the historical account of how this came about. One important issue is that Freud and the medical men in his inner circle welcomed women from early in the 20th century. Another important point is that Karen Horney was able to challenge Freud on the issue of female sexuality and to become a leader in the psychoanalytic world early on. And a third point is that the male hegemony in psychoanalysis allowed in women physicians trained during World War II when medical schools had too few male candidates and allowed women to train as doctors. Women like the founders of IPTAR and the all women education committee of New York Psychoanalytic Institute, as well as such great contributors as Annie Reich and Frieda Fromm Reichman spoke up in favor of understanding psychopathology as including relations with early "objects." Reading case reports from the mid-century and after, there are many descriptions of relations to early caretakers and how they, and their treatment of the children they raised, influenced patients' lives. Similarly, Anna Freud's exhaustive records of the early experiences and the fantasies of patients paid much attention to the relationships with parents and caregivers.

What was new in the relational turn was initiated by men, notably Steven Mitchell and Jay Greenberg. Women were not the initiators, but were receptive to the emphasis on relations between patient and analyst as well as patient and early caregivers. So equating the female with the relational is, I think, a bit of a stretch. We have all known warm, nurturing men and many of us have known cold, demanding, authoritative women. I agree with the notion that we do not need another round of "Anatomy is destiny," but I think we do need a way of understanding the relationship between mind and body that frees us to deal with the current revolution in gender in which the binary is totally rejected and the spectrum first envisioned by Freud has come to mind-bending reality.

CHAPTER 7

Increasing psychic space to see something new, to think something new, to be part of a new thought collective: Discovering the Female Cervix

Nancy R. Goodman

A note about writing during COVID 19: The beginning of the new, the ideas that generate all that can be thought, may be when the psyche and the world are shaken up, almost destroyed. My hope is that the terrible amount of death and grief occurring now will eventually engender transformations in our psychoanalytic thinking and clinical models. It is particularly moving to be part of this group of thinkers about Arlene Kramer Richards' paper as we live through the present terrors and rage—thinking together helps create resilience.

(May 26, 2020)

It takes chutzpah to break away from a thought collective that hides from new knowledge, and then to lay down the groundwork for a new thought collective. Chutzpah is a Yiddish word defined as shameless audacity, impudence, personal conviction, and courage. The description on YouTube of a Ted Talk by Jonathan Howard (The Art of Chutzpah: what blocks us from creative thinking?) states that "...cultivating chutzpah is a powerful way to think about inner boundaries that block our creativity." In other words, one needs chutzpah to break the block, to create and to join with others in the act of creation. Gathering the strength to be creative requires being able to feel rage, to honor its psychic reality, and to have others who join in recognition of rage. Creative use of rage is the opposite of destructive envy, attack, and perversion. A block in psychoanalytic thought defeats the process of psychoanalysis that always involves layers of the mind and the unconscious fantasies that accompany all of our awareness and thinking. It seems to me that belonging with a group can augment the chutzpah of oneself and become the chutzpah of the group determined to work with the rage. Being invited to comment on Arlene Kramer Richards' paper and accepting to take part in the writing of commentaries gives me more courage to remember what has enraged me about blind spots toward women (Goodman, 2018, 2019) in society and psychoanalysis. It is important to feel rage when there is basic misunderstanding of female, the female psychic body, and the full dimensions of unconscious fantasy about female. Throughout my experience as a psychoanalyst I have been working on how to understand the way deep overwhelming traumas enter the mind as dead spaces and how discovering and creating living spaces through symbolism brings resilience to the mind (Goodman, 2012). Being part of this commentary group increases the psychic space for making symbolic and meaningful knowledge where nothingness of dead theory, in need of rage reaction, had resided. I am thankful to be part of this thought collective.

In writing about "Rage and Creativity", Arlene Kramer Richards introduces the thinking of Fleck (1979) who describes "thought style" of a particular time and place that "generates all the concepts capable of being thought" leading to a "thought collective". Arlene explains that this arises within a group of people who have contact—"through any medium" resulting in a shift of thought. She demonstrates the process by recounting the influences of second generation feminists on the field of psychoanalysis. What would Fleck say about collectives not only gathering together all of the thoughts in a community but then, (I emphasize the 'then') having these thoughts lead to new open un-defined psychic space birthing ever generating multiple thought collectives? In other words I suggest that there are continuous patterns in which a group synergistically produces new thoughts and makes new space as long as the thoughts have a sense of truth and usefulness. There is never one event, but there is a process. By defining a thought collective as a process there is a way, a method for approaching thinking about something. The drum beat heard loudly through the words of Arlene's title: "Rage and Creativity" can be felt as the floor vibrates with the sound. The transmission of anger and creativity influences my taking in and working with this paper. I see the process beginning with a disturbance causing one to fear falling through the earth until stabilization ensues.

The hypothesis I take away from Arlene Kramer Richards' paper is that rage, when able to be felt, especially with others, awakens creativity bringing about new thinking. Rage equals a felt earthquake and creativity provides recovery. Unending rage, especially when turned against oneself does not open the new possibility, so the ingredient of recognizing with others provides the useful fertility of mind.

I identify, not only that the something new takes on a powerful force for a group, but that the way to find the new is part of the potency producing the thought collective. In other words, a methodology is born and is central to the process of finding what had not previously been found. I have written about "finding" unconscious fantasy (Ellman and Goodman, 2017) and here continue to emphasize the import of "finding" in my response to Arlene's paper; that is, the finding of models of thinking that hold validity and appeal to a group that then continually expand the central compelling and useful ideas.

I have decided to concentrate on two events involving the female body that hold the feel of earthquakes taking place. Since both are centered on something opening, I use the image of the speculum as both an actual instrument and as a metaphoric psychic instrument that allows new concepts to be seen and discovered. In Latin, speculum means mirror and it is this new mirror that reflects what had previously been covered over, consciously and unconsciously.

Seeing the cervix: Consciousness raising groups and the speculum

My first association to the topic of Arlene's paper was to this Second Wave feminist revolution which took place in New Haven, Connecticut in 1971, when women (both Yale associated and community members) went to meetings where they each received a speculum in order to be able to see that inner private place—the cervix. The anger of the early 1970s led to claiming of the interior female body through collective acts of consciousness raising groups. A background of restriction, discrimination, and being treated as invisible under the elm trees of the Yale campus moved from identifications with the aggressor ("of course we will not cause trouble") to intensification of a protest movement. Women had recently been admitted to Yale College as undergraduates receiving tremendous backing by faculty. Women in the community and women who were the wives of faculty and graduate students were still considered a pariah for the campus—"you can take a class on cooking, but cannot sit in on any academics" and to those applying to the graduate programs—"stop trying to sneak through the backdoor because your husband is on the faculty".

In 1971 women who had been meeting in consciousness raising groups gathered in a large room filled with tables, a speaker's podium, and a film screen. Upon entering the room each woman was handed a plastic speculum in protective wrapping. The main speakers explained that many women were afraid to look at their genitals, so slides of photos of female genitalia were accompanying the presenter's remarks, including naming the features of the female genital. One of the topics was about the recent findings of Masters and Johnson in *Human Sexual Response and Human Sexual Inadequacy* (published in 1966 and 1970), which legitimized the equality of orgasms from intercourse and from clitoral stimulation alone. Photos of the outer genital were displayed in a slide show as the speaker told of a survey in which many women were sure there was something wrong with their genitals—labia too large, labia too small, etc. The next step was the opportunity to lie on the table with a small group of other women and to show how a speculum could be inserted and opened while holding a mirror to see one's own cervix. This passageway provides an outlet for intimate inner secretions, including menstruation, to flow out. The cervix also marks the place where sperm can enter on a quest to find the ovum and make a baby. And, of crucial importance, the cervix softens and opens (effacement) during labor providing the gateway for birthing. For most of the women in the crowded room, the name cervix was learned in relation to the pap tests done by doctors to rule out disease and through their pregnancies when doctors would pronounce that the cervix was fully dilated and pushing to deliver one's baby could take place. As women revealed this important precious tissue to view, they also admitted that pressure against the cervix provided sexual pleasure—another internal presence that may have been held secret. Not only was the rounded protruding cervix with a small hole in its middle now visible but the means for access belonged to each woman.

The medicalization of female body and the misogynistic attitude that only the physician had visual access was breaking down as women took possession of their full genital, their association with other women, and their anger. As women met, creativity was exploding, including the writing of *Our Bodies Ourselves* that grew out of 12 women meeting in a women's liberation conference in Boston in 1969 bringing about the publication in 1971. The work was to provide knowledge to women about the female body enabling women to claim their own bodies with information removing reliance on the medical establishment. The volume has continued to be updated and the original is referred to as a feminist classic. Women were overriding stereotypes with their own experiential knowledge symbolized by the page content being overlaid against a background of newsprint. A new message was born.

A statement was being made that women lived in bodies that belonged to them, including the cervix and ownership of choices around fertility, birth control and abortion. The act of possessing the means for sight arose from anger within a group thus starting the demarcation of a new thought collective. This thought collective was about women, about power, and about body and psyche. Identifications with a paternalistic social order were being questioned and replaced in concert with the political protests also taking place in New

Haven (the Bobby Seal trial vigils on the town Green and the anti-war rallies). Later other barriers came down because of the brewing of rage among psychologists and non-medical therapists to bring about a way to have psychoanalytic training which had been considered privy to only psychiatrists. The famous psychoanalytic lawsuit against the American Psychoanalytic Association's training only of psychiatrists, of which Arlene Kramer Richards was an active participant, was initiated in 1985 and settled in 1988 allowing training for many more women. Could momentum have begun because women had access to the new method of seeing inside, the speculum?

Listening to primary femininity: a psychic speculum for transforming the blind spot of bedrock

As with the women who were gaining access to seeing their inner genital, the cervix; psychoanalysis took a turn which expanded the ability to see the feminine psyche (and the male psyche) by doing away with penis envy as bedrock and expanding psychoanalytic listening to include primary femininity. The development of this line of thinking and the attraction of clinical and theoretical interest produced the ground swell of innovative thoughts defining a new thought collective in regard to the feminine. The new thought collective could now listen for depth of mind, for unconscious fantasies previously covered over, and for compromise formations involving uniquely female form of desire and fear. Bedrock was replaced; new space was opened for understanding of all minds.

Historically Freud had provided a way to deeply know the mind, including motivations, instinctual forces, and fantasy compromises involving wish, fear, and punishment. A male paradigm developed in which the boy's wish to marry mother was accompanied by fear of castration as retaliation for killing off of the father function. Freud admitted he did not understand the feminine and that it would be women who would eventually discover the mysteries of femininity. I have a vivid recollection of when I read Nancy Chodorow's Feminism and Psychoanalytic Theory (1989) and could feel more settled that I could love psychoanalysis and its exploration of deep experience and also be a feminist in approaching the blind spots embedded in psychoanalysis in regard to women. I am still thankful for her revelation of how to manage both. As I see it, the new arose from creativity ignited from rage turned into the defining of primary femininity which then became the speculum for the mind to open to new spaces and new psychoanalytic vision.

Primary femininity: the thought collective centered on the new capacity to see the body

The term 'primary femininity' came into prominence, and with writings by Stoller (1976) highlighted that the female baby/child has a sense of her femaleness and knowledge of her own body as gender specific. The girl knows she is a girl rather than a boy who has been made into a girl through castration. While patients might themselves may have such a fantasy, it is not a theoretical truth. The concept of primary femininity became central to a new thought collective publishing a body of literature centered on seeing the female body, including the psychic reality of impressions, representations, and unconscious fantasies. The new concept, like a speculum, had the ability to open new vistas in the entire field of psychoanalysis. Not only could women psychoanalysts obtain the freedom to listen to patients and their own minds in new ways, but psychoanalysis could be organized to open theory and thus increase the effectiveness of psycho-analytic listening. The model of mind without bedrock could now be seen as layered and continually in process with one fantasy defending against others and also leading to others, thus expanding the psychoanalytic clinical action of finding unconscious fantasy (Ellman and Goodman, 2017). The unconscious is iterative, not formulaic.

Equivalence of a basic fantasy could move in multiple directions and be listened for by analyst and patient. A new potent form of listening evolved within the expanding membership of a new thought collective that could make use of the idea of primary femininity to hear more truths of the female psyche.

It takes courage to corral the energy to turn rage into creativity. I discovered how tempting it is to retain allegiance to the enraging paradigm, consciously and unconsciously, when researching primary femininity with a group of colleagues. We discovered a lag between our theoretical knowledge and the clinical use of it. When the rage about being constricted in thought does not have a group, the movement forward to develop more useful thoughts can easily close down. The title of our paper, "Hearing what cannot be seen: A psychoanalytic research group's inquiry into female sexuality" (Basseches, et.al. 1996) emphasized that listening to both theory and practice could address the vacuum that is created when the old set of knowledge—the old thought collective—has fragmented under the force of the new. We identified a lag in translating the new theoretical to the clinical, which resulted in enriching our self-reflection on the vicissitudes of shifting attention needed for working with the new thought collective. I felt I had joined and helped to make the new thought collective able to use listening in a more complete way. This ongoing psychoanalytic self-reflection continued in Margarita Cereijido's edited volume, *Changing Notions of the Feminine* (2019) in which analysts reflected on the blind spots in their own thinking that have evolved into their current understanding about the feminine psyche.

Creating a literature: psychic work on the female body

I highlight here some of the authors who have provided the intellectual groundwork for the new thought collective through emphasis on the soma and psyche of the feminine. Each of these papers is meaningful to me in the way they have used the psychic speculum of listening to primary femininity—of making use of rage with creative insight. Elizabeth Mayer (1991) expanded on the work of Erikson (1950, 1964), who had observed that boys tended to make block designs of towers while girls built more encompassing circular surrounds. She devised a study asking girls to respond to drawings of blocks in various configurations, reporting that girls chose the circular block designs as their favorites. She speculated that both sexes are practicing with representations of their genitals, demonstrating that girls had a sense about their own genital formation. Galenson and Roiphe (1976) observed genital awareness in little boys and girls between the ages of 15-19 months. Kestenberg (1982) gave name to the inner-genital phase of development for little girls, adding another concept to the phase Freud called the phallic stage of development. Indeed, naming (Lerner, 1976) holds import for mentalization and the sense that one's body is worth knowing. When the mother does not name the little girl's genitals, including labia and clitoris, it can be construed as a wish for the girl to not know herself or to not have sexual awareness. Kulish (1991) addressed the absence in psychoanalytic thought of the representation of the clitoris considered dominant as a place of pleasure for girls and for many women. Holtzman and Kulish (1996) observed that until their paper, "Nevermore: The hymen and the loss of virginity," there was little attention to the hymen either in psychoanalytic clinical writings or in theory, even though first sexual intercourse was so important to women. Female psychoanalytic writers articulated that women have fears of genital harm which had been overlooked by only speaking of castration. And Kalinich (1993) demonstrated clinically that these fears and resulting compromises could be displaced to compromises around mental functions such as the woman feeling her mind is spacey or empty or damaged, representing the fantasy of her superego punishment. All of these authors have brought enlightenment to the therapeutic action of analyzing women.

I witnessed how Arlene Kramer Richards turned rage into creativity one evening at a scientific program of the newly founded Washington DC branch of the New York Freudian Society. Arlene took up a topic which had been previously ignored, namely that girls do have inner genital sensation. She used theoretical and clinical material to illustrate the main thesis of her paper that the little girl realizes the presence of her inner genital, discovering sensations through sphincter sensations of urethral and anal functions. She later published this paper with the title: The Influence of Sphincter Control and Genital Sensation on Body Image and Gender Identity in Women (1992). Her compelling paper relating the influence of sphincter control and genital sensation on psychic truths for women was greeted by many men, members of the old thought collective, with disdain. Rather than being haunted by castration anxieties, women now could be seen as in possession of their own set of genital fears, such as having the vagina closed up, or not being able to have a baby, or of being raped. These imaginings were based in the knowledge of pleasurable genital sensations, including orgasm. Arlene received a number of questions and comments directly confronting her thinking, such as, "How do you know that girls have inner sensations?"; and "Isn't this your fantasy? Girls often report thinking of themselves as boys and feeling envy and you are saying they know they are girls." Arlene listened and asked if there were other comments and thoughts; and she continued to be treated as if she were making it up. With directness and a clear voice, she said she was a woman living in a woman's body and that she listened to her female patients who talked about their bodies. She added that men were free to write about what they knew from their body sensations. To me and to others in the room this was a wonderfully earth-shaking moment—a shift in thought was now a magnet for a new thought collective. Through Arlene's proclamation, a kind of revolution was taking place. And, rage at being up against a brick wall had turned into creativity.

Mothers, Birthing, and more about being able to see the cervix

The figure of woman as mother and of becoming mother is taken up by Rosemary Balsam in the volume *Women's Bodies in Psychoanalysis* (2012). I delved into the pages of this book for this essay, discovering the body and the resistance of culture and psychoanalysis to know the full force of the pregnant female body and birthing (just an inverted male body). Having decided to write about the gathering rage of feminism in New Haven in 1971 and the (outrageous) handing out of speculums so women, with other women, could own the sight of the cervix, I called Rosemary to ask if she knew of psychoanalytic papers referring to imaginings and fantasies about the cervix. We could not think of any papers and discussed her idea that following the feminist revolution of thinking about female passion, body, and fantasy life, something closed down. There is more writing about early attachments and less writing about female erotic life and purely feminine fears about genital harm for wishes, competitions, and orgasms.

There are many ways that fear of female birthing power and orgasmic power can get erased from the mind. Why have I not interpreted the presence of cervix in the mind, a special feminine powerful passage for birth and pleasure? How often have I heard dream material about two spaces being discovered in a house and never thought of naming the cervix as a connector with almost magical features. As in my research group's discovery of a lag in turning theory into clinical interventions, I am now conscious of what I could not think and now will be able to use the cervix imagery and wonder at the compromise formations that had covered it over—the fear of having a pleasure place removed, once known. I now will be able to conceptualize interpretations and name this ever so feminine birthing place with its symbolic meanings.

Gathering around the mirror, the speculum

Concluding my associations to Arlene Kramer Richards paper, "Rage and Creativity: How Second Generation Feminist Thought Collective Influenced Psychoanalysis", I think about Nancy Chicago's *The Dinner Party* (1974) and imagine us all seated at the triangular table, each at our own vulva shaped place setting. She honored historic female figures with place settings, then commandeering friends and colleagues to help make the installation which continues to be exhibited in museums. There are 39 place settings and each place setting includes a shape of a vulva with the name of a female historic figure. As written in Wikipedia's descriptions, Nancy Chicago, described as the first feminist artist, was inspired to create her dinner party after attending a real dinner party. "The men at the table were all professors," she recalled, "and the women all had doctorates but weren't professors. The women had all the talent, and they sat there silent while the men held forth. I started thinking that women have never had a Last Supper, but they have had dinner parties." You can feel her rage and her creative force.

The Second Wave feminist rage of the 1970s led to use of a speculum for seeing within the female genital. The rage of psychoanalysts about the blind spots related to the idea of penis envy as bedrock led to use of listening to primary femininity as a psychic speculum to open the unconscious representations and fantasies about the feminine, including the genital, orgasm, and the making of babies. Many of the "new" papers focused on seeing evidence of the girl's knowledge about female body experience clarifying the presence of body representation and desire for erotic pleasure releasing theory from the idea that women must accept inferiority and adaptation to it. Naming what is being seen, that had not previously been seen, begins a possibility for further discovery able to draw together a movement, a group becoming identified with the discovery and with the discovery process. Most importantly the "new" enters thought, often with anxiety and excitement, and then can ignite a way to know more, to find more about unconscious fantasy.

Bringing the female body out of the dark continent into the light formed the thought collective that was and is listening to the full psychic experience of women. However, the dark continent ideation is appealing to those who cannot bear to use the speculum to see inner woman. The new thought collective could collapse if there is not continued courage and creative use of rage. The new thought collective receives nurturance through Arlene Kramer Richards' paper and the group that can tolerate the excitement of seeing together.

References

Balsam, R. M. (2012). *Women's Bodies in Psychoanalysis*. London: Routledge.

Basseches, H., Ellman, P., Elmendorf, S., Fritsch E., Goodman, N., Helm, F., & Rockwell, S. (1996). Hearing what cannot be seen: A psychoanalytic research group's inquiry into female sexuality. *Journal of the American Psychoanalytic Association* 44S: 511–528.

Cereijido, M. (2019). *Changing Notions of the Feminine: Confronting Psychoanalysts' Prejudices*. New York: Routledge.

Chicago, N. (1974-1979). The Dinner Party Installation.

Chodorow, N. J. (1989). *Feminism and Psychoanalytic Theory*. New Haven: Yale University Press

Ellman, P. L. & Goodman, N. R. (Eds.) (2017). *Finding Unconscious Fantasy in Narrative, Trauma, and Body Pain: A Clinical Guide*. London: Routledge.

Erikson, E. H. (1950). *Childhood and Society, Second Ed.* New York: Norton.

Erikson, E. H. (1964). The inner and the outer space: Reflections on womanhood. *Daedelus* XCII, 2: 582-606.

Fleck, L. (1979). *Genesis and Development of a Scientific Fact*. Chicago: U. Chicago Press.

Goodman, N.R. (2012). The power of Witnessing. In N R Goodman & M B Meyers (Eds). *The Power of Witnessing: Reflections, Reverberations, and Traces of the Holocaust-trauma, Psychoanalysis, and the Living Mind.* (pp. 3-26). New York: Routledge.

Goodman, N. R. (2017). The "Finding Theater": A schema for finding unconscious fantasy. In P. L. Ellman & N. R. Goodman (Eds.), *Finding Unconscious Fantasy in Narrative, Trauma, and Body Pain: A Clinical Guide* (pp. 22–34). London: Routledge.

Goodman, N. R. (2019). "Finding unconscious fantasy in the female psyche: removing the blind eye", paper at the 2019 International Psychoanalytic Association Congress in London.

Goodman, N.R. (2019). Femininity: transforming prejudices in society and in psychoanalytic thought in Cereijido, M. (ed.) *Changing Notions of the Feminine: Confronting Psychoanalysts' Prejudices.* (pp. 83-94). New York: Routledge.

Galenson, E. & Roiphe, H. (1976). Some suggested revisions concerning early female development. *Journal of the American Psychoanalytic Association* 24(Suppl.):29-57.

Kalinich, L.J. (1993). On the sense of absence: a perspective on womanly issues. *Psychoanal. Q.* 62:206-228.

Kestenberg, J. (1982) The inner-genital phaseprephallic and preoedipal. In *Early Female Development: Current Psychoanalytic Views*, ed. D. Mendell. New York: Spectrum.

Lerner, H. (1976). Parental mislabeling of female genitals as a determinant of penis envy and learning inhibitions in women. *Journal of the American Psychoanalytic Association* 24: 269-293.

Mayer, E. L. (1991). Towers and enclosed spaces: a preliminary report on gender differences in children's reactions to block structures. *Psychoanalytic Inquiry* 11: 480-510

Masters, W.H.; Johnson, V.E. (1966). *Human Sexual Response.* Toronto; New York: Bantam Books

Masters, W.H.; Johnson, V.E. (1970). *Human Sexual Inadequacy.* Toronto; New York: Bantam Books.

Kulish, N.M. (1991). The mental representation of the clitoris: the fear of female sexuality. *Psychoanalytic Inquiry* 11:511-536.

Lerner, H. (1976). Parental mislabeling of female genitals as a determinant of penis envy and learning in women. *Journal of the American Psychoanalytic Association.* 24:269-283.

Mayer, E. L. (1991). Towers and enclosed spaces: A preliminary report on gender differences in children's reactions to block structures. *Psychoanalytic Inquiry* 11: 480–510.

Richards, A. K. (1992). The influence of sphincter control and genital sensation on body image and gender identity in women. *Psychoanalytic Quarterly* 61: 331–351.

Richards, A. K. (1996). Primary femininity and female genital anxiety. *Journal of the American Psychoanalytic Association* 44: 261–282.

Stoller, R. J. (1976). Primary femininity. *Journal of the American Psychoanalytic Association* 24S: 58–78.

The Boston Women's Collective (1970). Our Bodies Ourselves: A Book by and for Women.

Section I: *Essay and Discussions: Rage and Creativity*

Response to Nancy Goodman

Arlene Kramer Richards

Thank you Nancy for getting the point of the whole discussion in such a clear-headed and personal way. One way of characterizing the issue of feminism is in terms of the Mind-Body problem. How do we know what we are? Does the body lead the mind? Or does the mind create the body image? Do minds matter absolutely? How does the body impact on the mind and how does the mind impact on the body? After reading your account of discovering your cervix, I recalled the mirror showing my vulva and thinking it awesome and wanting to celebrate it. Such experiences change the way we think.

So it appears that the mind structures the body. Descartes' view was just that: Asking the question implies the answer. Crudely put: "I think, therefore I am." An adolescent patient wrestling with his identity told me a joke. "An airline stewardess asks Descartes, 'Would you like a drink?' Descartes says: 'I don't think...' Poof. He's gone." Since empirical science has addressed this question, thinking has gone in the direction that the brain, not the mind, is what directs the body. But the mind is the workings of the brain. No brain; no mind. So we touch electrodes to parts of the brain and the mind produces memories. We induce pain in the right hand; the left side of the brain produces electrical current. We smile at a newborn infant, the part of the brain that will light up when he smiles lights up at the sight of the mother's smile.

When we look at a part of the body that produces pleasure, we feel good about ourselves. Pain, pleasure, and relatedness are all part of the function of the brain. On the other hand, we lose someone we love; tears come and fall. The brain is affected by our experience of loss. Our pity for an innocent man choked to death by police engenders rage. The rage engenders fear in politicians. And so it goes with interconnections at every level, including body, brain, mind, social interaction. Intellectual understanding and emotional meaning of events is mediated by what other people think and what other people want us to think. In this sense, science is a conversation among scientists and what we want to be true is shaped by the ideas and opinions of the scientists we respect.

What we think in psychoanalysis has undergone a profound change since the inception of second generation feminism. The conversations among feminists outside of psychoanalysis affected the conversations within our field. The experiences of our own bodies overruled the ideas of male analysts. Your profound tracing of your own experience in the process of becoming a leader in the analytic conversation, in print and in person, has led me to understand a similar process in myself and in our female analytic collective.

In this regard, the establishment of IPTAR, the Contemporary Freudian Society, analytic training centers in several cities across the country, and the formation of Division 39 of the American Psychological Association, CIPS, and other institutions for the development and refinement of psychoanalytic thinking have given our field a new vibrancy as they have established groups thinking about analysis, practicing it, and promulgating its ever-changing ideas.

CHAPTER 8

Towards a "Female Paradigm" in Psychoanalysis

Cordelia Schmidt-Hellerau

When I started my psychoanalytic training in the 1980s, psychoanalysis was still a male dominated profession. Today, when I go to psychoanalytic meetings, it is highly visible that the majority of my colleagues are women. However, the assignments of keynote speakers and panel contributors seem to continue a preference for male colleagues. Is this cultural, psychological, or merely accidental? Anyhow, 107 years after its formation the members of the IPA elected its first female president in 2017, Virginia Ungar from Buenos Aires.

I learned a lot from Arlene Kramer Richards' paper on how a Second Generation Feminist Thought Collective Influenced Psychoanalysis. Even the notion of a Feminist Thought Collective was new to me; and so was the amazing fact that it was only (or first) in psychoanalysis, that women were able to form a mutually supportive, inspiring, and enduring collective. This is good to know, because despite the lingering idea that it is the exceptional individual (man) who makes and breaks history, it is the power of collectives that decide over the endurance of conventions as well as the acceptance of innovations. To bond in collectives inherently increases the power of women, and the question is: how does their influence show and what does it achieve?

Collectives can be characterized by a particular "thought-style," they are, what Kramer Richards references with Fleck's term, "thought collectives," a notion that reminds me of Thomas Kuhn's studies on paradigms. Kuhn saw the readiness for change in purely rational terms: when a guiding scientific paradigm has grown inadequate to solve emerging problems, it will eventually be overthrown by a new paradigm, which enables better results, thus be more satisfying for the researchers, which helps them to eventually move towards working under the new paradigm. In a long-term perspective we may observe something similar in psychoanalysis: a focus-shift from Oedipus to Narcissus to Object-Relations to Container to Alpha/Beta, which is not quite as scientific and superseding as Kuhn had it, but fits the principle of building new thought collectives—commonly called psychoanalytic "schools (of thought)." These new schools, after first being exciting and attractive, tend to petrify or wilt when they defensively conserve their way of thinking by excluding "deviant" colleagues, those who think "outside the box." If feminist thought-collectives set out to open psychoanalysis towards a specifically female "thought-style" and content, we may gather that the paradigm change they achieved has at no point been an easy feat. Kramer Richards explores how feminist "thought-collectives," overcoming the barriers of prejudice, culture, convention, and competition, gained the necessary self-assertion to make meaningful change in psychoanalysis.

To my delight, Kramer Richards, a declared "equality of opportunity feminist" values, Freud's "feminist position," which feminists themselves often cast into doubt. Of course, Freud grew up in the cultural climate of Vienna's turn of the century, and he could be called a "patriarch" in his Vienna Psychoanalytic Society. But even though he was (as we all are) a child of his time, he more importantly was a proponent of the Enlightenment and as such much too interested in all aspects of the human mind to disregard women and their thinking. His letters to Martha and his daughters show a great deal of respect, curiosity, admiration, and affection. He did admit that his understanding of female sexuality hadn't gotten very far, and his normative statements about the maturity of vaginal orgasm seem to have be more a brain-child than related to his psychoanalytic explorations. But what earned him the feminists' resentment was the notion of "penis envy."

It always seemed unfortunate to me that this notion was taken by its critics as an offense to women. The painful "ugliness" of envy, and the idea that envying the penis confirmed the inferiority of the female genitals (which effectively was how this concept was used by generations of analysts) contributed to the widespread outrage it drew in feminist circles. But here is how Freud, comparing both sexes, saw it: The little boy, when he catches sight of a girl's genitals, "sees nothing or disavows what he sees" (1925, p.252), which eventually leads him to belief in the threat of castration.

"A little girl behaves differently. She makes her judgement and her decision in a flash. She has seen it, knows that she doesn't have it, and *wants to have it*." (ibid. my italics)

This immediate wish to have what another has is a totally natural urge in every child. Also, it is easy to see the penis and hard to discover and picture the hidden vagina. Nowadays, parents do a better job in explaining the visible and the invisible, which helps—but does it eliminate penis envy? Taken as a metaphor, penis envy still represents socially or culturally engraved gender norms and expectations, the very thing the feminists have been fighting against for decades. When a patient of mine complained: "Why was my brother allowed to climb a tree and I was not?" she spoke of the inequality of opportunity based on the only tangible difference between her and her brother. Needless to say, one doesn't climb a tree with the penis, but that's what the parental verdict seemed to claim. She envied him for the greater freedom and the more adventurous life he was granted. We can call this "penis envy." Envy always embraces a high valuation of something one lacks, combined with a sense of injustice. Psychoanalysis can transform neurotic impotence, helplessness, and shame that is stuck in penis envy into authentic self-confidences, pride, and goal oriented creativity—the recognition that, sure, a girl can climb a tree and much more. Thus the penis in "penis envy" is a shortcut or denominator for everything that stands in the way of realizing equal opportunity, while remaining an object of desire. Anger and rage related to penis envy express self-assertion, the energy that wants to ascertain equal opportunity. I agree with Kramer Richards that penis envy should no longer be regarded as "the bedrock of femininity," and Freud's subsequent deduction of the inferiority of the female superego even turned things on its head (if anything women tend to be more superegoish than men). But to delete the notion of "penis envy" from the psychoanalytic literature would seem to me more a conceptual loss than a win.

Fortunately, there are differences between men and women (beyond penis and vagina), the emphasis of which Kramer Richards associates to the Second Wave feminists, who focus on connectivity, "concern for the welfare and feelings of others" and the value of caretaking. The idea had to be broached that these capacities are not "girly things", that boys too need to develop concern and care for the other. But as I have elaborated elsewhere (Schmidt-Hellerau, 2006), there may be different ways and means to connect and take care. O'Connell (2005) describes how he and his wife took care of their little daughter when she stepped in a bee's nest and was stung many times: besides tending to the hurt the mother soothed her daughter's pain and anxiety by staying up with her at night and talking about all aspects of the terrifying experience, while the father started to plot and eventually executed with the little girl a plan (a "military operation") to take out the bee nest. These are two necessary and complementary ways of taking care of the child and thereby teaching her how to take care of herself. As the example shows, the maternal care was focused more on the body and the inner world of the child, while the paternal care strategized with the girl how to defend herself in the external world. Does this sound like a stone-age cross-cultural tale of women tending the hut and men hunting for food? What the example shows is a predilection, an inclination, not a limitation. Freud, distinguishing the biological and sociological differences between men and women concluded "that in human beings pure masculinity or femininity is not to be found either in a psychological or a biological sense. Every individual on the contrary displays a mixture of the character-traits belonging to his own and to the opposite sex" (1905, p. 220). Acknowledging the differences and their mixtures, Freud conceded that certain fixed gender role assignments are imposed by societies, but he suggested that in the long run they can only be maintained if they are met by some somatic compliance, an innate/biological tendency that goes along with them. Thus, the aim cannot be to deny such differences (as Kramer Richards quotes Jean Stafford: "there is nothing worse for a woman than to be deprived of her womanliness"), the aim has to be of valuing male and female qualities equally—in fact, appreciating that the one group of qualities (male or female) would fail if it were not complemented by the other. Thus if women in order to succeed would try to copy men or be even more macho than their male colleagues, they would not only discredit their womanliness, they would also devalue and forego the specific contribution they can make in any field.

As a case in point, let me add the example of my particular area of research, a revision of Freud's drive theory (Schmidt-Hellerau, 2018), namely the concepts of the death drive, aggression, and the disappearance of Freud's self-preservative drive. Retrieving and repositioning the concept of a preservative drive, I posit that humans are not only driven to have sex, they are also driven to rescue, nurture, and protect themselves as well as their objects, to connect with others in concern for their welfare and the wish to take care of them. My conceptual revision of Freud's drive theory followed rational criteria, and, I always felt, anyone could have done this work—but clearly it would have to be a woman. Because a woman has a greater awareness of and interest in the issues of self- and object-preservative needs.

Freud, the man, who started out with a self-preservative and a sexual drive, had focused most of his explorations on sexuality, and in his 1920 revision he almost dropped his self-preservative drive and left us with sexuality and aggression as the two basic drives. We could call this the male tilt of psychoanalysis. I always thought that Freud would have agreed with my resurrection and reconceptualization of his self-preservative drive and all it entailed. Still to open my colleagues to this new "female paradigm" has not been easy. That caretaking is on equal footing with lovemaking, equally valuable and necessary—and always part of it—seems to be a notion senior colleagues who grew up under Freud's male paradigm are reluctant to accept.

Change is achieved with snail's pace, as the saying goes. Slowly but surely women, once encouraged by psychoanalysis to raise their voices, have eventually made themselves heard in psychoanalysis. "Feminism has a debt to psychoanalysis, but analysis is also indebted to feminism," as Kramer Richards writes, and she adds that "rage fueled by injustice has been a spur to creativity in the analytic world." When a woman's "soft voice of reason" is ignored, rage screams, an emphasis on what she has and wants to contribute. And now and then she is heard here and there. Over time the predominantly female theme of self-and object-preservation is establishing itself in psychoanalysis. The need to take care of oneself, the other, and the environment has to be considered—pathological preoccupation / obsession with, or negligence of, preservative issues should be analyzed and worked through. It is necessary to do this within the female paradigm, on a par with, not as a fallout of the male paradigm. The perseverance of the feminist thought collective has worked the ground and opened the intellectual and emotional space in psychoanalysis to perceive and study this in new ways.

References

Freud, S. (1905). Three essays on the theory of sexuality. *SE 7*.

Freud, S. (1925). Some psychical consequences of the anatomical distinction between the sexes. *SE 19*.

O'Connell, M. (2005). *The Good Father. On Men, Masculinity and Life in the Family.* New York: Scribner.

Schmidt-Hellerau, C. (2006). Fighting with Spoons. On caretaking rivalry between mothers and daughters. *Psychoanalytic Inquiry*, 26 (1): 32-55.

Schmidt-Hellerau, C. (2018). *Driven To Survive. Selected Papers on Psychoanalysis.* New York: International Psychoanalytic Books.

Reply to Cordelia Schmidt-Hellerau

Arlene Kramer Richards

Thank you Cordelia for your great appreciation of the feminist collective and the psychoanalytic feminist collective inspired by it. All the brave women who dared to say what thy experienced in the sort of analysis that ended with an interpretation of penis envy, and then either walked out of the analysis or got married and lived happily ever after, gave voice to each other. We ended the fifty year stretch in which analysis meant insisting to the patient that penis envy was her deepest level of feeling. That view meant that women were built around a core of resentment, hatred, and, especially, envy. Even when Melanie Klein retaliated with a theory that both men and women were built around a core of envy, women were still seen as even more envious than men. Women envied the breast as men did, but they also envied the penis. That invidious view of women could only be objected to by women who were not themselves analysts or planning to become analysts or by women who were extraordinarily brave.

The view of women that sees us as caretakers of the body and the feelings is the view that encouraged women to become nurses, teachers, mothers, and social workers. As several male analysts of the 50's and 60's complained, once analytic training was open to psychologists and social workers, the field would be flooded with women. Furthermore they claimed women would lower the fees and the prestige of what they regarded as their field. And they were correct. Women have flooded the field, and fees are no longer as high as they were in those earlier times. Both of these outcomes have been, in my opinion, to the good.

Your emphasis on the instinct for survival as a female way of thinking is most interesting and is borne out by our recent experience of those countries headed by women having survived the virus better than those headed by men. Women leaders took the threat more seriously, moved faster to combat the virus, and lost a smaller percentage of their counties' population.

I am grateful for your addition of this important conceptualization of the difference between men's and women's way of thinking. I think it comes from a different value system in which women think about the consequences to others as a measure of the good while men tend to think of the moral judgements in a hierarchical system which are the highest values. This is difference feminism. But you also stress accepting that women's way of thinking is of equal value as men's and this is equality feminism. I think that both kinds of feminism are useful and both are needed if we are to have respect for one another as fellow humans. Your own example as a women who thinks like a woman and succeeds like a man is inspiring to us all.

CHAPTER 9

Feminism Revisited:
A Rejoinder to Arlene Kramer Richards'
Examination of the Impact of
Feminism on Psychoanalysis

Dorothy Evans Holmes

Richards valuably reprises the works of generations of feminist writers who, through the power of their thought collectives, have dislodged from psychoanalytic thinking organizing concepts that trapped women in "idealized unhappiness" (Schafer, 1984). Principal among such concepts is penis envy. It took the work of the writers Richards mentions, and others, to identify the odiousness of the concept and its destructiveness to women's wellbeing. So, it is refreshing to read again that it took waves of feminist writers to help psychoanalysis come closer to its ideal self: as a radical discipline that aims for progress by upsetting the status quo. Implicit in Richards' paper is the fact that it took radical women writing feminist literature, to help psychoanalysis claim more of its radical identity in its theoretical framings of what it means to be a woman.

It is instructive to know that feminist writing comes in different flavors. As Richards notes, there are the "equality" feminists, and there are the "difference" feminists. Each collective of feminists focused on critically important issues. For example, equality feminists recognized and promulgated the right of women to seek equal education and employment, irrespective of the state of the economy in terms of men returning home from wars. In this regard, it is important to note that society fabricated role definitions for women (housewife, mother, and women's professions, such as nurse and teacher) to make room for men to be men, meaning that high status jobs would be reserved for them. Psychoanalysts were in cahoots with this configuration, as Richards points out. That is, the psychology that was to be analyzed was that a woman's unhappiness was to be interpreted as her neurosis, the kernel of which was penis envy. Here is a place to make more explicit my reference above to Schafer's notion of "idealized unhappiness" in women. His 1984 paper is in fact an insufficiently heralded feminist paper. He pointed out that analysts tend to foster women's unhappiness rather than analyze it, lest a woman's fury be unleashed, which, of course, would need to enter the transference-countertransference reactions of the work, perhaps feared by the analyst and patient. Schafer makes a cogent and spirited argument that such work is necessary, of course, so that women are liberated to actualize their true selves, free of constricted and preformed, male-determined roles.

It seems to me that one potential pitfall for the equality feminist point of view is that it can be misinterpreted to mean that a woman is equal to the extent that she identifies with men. An anecdotal experience from my midcareer days makes clear that such a distortion can be put into practice. A famed surgeon in the hospital in which I worked as chief psychologist did accept women into his residency training program, but he was famous (infamous) for saying that all of the surgery residents (including the women) on his team were men. Richards alludes to this possible distortion in her reference to Heilbrun's work. This corruption of equality feminist writing perhaps hides a male point of view that women who pursue equal opportunity are really engaged in penis envy.

What is critical to the "Difference" feminist point of view? I think it is to delink authenticity as a woman from all fixed gender-based notions such as "vaginal orgasm" or the assumed high importance of sexual experience in the hierarchy of a woman's life experiences. In this regard, I found myself curious about Richards' assertion that some feminists devalued sex (p. 8). Did they devalue sex, or did they devalue the fixed and high importance placed on sex in male-dominated points of view? Certainly, a modern psychoanalytic point of view would require the psychoanalyst to be openly curious about the value of sex in each person's identity, a point of view held by Freud, at least in his consideration of sexuality. His point was that analysis helps one to determine the correct psychical weight to be attached to one's sexual strivings—"correct" to be delineated in terms of each person's psyche and aspirations, not in terms of some pre-determined notion.

"Equality" and "difference" feminists can be caricatured, the former as blindly pursuing being just like men, the latter as blindly eschewing and hating men. Neither is true in relation to the compelling bodies of literature summarized by Richards, but they are pitfalls that may be seized upon by anti-feminists or those fearful of powerful women. Here again I will reference Schafer's seminal paper. He opined that analysts tended not to take up women's unhappiness in terms of its sexist and misogynistic determinants, lest intense anger be unleashed that will lead to lively critiques of self, the analyst, and oppressive society.

I would like to discuss the intense anger that may underlie women's unhappiness in terms of the first word in the title to Richards' paper, namely, "rage." Whose rage, I ask? My own point of view is that we need another way of understanding the creative and systematic ways in which feminists have caused psychoanalysts to have to redo our conceptual bases for looking at women and gender development. "Rage" is disorganized and destructive. Not that feminists cannot or should not feel that way, but our debt to them is that they, perhaps through the organizing effects of their collectives, developed enough scaffolding to hold the rage and to convert it to an organized, creative energy.

I think the rage that needs to attract our attention is the rage of men in society who cannot abide the power of women. It is still a force among us in this very time, and in high places in government. The feminist fight against that rage is operationalized in the "Me Too" movement. There will always be a need for feminist writers and their impact on social institutions including, but not limited to, psychoanalysis, because we are haunted by ghosts. The ghost of the base and concrete meaning of "all men are created equal" in the Declaration of Independence is a ghost that still haunts us, for example. That is, we are still haunted by the disavowed governing notion that equality, power, rights, privileges and unbridled happiness should reside in and be reserved for and controlled by men. Elizabeth Janeway, a 1970's feminist, in her book, "Man's World; Woman's Place" (1971), cogently opined about men's reaction in response to women who seek to have increased presence in positions of dominance. She said (p. 125), that "the reaction of men would be to increase the dominance they wield already until their power grows so great they are answerable to no one. The shadow role of the dominant male is ogre."

As psychoanalysts we need to face this deep psychological issue. Feminist critiques of psychoanalysis are helpful in keeping us as a discipline from being contaminated by the baser aspects of our founding societal precepts. Clearly, we have been so affected, as in embracing concepts like penis envy and clinging to them too long. We are not permanently immune from such influences, to wit, the value of reviews such as the one offered by Richards. However, I say that we, psychoanalysts, need to self-engage our responsibilities to conceptualize the underlying rage of men towards women, and to analyze it in our male patients, and the effects in our female patients, and to offer expert psychoanalytic opinion when we see its effects in society. In that regard, I was intrigued by Richards' references to the complexities of family life in Appalachia after the coal industry imploded there. Clearly, the psychological infrastructure of many men in that region is worthy of reflection. While some men have ably adapted to housefather roles efficaciously and productively, others resent the roles and are deeply unhappy. In part, does this mimic what happened to women when we felt trapped at home? When man or woman cannot exercise his or her true calling, misery is an outcome, and poor adaptations such as drug addiction, an affliction that permeates Appalachia, can happen. There is a darker possibility here, as well. To what extent are some Appalachian men afflicted with the view that just because they are men they, not women, are entitled to be the powerful ones? To what extent is their helplessness and haplessness to be housefathers, and their resentments of their more efficacious wives, some of whom returned to school and lifted themselves out of abject poverty, a smoldering rage that they act out in passive-aggressiveness or try to quell with drug addiction?

So, feminists continue to write. May there be more of the

likes of Arlene Kramer Richards to keep us focused on, and up to date about, such worthy contributions. Have we as psychoanalysts gained enough from feminism to stand on more solid ground in our analytic thinking, writing, scholarship and clinical work? What is that solid ground? For me it is wide openness to and curiosity about a woman being and becoming who she is, self-determinedly free of internal and external pressure and predetermination. This is easier said than done since as analysts we are part of the larger social order that is persistently tempted by and falls into significant prejudices and "isms" that limit our better selves. Feminist thought collectives have often given feminist points of view the heft they have needed to keep making their points whenever society needs them. I wonder if even they are strained to the hilt, as they continue to have constructive impact, as may be reflected in Richards' comments about third wave feminists whose tools are "anger, profanity, ambition, power, violence" (p. 15)? Is this approach an index of how desperate the struggle is against patriarchy and its weapons of sexism and misogyny? How much is this third wave an identification with the aggressor? Is it a byproduct of patriarchy's capability to ensnare its targets (including feminists) in its web of hatred, forcing them to use the destructive tools of the patriarchal ogres? A case in point: In the much heralded novel, *Where the Crawdads Sing* (Owens, 2018), the heroine, Kya (aka "Swamp Girl"), is rejected (abandoned) by her whole family and by the community on the outskirts of which she lived. Kya became a brilliant, wildlife expert, entirely without formal schooling. In that sense, and in being able to sustain a love relationship with the man who had taught her to read in her youth, she triumphed. She was able to accept him as a life partner, even though he, too, had abandoned her when he could not reconcile his love for her with his own ambitions;

but he came back to her, worked assiduously to regain her trust, and they formed a lasting love relationship. Even with these triumphs in her life, the early and chronic mistreatments that the "Swamp Girl" had endured took their toll. She came to stand trial for murder. As her lawyer said to the jury (p. 340):

> But ladies and gentlemen, did we exclude Miss Clark because she was different, or was she different because we excluded her?... If we had fed, clothed, and loved her, invited her into our churches and homes, we wouldn't be prejudiced against her. And I believe she would not be sitting here today accused of a crime.

The crime of patriarchy that has incited feminist writing is its insistent and persistent determination, by any means necessary, including violent means, to undermine women, to take from us our powers to define ourselves and to live fruitfully based on those powers. I am concerned about a trend in writing that would have us join the perpetrators in the use of their tools, lest they win still again. One might argue that "the Swamp Girl," Kya, was a third wave feminist, one who ultimately killed predation by killing her predator. There is a further argument to be made that her crime was an effective solution for her, but it did not resolve the structural societal hatred of, and rage towards, women. Feminist writing that attacks structural elements in society at large and in psychoanalysis must continue. In the fight against the embedded societal and intrapsychic forces that hold women back, feminist writings of all eras are a powerful tool that can undo some damaging aspects of patriarchy in psychoanalysis, such as the insidious use of the concept of penis envy to define the essence of women's strivings. Such writings are a necessary component of the armamentarium of tools necessary to advance women's rights. My own preference is to combine those writings with political action, rather than turning to violence, to contain the inevitable pushback against such rights (e.g., the Feminist movement of the 1960's, Roe v. Wade, 1973, and the current Me Too Movement).

References

Janeway, E. (1971). *Man's World, Woman's Place.* New York: Dell Publishers.

Owens, D. (2018). *Where the Crawdads Sing.* G. P. Putnam's Sons.

Schafer, R. (1984). The pursuit of failure and the idealization of unhappiness. *American Psychologist.* 39: pp. 398-405.

Response to Dorothy Evans Holmes

Arlene Kramer Richards

Having the intellectual heft and perspective that Dorothy Evans Holmes adds to our discussion is a great honor. Thank you Dorothy. She contributes a sense of the desperate and often violent defense of male feelings of power that leads to devaluation of women, women's feelings, and women's contributions to knowledge. Having someone to feel better than and superior to is so valuable to many, if not all, people that we all find the flaws in others that we reject in ourselves. If we feel weak, they are the weaker ones, if we feel dumb, they are dumber, and if we fear our own aggressive wishes, they are the provocateurs who unleash aggression.

Dorothy's deep understanding of the novel *Where The Crawdads Sing* speaks to her understanding of the rejection of the victim. In order to relieve our guilt at victimizing we need to think of those we hurt as not deserving our sympathy or help. We need to think of them as less human than we are and less deserving of our consideration.

I too loved that novel especially because the victim was rejected and deserted by her own family first. That made her unable to trust the few people who wanted to help her. Her bitter disappointment by a man who seemed to love her led to her killing him. And, I believe, that it was only after she deliberately murdered him that she could free herself of distrust enough to love someone else. The man she loved and married had also disappointed her, but he had not only taught her to read, he also taught her to value herself by respecting her scientific achievement. It was the respect that, I believe, enabled her to go on with her life. The wonderful achievement led her to accept the respect of others, to trust and to nurture. In this way the novel depicted the change in the coal miners wives when they became able to be the breadwinners in their families.

Why are women more resilient in their self-image than men? Why do men need to devalue women? I think that psychoanalytic theory has a potential answer. The first person a baby attached to is almost always the mother or a female mother substitute. The mother has all the power. A girl can identify with this powerful mother. As he grows up, a boy must dis-identify with her in order to assert his masculinity. I think this is true in all societies we know of and that it may account for the almost universal devaluation of the feminine. For me, the riddle is why we women put up with it.

Here Janeway's assertion that men's response to feminine rage must be increased push for dominance, intensified attempts to devalue and denigrate women who stand up for ourselves and who make it clear that we want to be heard, listened to and responded to as people who are equally interesting and from whom others can learn. Dorothy has given us an example of the voice of a woman worth listening to and learning from.

CHAPTER 10

Affirming the Self Across Divisions of Gender and Race: Response to Arlene Kramer Richards' Paper, "Rage and Creativity.."

Lee Jenkins

I am an African American man who has been the beneficiary of a middle-class upbringing, emphasizing the reality of aspiration and accomplishment, as seen and demonstrated in family members, peers and leaders who shared similar impediments as a consequence of their racial identity. The idea that one could achieve something in the world was taken for granted, in my environment, in spite of the omnipresent social and legal obstacles confronting me, the racism that consigned me to a second-class citizenship, the racially assigned place for me as an inferior lacking intellectual capacity, refinement and discriminating abilities to think and function as an equal among whites.

There has always been a struggle in the mind, at whatever level of intensity or depth, between the right to self-assertion and fulfillment, and all the forces, internal and external, militating against such self-realization. Internal constraints are the ones confronting everyone as a result of the vicissitudes of their upbringing: internalized conceptions of unworthiness (for me exacerbated by racist enforcements); the way that adaptation to the needs of early love objects laid down notions of dependence or narcissistic defensiveness; the way the interactions of these factors promoted fears of competence and adequacy.

One can have been loved and accepted, for the most part, and act in accordance with such an inheritance, or one can have learned to basically be fearful, defiant, depressed, or angry, basically distrusting of the motives or sincerity of others. Learning to trust and have empathic connections with others might be a life-long effort. When developmental experiences such as these are combined with the legacy of racist denial of the worth or even humanity of a black person, life can be a difficult or agonizing thing, at the same time that one keeps trying to meet the inner spiritual imperative to embrace self-acceptance, self-adequacy, dare we even call it self-love— or at least a sense of the need to continue to endure, live, and, perhaps, one day to prevail.

Arlene Kramer Richards' penetrating, thought-provoking essay—"Rage and Creativity: How Second Generation Feminist Thought Collective Influenced Psychoanalysis"— brought into focus for me some of the similarities and contrasts of the struggle for women's liberation and that of people of color. It is a huge, fascinating topic. What I want to reflect on here is the unusual subject of some of the ways the struggle for liberation of white women and black men intersect.

Psychoanalysis always appealed to me as a discipline that had the greatest depth in exploring the psychological functioning of the mind. This was of particular interest to me because of the mental disorder in my family (my father drank and my mother had schizophrenia). They were wounded in so many ways, yet I admired and looked up to them. My father was a contractor who built houses (our own two-story house an example) and made fine furniture. When he be-came ill with a respiratory disorder, he entered the business world, eventually becoming district manager of an insur-ance company. My mother was a primary school teacher. She struggled with her mental illness, afflicted yet incredibly functional, with indefatigable energy and an independence of spirit. Her family were successful farmers on a reputed 100 acres given the family by their slave owners, with whom they had interbred. (They had skirmishes with the Ku Klux Klan, who wanted to suppress their self-sufficiency.) My mother was the youngest child of eight and the first one to graduate from college and do graduate work. My father's family was academically accomplished, with a school principal and col-lege professor. I grew up near the campus of Florida A. and M. University, in Tallahassee, Florida, the state Capitol, ben-efiting from the progressive cultural and social uplift of that environment.

As can so easily happen, you can be an adult before a full realization sets in of the psychic burden you're carrying and the need to explore or address it. This led to my becoming a psychoanalyst, after receiving the Ph.D. degree in English and Comparative Literature from Columbia. Just as white women have had to assume their place in the hierarchy of white male dominance, so have black men and women. Each has had to deal with intrusive and limiting conceptions of their nature and place in life. In her extraordinary study, *Caste* (2020), Isabel Wilkerson, in discussing the hierarchy of caste des-ignations, lists this category among others: "*Marginalized people* in addition to, or instead of, women of any race, or minorities of any kind" (p. 29).

Psychoanalysis, a discipline that purported to under-stand the operation of the human psyche, and the nature of intrapsychic and psycho-social interactions, did not always view women or blacks with clarity or accuracy with regard to conceptions of their biological or social difference from white men. Constraining or belittling factors were always present regarding how these two groups were viewed. Arlene Richards forcefully shows how women in psychoanalysis have brought about changes in the discipline that are more humane in the conceptions of what men and women have in common and how they differ. This was brought about through the contributions of female thinkers theorizing on their own and protesting distorted ideas about women's functioning—as in the debunking of the idea of penis envy and in a reconsideration of the superego "to account for the moral integrity of women based on their concern for human values and people's feelings..." (Richards, A., p. 19). This seems to me an extraordinary contribution, of immense proportions, affirming the humanity shared by both men and women, beyond conventional notions of gender roles, that seems to have been so incredibly overlooked.

Trying to be a proponent of one's own selfhood and protesting others' limiting conceptions of oneself have always been concerns of black people who have been subject to such inhumane treatment and who are highly sensitive to the absence of empathic black/white interactions in everyday life. The Rage and Creativity that are being expressed in today's protests against racial injustice highlight the many ways that inhumane treatment seems a common feature of the status quo.

Psychoanalytic talking about fears and wishes rather than the suppressing of them is one of the great therapeutic innovations of psychoanalysis. The statement, "rape is the female fear equivalent to male castration fear" (p. 19), seems completely accurate to me. A black man would expand that to the fear of lynching, the ultimate castration, literally or metaphorically carried out. For white and black women and the black man, it would be the ultimate silencing, the effect of the internalized prohibition against self-assertion and the assuming of a self-respecting command of oneself. In spite of being looked down on and castigated, black women have been able to announce more of their rage and engage in insubordinate acts, as is recognized in the stereotype of the Angry Black Woman.

The white woman may not be interested in asserting herself in terms only recognized as similar to what men do; she may want to abandon the idea that assertion can only be male-like and not a natural expression of psychic female forcefulness that would be a female prerogative that is not bound by patriarchal notions of assertiveness. I think a similar position is true of black women.

Black men might also be struggling to acquire a natural assertiveness freed of the defensive need to prove themselves against the white denial of their manhood and competency. This mutual struggle may be involved in the sometimes muted attraction white women and black men can have for each other, for good and ill: the desire of a white woman to dominate a man; or have a man to whom she can narcissistically subject herself but still feel superior to as a member of the dominant group; or, on the contrary, cast off the shackles of white male patriarchy and feel free to make not a defiant choice but one consistent with the prerogatives of her own choosing.

For the black man, the situation might be to make the choice of a white woman not simply to defy the prohibition against doing so, or elevate his self-esteem, claiming for himself the privileges of white male authority by appropriating for himself the prized white female; but, rather, to be free enough in his own conscious mind to claim the right to choose a woman of his own desire. This assumes, of course, that *any* choice we make is an interaction between conscious and unconscious imperatives, compensatory urges, realistic assessments which, in the end, make or do not make for a successful union.

To dramatize some of the ideas I'm considering, I have enclosed a section from my novel, *Right of Passage* (2018), which presents a scene showing the romantic involvement of a black man and white woman. They are vacationing on Martha's Vineyard and have arrived at a secluded stretch of beach:

"'I always wanted to do this,' she said....She took off her clothes and walked nude into the water. 'Aren't you coming?' I didn't reply. I looked back up the road and could see our car, waiting, its two headlamps like eyes observing us. I watched her back and rumpled thighs, the flesh of which rippled as she walked. Granules of sand adhered to her skin, giving the appearance of a fine satin garment. I thought how the merest stitch of clothing made one clothed, compared to its absence altogether. She sat still in the water, like an idol, almost as if she were at prayer, giving the impression of an indescribable aloneness, nothing in it of the serenity, for instance, of a meditative yoga pose. To me there was also in it something of a sadness, a need...

"I didn't want to join her. It answered no need in me... and I thought that one reason she was able to do it was that she was with me, empowered by whatever it was I represented. I, however, didn't want it thought that there was something about myself that I wished to reveal—some statement I wished to make—that could only be made through the public exposure of my body. The impulse to do so seemed trivial to me, unless it were a case in which you were naturally called upon to be naked, whereas she seemed most concerned about providing for herself the experience of having done so, in the absence of which there could be no substitute. She seemed to want to prove to herself the right to be able to do so. I didn't feel that you ought to have personally felt any constraint regarding doing so in the first place. But why not just get naked for the hell of it because she wanted me to? Then why wear any clothes at all in public if that turned you on? Yet I was the one who went naked in our apartment and walked past windows, and even looked out of them, something she would never do. The thoughts keep pressing in on me. Where else would it have been appropriate to be naked, if not at a beach? But for her was this so because she was with me, the dark-skinned nature boy, the naked one? If this empowered her, why couldn't it empower me? And wasn't there for me something empowering about her being white? A difference of the drawing room or the jungle. What did I imagine I was doing, eating this vanilla Swiss almond? It certainly wasn't chocolate fudge! And liking it wasn't the same as accepting it.

I sat down in the sand with an image of the scene, a tableau, the sight of which hurt and oppressed me. As I watched her, she rose from her reverie and emerged strong and dripping from the sea. She approached me with a smile but also a queer luminosity, a certain triumph of resolve that seemed to focus on me. It seemed to me she wished to convey a sense of herself as carrying a power greater than my own, a will both to honor and subdue the opposing male in me, a side of her I had not seen before. She came to me, kneeled, and reclined, with me, on the sand in a motion that seemed to compel. I didn't like the chill of her body, its wet, gritty feel. The strength of her resolve seemed to clarify the need for my resistance, and so I held her, by force, in an embattled embrace, until her own struggling was stilled. I held her this way until my grip was relaxed, but neither of us disengaged from the other, holding on to something still…

"'Is this what we want?' I said, with effort.

"Her eyes were closed, as if she were wondering, or sighing.

"There had been something in it of everything: man against woman, boy against girl, black against white, Jew against Gentile, male against female, your discrete separate inexorable uncompromising self in opposition to mine. *There* was something truly overly-determined. We got up and went back to the car, as if nothing had happened, not being able to say what had happened, or what it meant. By the time we reached the ferry we had gained composure.

"'That was interesting!' she said. 'I don't know what came over me. I wanted to wipe you out.'

" 'I know,' I said.

"'I didn't think you'd resist.'

" 'Did I have a choice?'

" 'There's a grievance in women,' she said.

" 'To be on top,' I said.

" 'That's a man's way of saying it.'

" 'Of things,' I said. She just continued to look at me, saying nothing.

"Then she said, 'Not to be hindered.'

" 'Yes,' I said. 'Respected, wanted for yourself only. Maybe that's a black's way of saying it.'

" 'That's what women used to say to men.'

" 'Used to?'

" 'But you're not a woman.'

" 'You're not a man.'

" 'I *am* a white female. Doesn't that factor in? Why must it always be something bad?'

" 'History doesn't stop just because we want it to.'

" 'Then we have to continue to write it.' I didn't have anything to say to that. Soon we were in the car again and on our way back to Manhattan" (pp. 283-286).

References

Jenkins, L. *Right of Passage.* (2018). London: Sphinxbooks.co.uk

Wilkerson, Isabel. *Caste.* (2020). New York: Random House

Section I: *Essay and Discussions: Rage and Creativity*

Response to Lee Jenkins

Arlene Kramer Richards

Thank you for bringing up an important issue. I think that racism and anti-feminism are similar in important ways. Both define an other person as "other". They both devalue the "other". And they both engender feelings of low self worth in the "other". So both need to be countered with the concept of humanness.

One way of countering the devaluation is to define one's self as a member of a group all of whose members value each other. Taken to its logical conclusion, such a group is sexist or racist itself. It accepts the definition as other, it even defends its borders while insisting that the group itself define its name, its membership requirements and its code of conduct. I encountered this when the Black Power movement rid itself of white collaborators in the civil rights movement. It also happened when some feminists insisted that only lesbians could be totally loyal to feminist goals. The separatist and self definition requirement that black people reject white people and that feminists reject men's led and still leads to an impoverishment of the humanity of those who reject. I believe that this is just as true of the formerly discriminated against as it is of the dominant power groups.

In both of these instances friendships and love relationships with those outside the group are devalued or even forbidden. The individual's choices are eliminated and the group becomes dominated by the biggest bullies in it. An unfortunate example is the current political scene in the United States. Separatists of all stripes have empowered the biggest bully. We need to recognize the right of each human to have her own mind, choose her own way of life as long as it does not harm others, and pursue her own goals.

So choosing to belong to a collective that shares ideas and values has to be balanced by asserting one's own selfhood in all of its complexity. I think that your beautiful statement of this in the beach scene from your novel moved me so much because you located it in nature, in the human body, and in the interplay between the observer and the observed, the actor and the narrator, and the tension between love and self preservation. Thank you for all of that.

CHAPTER 11

A Discussion Prompted by Arlene Kramer Richards' "Rage and Creativity: How Second Generation Feminist Thought Collective Influenced Psychoanalysis"

Kimberly Kleinman

Richards describes the "Rage and Creativity" that created the space to think about how genital differences, specifically the female experience of her gender, are conceptualized psychoanalytically. She begins with pointing out the rarity of a female thought collective in science, and then traces the steps that led to a mutual influence, a thought collective between feminists and psychoanalysts. She describes how the formation of a feminist thought collective created a productive change in feminist thought and also in psychoanalysis. The ultimate result of this process was the abandonment of penis envy as bedrock within the psychoanalytic thought collective as a whole. The paper inspired me to think, what else? What are other avenues where a mutual influence would be beneficial?

Recently I have been reading books and watching shows that depict women's lives in China, India, Korea, and the Satmar of Williamsburg, Brooklyn. What is clear is how ubiquitous it has been around the world that a woman is expected to leave her family, and to live with her in-laws where she is powerless and isolated. If she does not provide the family with a baby, she has no value. Even if she is horribly abused by her in-laws or husband, if she tries to return to where she lived before she married, she is turned away by her family of origin. Were Chinese women's feet bound to make running away close to impossible? Although modern marriage has provided alternate patterns for relationships and parenting, it is still an institution rife with difficulties. The primary form of marriage created a precarious situation for women, one that would not meet the standard of livability as Judith Butler defines it. Modern marriage continues to present a challenge to flourishing.

> Livability operates as a theoretical tool to illustrate that we cannot take the concept of the "human" or the idea of human life for granted, to do so is to fail to think critically and ethically about the consequential ways in which the human is produced, reproduced and deproduced in contexts of precarity, power and the ever present possibility of unlivable life. (McNeilly)

There are many theories about what conditions are needed to allow people to flourish together without the tyranny of being oppressed or being the oppressor. These include sexual liberation, freedom from pregnancy, ability to make a living, intellectual freedom, as well as controlling the means of production. What I propose is that we haven't thoroughly thought through the psychoanalytic conflicts and social controls around the means of reproduction.

There have been discussions about how women can be oppressed by pregnancy, childbirth and childcare. Women who have sex outside of marriage suffer societal rejection or are killed, honor killings being an example of that. There is an obvious link between these practices and sexual repression. Much has been written about how sexuality and pregnancy are regulated by the patriarchal system. Freud emphasized the detrimental effects of sexual repression on our psyche, bringing about a striving towards sexual liberation. Early psychoanalysis seemed to assert that women and men need orgasms to be free.

The dystopian novel, *The Handmaids Tale*, by Margaret Atwood, portrays the objectified woman as a childbearer rather than prostitute. We are familiar with a whore/Madonna split in culture. Atwood's story portrays a rare configuration that emphasizes pregnancy under control, which of course includes controls on sexual expression. Compare the prostitute with the handmaid. The prostitute's purpose is to meet the sexual needs of men. The handmaid's purpose is to meet the procreation needs of a specific man to whom they belong. What can this story tell us about the psychological and socio-political position of pregnancy? What if we focus on the control of pregnancy, if we think about it as the ownership of pregnancy and children as a frame for understanding the repression of women and children?

Early psychoanalysis described childhood sexuality. The buildup and release of tension was emphasized. But what about the reproductive function of our bodies and how it is registered in the mind of the child? As a child analyst I am constantly reminded of the intense curiosity children have around the question of where babies come from. Freud had children, he must have had to field questions from his boys and his girls. Why could he see that girls were fascinated by the penis, but he had a blind spot for the universal fascination with and envy of the pregnant belly? There is ample evidence of male envy of childbearing, starting with the fact that the leading cause of death for pregnant women is homicide.

I think it would be interesting to take a wider angle look at the female body, the pregnant body and reproduction. Richards (1992) wrote about a gender identity that originates from the girl's experience of her own body, not in contrast to the boy's body. Balsam (2003) writes about the lack of theory about the pregnant body. Why did it take so long to see this?

The Venus of Hohle Fels (Paleolithic Era, 40,000 and 35,000 years ago) is currently considered to be the oldest figurine that represents a human. An internet search for Venus figurines will demonstrate that there have been multiple figures found that are representations of similar round bellied full breasted woman. They look like they are pregnant or have been pregnant multiple times. Venus of Willendorf is another well-known example. We think these figurines were representations of goddesses and may have been worshipped. They could have been early pornography, dolls, or talismans to bring fertility. As psychoanalysts we can say that the pregnant female body was on the minds of the sculptors. These figures seem to me to convey power. I contrast them with current images of women like the Barbie doll, or the fashion model where the female body is represented absent of any sign of fecundity and seem to me to be as reduced and contained as a bound foot.

The Adam and Eve story is relatively recent in comparison with the paleolithic female figurines. What is the purpose of Eve being created from Adam's rib? There are of course many explanations given by religious scholars. In the spirit of multiple determination, could one reason for this be that this a male appropriation of birth? Could this be seen as men owning the first human birth, and women then take over that function in a disgraced state and in sorrow?

Richards mentions the 2019 documentary *One Child Nation*. The film, by Nanfu Wang and Jialing Zhang, details the implementation and impact of the one child policy. "The policy was a war on women, women's bodies, and, in particular against women's fertile bodies. It was a war against mothers and potential mothers." One of the filmmakers asks her grandfather why, in 2019, sons are still preferred. He tells her that grandsons stay in the family, granddaughters leave. This was a typical sentiment in old China, and apparently it persists in the countryside amongst the older generation. Although this sentiment is not consciously encouraged at in the present era, what are the generational sequelae of this practice? The grandfather is described preventing himself from getting attached to a girl grandchild, not because she has no value, but because she will leave the family. If the entire family resists getting attached to the girl, how does this ripple through the family of origin and family of procreation psychologically?

Richards' depiction of the coal miner's dilemma highlights that the gender issues are deeply woven into the psyche and society. When Mr. Rose says: "The way of life is changing so bad," he grew quiet. "You'll get overwhelmed if you think about it too hard."

Richards brings up another avenue to explore. She states, "A very important effect of feminist thinking has been in the area of understanding the importance, value, and potential of parenting so that the old idea that only mothers can be caregivers has been deleted from Freudian thought." This is so important. The idea that caring for a child is a gendered activity is unnecessary and has created havoc.

> Parenthood is a basic function, which includes the so-called maternal and paternal function. Typically, the father is thought of as the provider of a paternal function or thirdness, and the mother is thought of as providing support. In order to refrain from biological gender designations, I refer to these functions as support and thirdness, respectively... These functions can be staggered, shared or fixed. (Rotenberg, E., p. 107)

If caring for a child is feminine, it will be devalued. If caring for a child is feminine and devalued, many men will either feel awkward about caring for their children or they simply won't do it. The child of same sex parents adores his parents only to find that society devalues his two Moms or devalues the parenting her two Dads provided her. This is all to the detriment of the child who longs for love from both parents.

Developmentally, both boys and girls have fantasies of the fecal baby. If this fantasy persists into adulthood it bodes poorly for the actual babies born to the people who think they are crap. Entering a grownup world where gender roles involve becoming the oppressed or the oppressor would certainly create difficulties in creating a reality-based understanding of one's body and therefore one's gender. Patriarchal control of women and children is a dominant contributing factor creating the repetitive expression of misogyny and childism, generation after generation. As psychoanalysts we understand that these generational patterns cannot be eradicated through conscious decision making. They have to be changed through a working through process that involves a constant recognition of blind spots. Perhaps Foucault's concepts of biopower, where he discusses how people are organized around creating order around biological processes, including reproduction, will help us continue to think creatively and to employ our rage to empower continued change.

References

Balsam, R. (2003). The Vanished Pregnant Body in Psychoanalytic Female Developmental Theory. *Journal of the American Psychoanalytic Association*, 51(4):1153–1179.

Richards, A (1992). The Influence of Sphincter Control and Genital Sensation on Body Image and Gender Identity in Women. *Psychoanalytic Quarterly*, 61:331–351.

Michel Foucault Biopolitics and Biopower, by Rachel Adams

https://criticallegalthinking.com/2017/05/10/ michel-foucault-biopolitics-biopower/

Livability: Notes on the Thought of Judith Butler, by Kathryn McNeilly https://criticallegalthinking.com/2016/05/26/livability-judith-butler/

Rotenberg, Eva. (2017). 'The True Self Parental Function,' the Basis of Ego Integration. In Seitler, B. Kleinman, K. (ed.), *Essays from Cradle to Couch in Honor of the Psychoanalytic Developmental Psychology of Sylvia Brody*. New York, New York: IPBooks.

Response to Kimberly Kleinman

Arlene Kramer Richards

Thank you Kim for your focus on the value of childbirth and child rearing and the corresponding evaluation of women and women's roles in society. I think the traditional devaluation of girls has roots not only in Chinese culture, but in all patriarchies. Because women were likely to die in childbirth, getting too attached to a woman meant risking loss. It was true that in China women married into and lived with and produced sons for the husband's family, thus not producing value for their family of origin. But husbands were expected to provide a bride price so women did have some value. I believe it was more the loss of a loved child that caused families to avoid attachment to their girl children.

It remains a puzzle to me to this day how women are caught up in devaluing women. How is it that women voted for Trump after he publicly devalued the women he molested? How can it be that there are loyal "Trumpettes"? Male envy of women's power to be pregnant and give birth is surely part of it. Fear of the seductive power of women is surely another part of it. But what about self-disregard? What about these women's beliefs that they are just decoration or just service providers? Or helpless butts of male power? Or powerful because they control powerful men?

Surely we can speculate about these ideas. Psychoanalytic

data on such questions is very hard to find. One of the most convincing papers I ever read in this vein is Annie Reich's paper A Contribution to the Psychoanalysis of Extreme Submissiveness in Women (1940). The mere title of the paper is startling even today. Thinking of submissive women as suffering from psychopathology is itself a statement. Reich's conclusion that these women give up their self-esteem in favor of attachment to a man whom they overvalue tells us a lot about how such women think and why they believe that their men are right to devalue them. The more men devalue women, the more some women are eager to attach themselves to a man they perceive as powerful. And the more feminists depict their men as powerless sissies the more such women hate feminism. Or am I being too blunt?

Lucille Spira pointed out to me the Eve story in your contribution as a myth about the danger of women. In the Adam and Eve story, it is Eve who tempts Adam into breaking God's law. The danger of being seduced into sin and guilt by a seductive woman is built into this misogynistic story. I believe that the story in which a woman is created out of a man's rib is a story about where babies come from that denies the female power to reproduce. It makes woman secondary, ancillary, unequal and dangerous. And at the root of it is the female power to reproduce.

This cultural trope is a response to biological reality. It counters the reality that women live longer than men, that women face greater pain and suffering in childbirth than men face in war. Not every soldier suffers pain and the danger of dying, but every woman who gives birth to a child does. Not every man has to be valiant in the face of pain and danger, but every woman who bears a child does. To imagine men as brave and powerful and women as weak and submissive counters the humiliation to men of this reality.

CHAPTER 12

Feminism and Psychoanalysis:
A Discussion of Arlene Kramer Richards'
"Rage and Creativity"

Discussion by Nancy Kulish

Arlene Richards has provided us with an interesting opportunity and challenge to think about how the second wave of feminists (post World War II) has influenced psychoanalytic thinking. As a starting point, she outlines the history of the movement and suggests its two major thrusts: equality for women and the recognition and valorization of women's differences from men.

I will begin my discussion of Richards' paper by a reflection on the early days of psychoanalysis, more than a half century before these social movements emerged. Following her lead, I will use the concept of penis envy as a way to organize my thoughts about the changes wrought by the feminist movement on psychoanalysis. Freud's theories about women and female development reflect the science and belief systems of his era and milieu—Vienna at the turn of the nineteenth century. From the beginning, these theories have been subject to critique from within and outside of psychoanalytic circles. Even then, many of the women who became psychoanalytic pioneers and studied under Freud, along with a few men, voiced their differences, modifications and objections to his views about women. Three of the most influential voices were Karen Horney, Melanie Klein, and Clara Thompson. In particular, Horney (1924, 1926, 1933) was astonishingly ahead of her times in her understandings of female development. She argued against Freud's insistence that little girls did not know they had vaginas—a thesis connected with his theories that positioned penis envy and a sense of lack as central to female psychosexual development. She also articulated other aspects of the way females felt about their bodies that rested on different assumptions, namely that females' psychology should be understood not in terms of terms of lack and inadequacy, in comparison to males' bodies. She asserted that her male colleagues were biased in their over-valuation of the penis, reflecting little boys' fears and fantasies. She argued further that penis envy was originally a passing phase in early female development, only to become significant as a possible defensive reaction later in the oedipal phase, a point taken up years later by Grossman and Stewart (1976). That is, a girl's wish to be a boy fights off fearful fantasies of vaginal injury from penetration from the father's penis. She also saw the wish for motherhood as primary in little girls, not as a substitution for a wished for penis, as Freud has suggested. Thus, her views anticipated later theoretical developments around ideas of primary femininity—an early explicitly feminine sense of self and body not simply the negative of masculinity. Melanie Klein (1928), I think, in emphasizing the importance of the early oral phase and the pre-oedipal period, indicated that girls have a dominant feminine instinctual disposition and that penis envy originates secondarily from oral envy of the maternal breast and mother's body and its contents. Children of both sexes share these phantasies. Thompson's ideas (1941, 1942) can be read as a reaction against the Freud's views of women as biologically destined. She described the cultural forces that affect women's attitudes toward themselves and their roles in society, including attitudes toward marriage, childbearing, genitals, and sexuality. She described herself and her female contemporaries as being in a period of transition, thus anticipating the feminist movements to come.

As the century proceeded, the feminist movement began to swell within and without psychoanalysis. The ideas from the feminist movement in the US, Britain, and France, as described by Richards, infused energy and new ways of thinking into the psychoanalytic thinking of the time. I believe that psychoanalytic feminists themselves, often with roots in other disciplines were influential voices in the over-all movement. Examples are Julia Kristeva, from linguistics and philosophy; Juliet Mitchell, from English studies and Nancy Chodorow, from sociology.

As Richards points out, the argument against the idea that penis envy and reactions to it are "bedrock" in a female's psychology has led to and is related to many other aspects of contemporary psychoanalytic understandings about female development. Grossman and Stewart discussed the differing conceptualizations and meanings of penis envy in contemporary thinking, stressing its different defensive functions and roles in development. While many child analysts write about their observations of penis envy in little girls, they speak of it differently: as accompanying other feelings more in line with a primary sense of femaleness. For example, Yanof (2000) asserted that the personal meaning of a girl's femininity can reflect whatever the girl perceives herself to have or to lack. Similarly, Wilkinson (1991) writes about penis envy as a temporary narcissistic reaction to sexual differences, reinforced if males are given preference in the family or in patriarchal societies. It has to be said, however, that in certain psycho-analytic theoretical frameworks and parts of the world the concepts of penis envy or castration hold a more complex position. For example, it seems to me that Lacan finds it hard to account for female subjectivity without the concept of lack, symbolized by the phallus. I would be interested to hear what other colleagues from around the world have to say about this in these discussions.

I will outline a few of these critical conceptual arenas related the changes in psychoanalytic change of thinking about penis envy as bedrock (Freud, 1937):

1. **Primary femininity:** Many of the newer ideas cluster around the idea of primary femininity; that is, that there is an early sense of femaleness tied both to body and to identifications. As mentioned above, these ideas originated in the contributions by Horney, followed by Jones (1927, 1933), who also regarded girls' femininity as primary. Jones accepted the importance of early receptive wishes based on an awareness of early vaginal sensations and believed that the phallic phase in girls is defensive. Later, Stoller (1968, 1976) referred to the term "primary femininity" in his studies of the development of core gender identity and disorders of gender identity. He argued that femininity was primary in the sense of embryology and for both females and males primary in another sense, in that the first object of identification for the infant is female, the mother. Elise (1997) and Kulish (2000) offered contemporary critiques of the concept.

Included here are a myriad of other ideas about the importance of a girl's uniquely female body. Noteworthy is the influential contribution from Bernstein (1990) who elaborated early female genital anxieties: fear of access, of penetration, and of diffusivity. Many others followed along these lines. Kulish (1991) explored the meanings of the clitoris, not in terms of a miniature penis as postulated by Freud, but as an organ of female sexual pleasure; Balsam (1996) pointed out how the body-to body comparisons that a little girl makes with her mother contribute to her primary sense of herself as a female; Richards (1992, 1996) explicitly elaborated her ideas about girls' experiences and conflicts about genital experiences in the context of primary femininity. (Earlier Mayer (1985) had proposed another primary feminine genital anxiety, with one foot still in more traditional views, traditionally labeled "female castration anxiety", which involved the feared loss or closing of the genital opening, and allied fears of the loss of openness as a trait of the personality.) I think that these kinds of female genital anxieties are more comparable to castration anxiety than is rape, as Richards suggests. Rape is a horrible reality that has been with us for centuries and in all societies, whereas castration anxiety is a psychic *fantasy*. As far as I know, castration except in certain situations in past eras is not a horror men routinely endure in real life.

Woven throughout these writings on primary femininity are ideas from a different frame of reference: the importance of girls' identifications with their mothers and other females in the development of an early sense of femininity and of the female body (Tyson, 1982; Tyson and Tyson, 1990). The emphasis of the closeness of daughters and mothers is in line with the conclusions of Chodorow (1978), Gilligan (1982), and Silverman (1987), who, from different vantages points stress the importance for girls in bonding and relatedness, rather than autonomy valued by boys.

2. Motherhood: A second set of ideas influenced by the feminist movement revolve around motherhood and women's desires for babies, understood as stemming primarily from

such identifications with their mothers and mothering functions and not as a substitute for a missing penis. Rosemary Balsam (1996, 2000) has been in the forefront in her writings about the importance of mothering and the maternal body in the internal world of girls and women. Her writings capture a female's subjective experience of internalization of experiences with her own mother as she encounters becoming and being a mother. Julia Kristeva, another prominent writer who ties experiences of femininity and female identity to the mother's body, has explored the desire to be a mother and the joys of motherhood (Moi, 1986; Kristeva, 2014).

3. **Super-ego:** A third set of ideas focuses on the development of the superego in girls. Freud suggested that castration anxiety impels boys to renounce oedipal longings and identify with their fathers thus solidifying the superego. Girls, in contrast, lacking such strong motivation, end up with weaker superegos. Contemporary psychoanalysts argue that female superegos are not weaker than those of males. Gilligan (1982) first pointed out that studies claiming girls possess "weaker" moral values than men had been formulated by men, using males' values as measuring sticks. Bernstein (1993) suggested that the superego can be considered in terms of its strength, contents and structure. She then argued that females' superegos may contain different contents, but are not weaker than those of males. Such arguments have morphed into reformulations about the superego development in general for both boys and girls. Contemporary theorists talk about superego development as a more gradual process, formed out of a build-up of identifications and internalizations and not simply based on fear of the (castrating) father but on love for the parent (Schafer, 1960; Lichtenberg, 2004).

4. **Psychosexual stages of development:** One of the major

criticisms of penis envy concerns its supposed role as the impetus for a girl's entering the triadic or oedipal phase, and as
the motivating wish to have babies. As the concept of penis
envy has become less an important cog in the forward movement of the developmental line toward femininity, so has the
thinking about psychosexual development for both sexes become less tied to a lock step linear development of psychosexual stages, as originally described by Freud. Even early on,
female analysts questioned the sequence, inevitability, and
the dynamics of the stages in female development moving
from the phallic phase, to the negative oedipal, to the positive
oedipal. Edgecumbe and her colleagues at the Hampstead
Clinic (1976) questioned the inevitability of the negative oedipal phase preceded the oedipal phase itself in girls. Later
many questioned the appropriateness of speaking of a phallic phase for girls in general. Glover and Mendell (1982), for
example, proposed that psychoanalysis re-conceptualize the
"phallic" stage as the "pre-oedipal genital" or "genital" stage.
Many others such as Parens (1990) made similar proposals.

Kulish and Holtzman (2008) re-examined the formulations about the female oedipal phase as first proposed by
Freud and argued that it was not analogous to the male oedipal stage in many crucial ways. They proposed a name change
as well—as the "Persephone Phase" to better describe its un-
folding and dynamics, its characteristic themes and preoccu-
pations, and its typical conflicts and defenses.

On examination of this burst of writings about female
psychology and body influenced by feminist thinking, I
would say that most fall into the category of asserting the differences, whether essential or a product of the environment,
between females and males. The French feminist and analyst
Irigary (1994) has built her work on the idea of difference;

she attacks the "myth of symmetry" which supposes that the females' bodies and minds are symmetrical with males' and thus in these differences are defined as inferior and flawed. She then uncovers the uniquely feminine hidden from view by this blind spot. In many ways, however, such writings that assert the differences in the sexes have paradoxically paved the way for ideas that more generally erase the differences.

The wave of thought has moved from generalities based on a binary model—"he has" and "she has not" to an appreciation of individual differences, and the complexity and non-linearity of gender development. Chodorow (1978, 1994), for example, whose work was revolutionary in the sense in showing that females' sense of gender arises from a reproduction of mothering and is generally marked by relatedness, now emphasizes individual differences: sexual-*ities*, femininities and masculinities. Kristeva (2004) speaks of pluralities of versions of femaleness. Thus the arc in psychoanalytic feminism has moved from difference to individuality and ultimately to certain notions of equality. From the emphasis on identification in the formation of gender which accounts for observed sexual differences, the next theoretical jump has been to the complexity of these identifications, and the multifaceted make–up of female and male identifications that go into an individual's gender identity.

Many contemporary psychoanalytic writings about the role of culture and the formation of gender echo the ideas and ideology of equality proposed by the second wave of the feminist movement. These psychoanalytic theorists have up-ended Freud's early theories about gender (a term which he did not use as such). I am thinking about Freud's famous equation of passivity with femininity and activity with masculinity (1937). Freud, here, was speaking of attitudes and positions which could be observed in both men and women on a continuum. These ideas were obviously influenced by the cultural surround as Schafer (1974) pointed out: "What is problematical is the patriarchal bias in Freudian conceptualization and emphasis, a bias involving taken-for-granted models of masculine and feminine roles in our society" (p. 468).

These ideas were advanced by Fast's influential (1979) on the earliest development of gender through differentiation from an original undifferentiated state. She argued that both little boys and little girls react to their first perceptions of differences in gender as narcissistic injuries. Harris (2005), who wrote that gender is socially constructed, contributed significantly to contemporary psychoanalytic thinking which rejects the idea of fixed and inborn feminine or masculine attributes.

Those psychoanalysts since Thompson who have emphasized the role of culture, in the form of patriarchy, on development echo the feminist movement's call for equality for women. Take Benjamin (1988), for example, who illuminates how women, under patriarchy, cannot find a model for, or a road to, the formation of a robust subjectivity. She is one of many psychoanalytic theorists who have pointed to the restraints on gender roles and the formation of rigid gender identities enforced by patriarchy. Analysts have argued that these restraints affect men and boys as much as women and girls. The insistence in the importance of penis envy in the formation of a girl's sense of herself is matched by an over-evaluation of phallic prowess and power in the identity of boys. Diamond (2015) speaks of the overvaluation of phallicity that both individuals and psychoanalytic theory places in considerations of masculinity. Corbett (2001a) points to the deleterious and misguided effects of the insistence on "normal" phallic measures of masculinity for boys and men. In speaking of rigid versus more open gender identities, Corbett (2001b) privileges mental freedom as the guideline for mental health. Moving away from the emphasis on castration and phallic concerns in men by psychoanalysis, Fogel (1998) articulates the notions of *inner* bodily aspects of male experience, usually labelled as "feminine".

As the decades passed, psychoanalysts and gender theorists writing from a psychoanalytic perspective have deconstructed gendered polarities. Instead of two magnetic poles pulling masculine aspects to one pole and feminine to the other, gender configurations have come to be pictured now as points anywhere on many intersecting lines to be combined in any one individual in millions of ways. Thus, the conception of gender viewed in dichotomous attributes such as active/passive, has shifted to multiple complex gender formations—to be viewed via a turning kaleidoscope rather than a fixed microscope.

Finally, in psychoanalytic institutions themselves, in the training programs, the societies, and the associations, the feminist movement's call for equality for women can be seen concretely in the number of women who are leaders of the field in all aspects. When I began my training, 50 years ago, in my own institute there were few female candidates, only one female training analyst, and none of the leaders were women. Similarly at the American Psychoanalytic Association I saw a sea of older (white) men in leadership. As a candidate, I joined a workshop at the meetings of APsaA called "Problems for Women in Training", formed by and run by the indomitable Helen Meyers from New York. I was astounded by what greeted me—a women in the corner nursing her baby, a packed room, run in a non-authoritarian manner, with everybody talking, interrupting—so much energy. The group was full of ideas which were put into action: research, such as Elizabeth Mayer's that showed conclusively that women analysts were not referred male patients in statistically significant numbers; the huge undertaking of the annotated bibliography edited by Eleanor Schuker and Nadine Levinson of psychoanalytic writings about women (1991); a mentor program to send female analysts around the US to give presentations and do consultations. In that workshop the women encouraged everyone who came to speak, and to speak up elsewhere, to write, to progress in our training and embrace our aspirations. It was one of the most significant experiences of my career. Many of the women I met there have become lifelong friends. I am sure my experience is not unique and that similar support groups were born in psychoanalytic circles across the world. These circles have reverberated from the world-wide feminist circles described by Richards.

References

Balsam, R. (1996). The pregnant mother and the body image of the daughter. *Journal of the American Psychoanalytic Association* 14: 401-427.

——— (2000). The mother within the mother. *Psychoanalytic Quarterly* 69:465-492

Benjamin, J. (1988). *The Bonds of Love: Psychoanalysis, Feminism and the Problem of Domination.* New York: Pantheon.

Bernstein, D. (1990). Female genital anxieties, conflicts, and typical mastery modes. *International Journal of Psychoanalysis* 71:151-165.

——— (1993). *Female Identity Conflict in Clinical Practice.* Northvale, NJ: Jason Aronson.

Chodorow, N. J. (1978). *The Reproduction of Mothering: Psychoanalysis and the Sociology of Gender.* Berkeley, CA: University of California Press.

———— (1994). *Femininities, Masculinities, Sexualities.* Lexington, Kentucky: University Press of Kentucky.

Corbett, K. (2001a) Faggot=loser. *Studies in Gender & Sexuality* 2:3-28.

—————— (2001b). More life: Centrality and marginality in human development. *Psychoanalytic Dialogues* 11:313-355.

Diamond, M. J. (2015). The elusiveness of masculinity: primordial vulnerability, lack, and the challenges of male development. (2015). *Psychoanalytic Quarterly* 84(1):47-102

Edgecumbe, R., Lunberg, S., Markowitz, R., & Salo, F. (1976). Some comments on the concept of the negative oedipal phase in girls. *The Psychoanalytic Study of the Child* 31:35-61.

Elise, D. (1997). Primary femininity, bisexuality, and the female ego ideal: a re-examination of female developmental theory. *The Psychoanalytic Quarterly* 46:489-517.

Fast, I. (1979). Developments in gender identity: gender differentiation in girls. *International Journal of Psychoanalysis* 60:443-45.

Fogel, G. (1998). Interiority and inner genital space in men: what else can be lost in castration? *Psychoanalytic Quarterly* 67:662-697

Freud, S. (1937). Analysis terminable and interminable. *Standard Edition* 23:211-253.

Gilligan, D. (1982). *In a Different Voice.* Cambridge: Harvard University Press.

Glover, L. & Mendell, D., (1982). A suggested developmental sequence for a preoedipal genital phase. In *Early Female Development*, ed. D. Mendell. New York: S. P. Medical and Scientific Books, pp. 127-174.

Grossman, W. I. and Stewart, W. A. (1976). Penis envy: From childhood wish to developmental metaphor. *Journal of the American Psychoanalytic Association* 24:193-213.

Harris, A. (2005). *Gender as Soft Assembly.* Hillsdale, NJ: The Analytic Press

Horney, K. (1924). On the genesis of the castration complex in women. *International Journal of Psychoanalysis* 5:50-65.

——— (1926). The flight from womanhood *International Journal of Psychoanalysis* 12:360-374.

——— (1933). The denial of the vagina. *International Journal of Psychoanalysis* 14:57-70.

Irigary, L. (1994). *Thinking the Difference*. New York: Routledge.

Jones, E. (1927). The early development of female sexuality. *International Journal of Psychoanalysis* 8:459-472.

——— (1933). The phallic phase. *International Journal of Psychoanalysis* 14:1-13.

Klein, M. (1928). Early stages of the Oedipus complex. In *Love, Guilt and Reparation and Other Works: The Writings of Melanie Klein*, V 1. London: Hogarth Press, 1975, pp. 186-198.

Kristeva, H. (2004). Some observations on female sexuality. *The Annual of Psychoanalysis*, 32:59-68

——— (2014). Reliance or maternal eroticism. *Journal of the American Psychoanalytic Association*, 62:69-85

Kulish, N. M. (1991). Mental representation of the clitoris: the fear of female sexuality. *Psychoanalytic Inquiry* 11:511-536.

——— (2000). Primary femininity: clinical advances and theoretical ambiguities. *Journal of the American Psychoanalytic Association*, 48:1355-1379.

——— & Holtzman, D. (2008). *A Story of her Own: the Female Oedipus complex Reexamined and Renamed*. Lanham, Maryland: Jason Aronson

Lichtenberg, J. (2004). Commentary on the superego –a vital or supplanted concept? *Psychoanalytic Inquiry* 24: 328-339

Mayer, E. L. (1995). The phallic castration complex and primary femininity: paired developmental lines toward female gender identity. *Journal of the American Psychoanalytic Association* 43:17-38.

Moi, T. (1986). *The Kristeva Reader*. London: Blackwell 187-213

Parens, H. (1990). On the girl's psychosexual development: reconsiderations suggested from direst observation. *Journal of the American Psychoanalytic Association* 38:743-772.

Richards, A. K. (1992). The influence of sphincter control and genital sensation on body image and gender identity in women. *Psychoanalytic Quarterly* 61:331-351.

——— (1996). Primary femininity and female genital anxiety. *Journal of the American Psychoanalytic Association* 44/S: 261-281.

Silverman, D. (1987). What are little girls made of? *Psychoanalytic Psychology* 4:315-334.

Schafer, R. (1960). The loving and beloved superego in Freud's structural theory. *Psychoanalytic Study Child* 15, 163-188

——— (1974). Problems in Freud's psychology of women. *Journal of the American Psychoanalytic Association* 22 459-485.

Schuker, E. and Levinson, N. A. (1991). *Female Psychology*. Hillsdale, N. J.: Analytic Press.

Stoller, R. (1968). The sense of femaleness. *Psychoanalytic Quarterly* 37:42-55.

——— (1976). Primary femininity. *Journal of the American Psychoanalytic Association* 24:59-78.

Thompson, C. (1941). The role of women of this culture. *Psychiatry*. 4: 1-8.

——— (1942). Cultural pressures on the psychology of women. *Psychiatry* 5:331-339

Tyson, P. (1982). A developmental line of gender identity, gender role, and choice of love object. *Journal of the American Psychoanalytic Association* 30:61:86.

——— & Tyson, R. (1990). Gender development: girls. In *Psychoanalytic Theories of Development: An Integration*. New haven, CT: Yale University Press, pp. 258-276.

Wilkinson, S.M. (1991). Penis envy: Libidinal metaphor and experiential metonym. *International Journal of Psychoanalysis* 72:335-346.

Yanof, J. A. (2000). Barbie and the tree of life: the multiple functions of gender in development. *Journal of the American Psychoanalytic Association* 48:1439-1465

Response to Nancy Kulish

Arlene Kramer Richards

I am very grateful for the very thoughtful, well documented, and serious response from Nancy Kulish. She provides a detailed history of female psychoanalysts who preceded the Second Wave feminists of the post-World War II era. Those analysts provided the foundation on which the female analysts of the 1970s and 80s built a new understanding of female psychology that influenced analytic practice in almost universal ways. As Kulish demonstrates, the knowledge was there. Primary female identity was convincingly argued by Karen Horney. I am proud to have been influenced by her ideas. But analysts in the 50s and 60s in the United States were still clinically practicing as if penis envy were universal bedrock for female development and the major reason for neurosis in women. It took the influence of the Second Wave feminists to change that.

Another important issue Kulish points out is the issue of rape fantasies in female psychology. I posited rape fears as important factors in female fantasies. This was the opposite of what was the standard doctrine at the time. My point was that women do not long for rape, we are afraid of it. And as Kulish points out, these fears are all too likely to be corroborated by dangers in reality, Many women are really raped. And rape is far more common than male castration in reality. So the idea that rape fears lead to rape fantasies does not imply that little girls are wanting to be raped. Just the opposite. And it is the Third Wave feminists of our time who have documented date rape, campus rape, fraternity gang rape and other horrors perpetrated on young women.

The issue of equality for women is one in which the analytic world has followed rather than led in our understanding of women. I think that such issues as child care, maternity leave, equal pay for equal work, respect for "women's work," like nursing, social work, nursery and primary school teaching, and ending sexual harassment in the workplace have come mainly from outside our field. These issues have a profound influence on identity and self-respect. They have been addressed mostly by critics of psychoanalysis as it was in the 1950s. Now analysts are taking note of them. And they are being addressed in clinical practice.

I am especially grateful for Kulish's description of the women's group in psychoanalysis she attended. It was certainly helpful in both creating sisterhood within the group and publicizing the ideas of the women writing about female psychology at that time. And I believe that it encouraged her seminal (maybe I should say ovarian) idea of the Persephone Fantasy. That was a first: a real challenge to the idea that everyone's life fits the Oedipus myth. It was an explication of a fantasy constructed in the face of a conflict between wanting to remain a mother's best beloved and wanting to become an adult woman relating to a best beloved man. At the time it was viewed as a separation-individuation conflict. But the point was that we could look at other fantasies as well as the Oedipal one and understand the conflicts that our current women patients have in terms of their own experiences as well as the universal issues all humans have. So the Difference Feminist view received a major support from this line of thinking. We can now understand our patients better because of this contribution.

Section I: *Essay and Discussions: Rage and Creativity*

CHAPTER 13

To Be A Feminist and To Be a Psychoanalyst, That is an Answered Question
Response to Arlene Kramer Richards' paper, "Rage and Creativity: How Second Generation Feminist Thought Collective Influenced Psychoanalysis"

Merle Molofsky

On reading this thoughtful, scholarly paper, I was aware that the author, like myself, is a psychoanalyst, and that we both remember, and experienced, the impact of the second generation feminist wave on our lives, on our ways of conceptualizing and responding to the established social and political norms growing up, coming of age, and determining the arc of our adult lives.

To respond to this paper is to begin at the beginning, to remember what growing up female in Brooklyn in my family of origin was like, and to consider what the concept of a thought collective means to me.

Genesis: I was born in 1942, to working class Jewish parents who were self-educated and highly cultured, valuing art, music, literature, and politically ultra-left wing.

I was the first born child, a girl, and my brother was born just before I turned three years old. Thus I was born into a gendered situation.

There is a clichéd belief that in Judaism, since Jews are waiting for the Messiah, and there is no question that the Messiah is going to be male, Jewish parents favor their sons, since any Jewish boy could grow up to be the Messiah. I did not experience any sense of either my brother or myself being privileged by our parents for any reason. I was not privileged for being the elder, or for being female, and he was not privileged for being the younger, or for being male. We were treated equally.

Growing up in the 1940's, and becoming an adolescent in the 1950's, meant growing up and coming of age in a markedly sexist culture. But growing up and coming of age in my family provided an experience different from what I experienced in the larger society.

I grew up in an egalitarian family. My parents shared similar values, similar interests, made important decisions together, and they shared responsibility for the household and childcare equally. Since my father worked six days a week until he retired, my mother did somewhat more housework than he did, but he certainly did his share of the housework. He liked food preparation, and although the family had a limited budget, and our food was simple, he liked the visual aspect of preparing food, and would make very basic salads appealing, cutting green peppers into rings, and cutting lemons into wedges to be used to dress the salad, for instance. When my parents considered my brother and me mature enough to come home after school to an empty house, my mother got a job as well, to bolster the family income.

The neighborhood where we lived was primarily Jewish,

primarily lower middle class and working class, with a sprinkling of genuine middle middle class families, and the social norms were different from what I saw at home. People lived in two-family and three-family houses, often with extended families in those houses. Some houses had porches, some had stoops. On weekends, in fair weather, when people gathered outdoors, the men would talk about sports and cars. When I heard my father joining in, I was puzzled. He didn't really know much about cars, didn't like driving, and didn't care for sports. My parents' friends, who did not live in our neighborhood, but with whom we socialized frequently, since a husband and wife couple ran a salon every weekend, were intellectuals, and talked knowledgeably about politics, controversial issues, and culture. I asked him why he joined in the kind of conversation the men on our block favored. He answered that he did so to be sociable, not because he was interested in what they cared about. He cared about them, not their interests.

The women on our block didn't work. In fair weather, weekdays and weekends, they would gather on someone's porch, and play mahjong. Perhaps they played indoors in cold or inclement weather, but I wouldn't have known that. My mother detested gambling, detested card playing and mahjong, and of course did not join them. She considered games of chance a waste of time. She wanted intellectual companionship.

So I grew up aware of a social norm that divided activities by gender, different activities for men and women, and an alternative social norm in which men and women spent time together sharing ideas in serious conversation. Except—isn't there always an "except"? Except that the two dear friends of my parents who ran a salon every weekend, all weekend long seemed to be very gendered. She spent her time in a tiny galley kitchen, tending to food preparation. All weekend long she roasted turkeys and baked apple pies. No other food was served, but she rarely seemed to leave the kitchen, the galley kitchen that wasn't large enough to accommodate one chair for her to sit! And he socialized, mingled, talked, encouraged everyone else to talk. Nonetheless, men did not dominate the discussion. Everyone who had knowledge, or an opinion, talked. I was used to hearing women talk enthusiastically about ideas.

My father was a clerk in a bookstore. He loved his job, because he could talk literature, art, ideas, with the customers. And he could bring home books! When I was not yet a teenager, my father gave me *The Second Sex* by Simone de Beauvoir when it was first published in English in 1953. Why? We never talked about why. He gave me many books that he thought I might enjoy reading. But I sure could speculate why.

My father had five sisters, and he was the only boy. He told me that all his life he never saw his mother sleeping. She was up before anyone else in the household awoke, and even when he was a teenager and came home fairly late in the evening, she was still awake, still working. She cooked, she cleaned, she scrubbed. She ironed all the frilly dresses her daughters wore. His father was a plasterer, worked on construction sites, and came home with dirty clothes. His mother scrubbed his clothes clean in the bathtub, using a washboard.

There is a Yiddish word, "balabusta," derived from a Hebrew phrase báalat habáyit, which means mistress of the house. It is used as a form of praise, implying a hard-working woman who devotes herself to maintaining a well-run household. I know my aunts, my father's sisters, were proud of their mother's skills as a balabusta, and those of them who married

160

and had children when they were young devoted themselves to maintaining a well-run household. I think my father saw excess in the devotion to housework, and wanted something else for me!

Genesis ends with adolescence. In adolescence, the realities of social attitudes toward the behavior of women and men, girls and boys, became paramount. I learned that who I was did not fit the social norms of my peers, of the world outside my family, and I automatically conformed in a superficial way, and yet could not help being myself.

I shall draw a veil over the conflicts and rebellions and acting out of my adolescence, and address the issues Arlene raised by considering my frustrations of early adulthood, of marriage, childcare, and more. These experiences, like the experiences of childhood and adolescence, shaped the psychoanalyst I was going to become—although I did not know I could become a psychoanalyst until I was in my 30's.

The fact that abortion was illegal pre-Roe vs. Wade, when the Supreme Court's 1973 decision created the right for women to obtain an abortion, had bearing on my life. My short story, "Miriam 1960," in my collection of short fiction, *Necessary Voices*, published in 2019 by International Psychoanalytic Books, offers an utterly grim depiction of the process a pregnant, unmarried teenager went through, searching for, and finally obtaining, a backstreet abortion that sent her, nearly dead, to a city hospital emergency room. Fiction? The story is true.

In the 1970's, I was invited by friends to something I recently had had glimmers of, a "women's consciousness-raising meeting." I was curious, and wanted to go. What did I do? I asked my then "boyfriend"—"Honey, may I go to a women's consciousness-raising meeting tonight?" He exploded into a diatribe about "lesbian feminists." What did I do? I did not go.

Yet, the feminist movement was in the air.

Women who became psychoanalysts were learning an inspired and necessary discipline, theory and clinical practice, which sometimes was not commensurate with their own lived reality.

I remember an anecdote that I heard, midway through my formal psychoanalytic education, told in class by a faculty member. A feminist was referred by her husband's male analyst to another male analyst, who was told to "bring her to her senses." Instead, her analyst did what a good analyst does, and encouraged her to be true to herself. She became a well-known feminist. Fortunately, this outstanding male analyst listened to his analysand! And countless women benefitted from her activism.

The vocal leadership of feminists during that time, including the woman whose male analyst didn't try to "bring her to her senses," eventually influenced me sufficiently. Yes, I ditched the "boyfriend." Yes, I was learning to value my own thoughts and feelings.

Arlene, you cite Ludwig Fleck's ideas about thought collectives, "a thought collective exists wherever two or more persons are exchanging thoughts," (Fleck, L., 1979, p. 102). His contributions certainly are valuable, and he is an outstanding thinker. And yet, can we go beyond the specific thought collective that defines man and woman, masculinity and femininity, maleness and femaleness? Obviously, we have to do that!

When you described miners losing work, doing housework, and needing help, and when I read your discussion

162

of boys not wanting to do "girly things," I was reminded of a story I read when I was very young, a book my mother showed me. I believe it had illustrations by the noted artist Kathe Kollwitz. The story told of a peasant family where the husband and wife were arguing over whose work was harder, men's or women's. So they decided to change places to find out. Aha! Oh ho! Guess what! Yup, the husband could not keep up with what women's work entailed, while his wife easily did his work. Another instance of generalizations, of course, but it certainly created a sense of empowerment in me in the late 1940's.

Again, early in my psychoanalytic education, I took a class in the early writings of Sigmund Freud, in which we read the Dora case. I was disturbed by what I had read, and in class I asked, "Why would a 14-year-old girl be aroused by the embrace of a man in his 40's reeking of cigar smoke when she already expressed admiration for Madame K's 'adorable white body'?" I knew from my own life experience that I wouldn't have felt what Freud said Dora felt. A man in the class started referring to me as "the feminist," and a woman in the class insisted that I should read Juliet Mitchell's work so that I could understand that "Freud really loved women." Juliet Mitchell is a renowned feminist who made an effort to reconcile Freudian thought with feminism, using Marxist thought. Yes, I read her work, and no, I don't think that all of Freudian thought can be reconciled with feminism.

Fortunately, we are capable of independent thought!

Given that I can disagree with Juliet Mitchell, and she and I both are women, it seems we need to be very careful about generalizations, about reifying the notion that what men want is universal for men, what women want is universal for women.

The notorious quotation from Freud—"What do women want?"—may not have been said by Freud. Nonetheless, we need to question the question.

A well-known feminist drive theorist, Doris Bernstein, made wonderful contributions to psychoanalytic developmental theory. She did not try to answer the question, "What do women want?" but, rather, she explored the psyche of a little girl, and thus, the psyche of a woman, in new ways.

Perhaps the value we most need is to create balance, by adding connectivity to independence. I am very grateful that you, along with your co-editor Lucille Spira, chose to publish my chapter in your book, *Myths of Mighty Women: Their Application in Psychoanalysis* (Karnac, 2015) in which I explored the thoughts and feelings of women who do Japanese taiko drumming. They sought balance, a sense of connection a sense of independence, a sense of self-expression, and a sense of power. In my chapter I pointed out that, ironically, the best feminist films emerged from a very male-centered culture, Japan, all directed by Japanese men. These sensitive filmmakers recognized women oppressed by a patriarchal society had needs, and rights.

Perhaps we can be both challenged and inspired by the publication, in 2012, by The MIT Press, of *Doing Psychoanalysis in Tehran*, by Gohar Homayounpour. The author, Iranian-born, trained in the West as a psychoanalyst, moved back to the Islamic Republic of Iran to practice psychoanalysis. Of note: the great Iranian filmmaker, Abbas Kiarostami, wrote the Forward. Homayounpour writes poignantly about so many things, with a commitment to truth. "I feel more identified with everything and everybody in Tehran, which leads to a great deal more emotional exhaustion in all scenarios, including with patients. It is also emotionally loaded, for at times I despise how I identify with people here. I have spent years separating myself from them, because I am not supposed to be who I was when I left" (p. 98). She dreads the return of the repressed, and realizes she has to deal with the anxiety it generates (p. 99).

Perhaps we too have to deal with the return of the repressed, the lingering, sometimes overpowering vestiges of gender roles, of who we may have been, of who we actually may be. We may have to continue the struggle against patriarchal standards, both external and internalized, using our "rage and creativity" in the service of freedom for all.

Amen, Arlene, to your powerful vision of hope for us as we are emancipated from restrictive gender roles.

Section I: *Essay and Discussions: Rage and Creativity*

Response to Merle Molofsky

Arlene Kramer Richards

Thank you Merle for your thoughtful response to this paper and for your open use of your own experience to convey how you understand the world. One of the effects of the Second Wave feminists' insistence on the idea that "the personal is political" is awareness that personal experience shapes how we see the world around us. People who grew up knowing hunger have a different view of food than people who were pushed to eat as much as their parents imagined they could hold. Learning a second language in early childhood made for flexibility of thought. Speaking a single language that was the same as that of all the people one knew made for a sense of certainty and commonality with one's group. For children of the Depression, money was something to be careful of not wasting. For those brought up in a consumer society, spending was fun and virtuous.

What is thinkable depends on the thinker's previous experience. When men have experienced growing up in male bodies with social expectations of what it is to be a real man, they think differently from women. And the reverse is true as well. We can explain ourselves to each other, but we can never experience exactly what another person experiences. So we rely on empathy and mutuality of interests to help us understand each other.

All of which is to say that your basic experience of gender equality in your family, overlaid by your later experience of gander inequality in your adolescence and young adulthood, has given you a rich perspective. And your willingness to recognize this in yourself and share it with others took courage and conviction.

What I find most interesting in what you wrote is your vision for the present and future. Having a worldwide epidemic makes it clear how connected we all are. If women are repressed and maltreated as part of the culture in some places, how does that affect women in more open societies? Does it make us fearful? Do we have a responsibility to ask those places or those cultures to change their ways? What gives us the right to decide how others should live? Such questions come up around issues of female "circumcision," rights to equal schooling, abortion rights, and equal pay for equal work.

Not having the answers, but paying attention to the questions, seems to me to open up a possible and necessary conversation. Thank you for doing that.

CHAPTER 14

The Prejudice Within:
A Discussion of Arlene Kramer Richards'
"Rage and Creativity"

Jack Novick and Kerry Kelly Novick

We are deeply honored to be asked to respond to Arlene Richards' evocative and rich paper, as she raises the question of the impact of the feminist movement on current psychoanalytic theory. She cites the remark that the "personal is political" and shares some of her own history as it has contributed to her ways of thinking. This resonated deeply for us, as many of the topics she discusses link to our personal and shared histories as well.

We met when we were both studying child psychoanalysis with Anna Freud. As well as discovering many intellectual and political affinities, we found that, despite our disparate backgrounds, we could both consider ourselves "2nd-generation feminists." By this we mean that our parents already lived ideals of equality and collaboration. Jack's mother arrived as a 16-year-old immigrant in Montreal, and led her union out on strike as a shop steward 2 days later. When she and Jack's father married, they ran a series of corner grocery stores together and other businesses for the rest of their lives. Kerry's parents shared activities and responsibilities, including those of non-sexist child rearing, and supported her voice and that of other disenfranchised groups from the outset. So it wasn't surprising that we began writing papers and remodeling houses together.

That's all fun and interesting, but why were we in London in the first place and how does that relate to Arlene's paper? She draws on and evokes numerous deep and significant areas of thinking and understanding, each of which deserves its own discussion or detailed examination. Here we will select only one or two points for elaboration and raise questions and ideas for the ongoing discussion.

We had to travel to London to obtain psychoanalytic training because we could not train in the United States in the 1960s. Jack was a Ph.D. clinical psychologist, advised by members of the admissions committee at a prestigious American institute just to lie in signing the form promising never to treat patients. Let's note that corruption is often a feature of authoritarian systems, with hypocrisy practiced to bolster the status quo. Unwilling to lie and wishing for child training (which was also then unavailable in its own right), Jack left the country. Kerry was a non-medical woman, equally interested in child analysis, who discovered that there was no chance of training in America, and went to the epicenter of the field in London.

There are some contextual factors that we find relevant. One is that the conflicts and tensions Arlene addresses apply mostly to American psychoanalysis, and specifically to the American Psychoanalytic Association as it was until 1989. Given that APsaA restricted its membership up till then to physicians, most of whom were the products of medical schools with strict racial, religious, and gender quotas, APsaA was a group of white men, inevitably subject to conscious and unconscious biases and ideas deriving from their very identities. Part of that history had also involved excluding child analysts, the majority of whom were women mental health professionals originally trained in other disciplines (note our reluctance to label them "non-medical," as if medical were the norm and standard, just as male development was considered by many psychoanalytic theorists to be the standard, with women as deviations. In many societies, adult analysis is 'normal' with child analysis an application or just absent). Sexism ran deep in establishment American psychoanalysis, as did other 'isms, perhaps even more deeply buried, like racism and antisemitism, as well as childism, so often linked with misogyny and sexism.

An alternative spirit sprang up in the "independent" North American societies, where people of different backgrounds were welcomed and encouraged and many female mental health professionals trained as psychoanalysts. This tradition finally was welcomed into the mainstream of international organized psychoanalysis, when the North American independent groups began to be recognized by the IPA in the 1980s. We could consider whether this represents another confluence of thought collectives, this time those of women analysts from different regions. The joining together of American women psychoanalysts from the independent societies with others from Europe and Latin America has borne wonderful fruit in the IPA's Committees on Women and Psychoanalysis (COWAP), Child and Adolescent Psychoanalysis (COCAP), Child Abuse, Refugees and more.

In Europe, there had always been many women analysts; in fact, Freud's early Vienna circle included as many women as men, and they played crucial roles in teaching and the development of theory and technique. Despite official exclusion from studies of medicine and other professions, powerful, effective women were drawn to Freud's theories and felt liberated by his views on sexuality in both men and women. For instance, Lou Andreas Salome was often consulted by Freud to increase his understanding of women's subjective sexual experience and for a time she was Anna Freud's analyst. She was married with a child, had affairs with prominent intellectuals like Nietzsche and Rilke, and wrote important contributions to psychoanalysis on female sexuality—indeed a prototype of a liberated woman, but not so unusual in the early years of European psychoanalysis.

When we accompanied an American colleague to his first IPA Congress in Rome in 1989, he was momentarily flabbergasted walking into the first plenary—"There are so many women!" he exclaimed. Not quite like APsaA meetings! We had had a similar experience in reverse, when we arrived in Michigan in 1977 to discover that the psychoanalytic society had only one full female member. APsaA did catch up, at least externally, so that now there are more women candidates than men, and more female members. But those many women who joined APsaA through the turn of the 20th century did not join as blank slates. Not only were they often well-trained, distinguished, and experienced already, but they were also the product of the times. They had been part of the feminist surge that generated fundamental examination of identity, development, relationships, our very grasp of bodies, minds, and beings who identified as female. They embodied the confluence of two thought collectives.

Arlene supplies an important corrective to the caricatured Freud so demonized by many American feminist thinkers and writers, but also notes those important female psychoanalytic thinkers marginalized in American psychoanalysis

172

over the first century. We would add to this list the work of Judith Kestenberg, an acute clinical observer of and staunch proponent of little girls' own subjective sexual sensations and experience, as well as an innovative theorist on mind-body relationships. Freud, in his discussion of the case of "Dora," and Anna Freud, in her first published paper, when she was in her twenties, discussed female masturbation. Anna Freud's paper was written only a few years after such luminaries as Ernest Jones were still stating as fact that masturbation was a harmful cause of neurasthenia! We wonder if mid-20th-century American psychoanalysis, still dominated by white men, had difficulty incorporating theories articulated by a non-medical woman, and even pushed some of Anna Freud's ideas to distorted extremes in aridly formulated "ego psychology."

If Freud had truly been such a male chauvinist denigrator of women, then his daughter Anna Freud would not have become the world-renowned figure she was. We were puzzled by Arlene's omitting her from the list. In an international survey of psychiatrists and psychoanalysts in 1971, Anna Freud was named their most outstanding colleague. Her 1936 book revolutionized psychoanalysis, pulling the field back from exclusive emphasis on drives and the unconscious to a richer, metapsychological formulation that encompassed the defenses, the ego and superego, and girls and women as agents of their own sexuality throughout development. Yet, as soon as ten years after her death in 1982, her work was rarely cited, taught, or acknowledged.

Anna Freud was not only a central figure in the history of psychoanalysis, but also made lasting contributions to "civilization," as Freud exhorted all analysts to do. Her work in the War Nurseries in London during the Blitz established that separation from parents was more traumatic for babies and children than the bombs. Her efforts to underscore the primacy of keeping parents and children together in stressful circumstances were extended to hospital settings; the impact of these ideas changed pediatric hospital practice throughout the world, so that now it is taken for granted that parents stay with their child as much as possible. The three volumes of "In the Best Interests of the Child" revolutionized the basis of legal approaches to child and family issues around the world. This was a woman born in 1895, the last of six children, the daughter of a world-famous Victorian man. Yet he was also the kind of man who encouraged, supported and did not interfere with her growing power and influence. When she died in 1982 she was the most important psychoanalyst in the world, but now very few American psychoanalysts refer to her.

What happened? Is it a continuation of the same anti-feminine and anti-child prejudice that dominated American APsaA psychoanalysis until the late 1980s? Arnie Richards has written a powerful exposition of the Communist affiliations of many of the American-born leaders of mid-20th-century American psychoanalysis. His work generates an intriguing hypothesis about the authoritarian bent shared by APsaA and the Communist Party. How do these relate and what might have been their impact on beliefs in hierarchy and their often accompanying sense of superiority to women and other populations seen as inferior?

The only psychoanalytic group ever to be disaffiliated by APsaA was the Michigan Psychoanalytic Institute. The story promoted was that Richard Sterba, a prominent analytic émigré, who had exemplified integrity when he had refused the Nazi invitation to head up the Vienna Society and the international psychoanalytic press (Verlag), was somehow misusing some funds. The reality was that both Richard Sterba and his non-medical wife Editha were close colleagues of Anna Freud. They had promoted her ideas about defense analysis and child work, and in Michigan they were analyzing non-medical people training to become psychoanalysts, people like Selma Fraiberg, Marvin Hyman, and Bertram Karon. These activities directly challenged and undermined the hegemony of APsaA, just as Anna Freud had challenged the adult-centric bias of the IPA in 1971. The New York psychoanalyst who spearheaded the disaffiliation is one of those identified by Arnold Richards as a Communist; that analyst also claimed the disaffiliation and reaffiliation, excluding the Sterbas, of the Michigan Society as the action he was most proud of in his career.

These historical events and issues bridge us to a further topic spurred by Arlene's paper. When we see the unequal treatment of any group with whatever designation (women, people of color, a variety of sexual orientations or identities, religion, children), we identify that as based on a prejudice— an unfounded belief that the target group is intrinsically different in some given biological way, inferior to the dominant group. Such a belief is used to justify the dominant group's efforts to own the others, to control and use them to serve their own needs. A psychoanalytic examination of prejudice should lead us to examine the motives of the dominant group, rather than focus on those characteristics of the target group used to justify the bias.

When psychoanalysts study the motives of prejudice, we invariably find a need to deal with one's own sense of helplessness or defectiveness by externalizing them and dominating others. In our work we have discerned underlying sadomasochistic dynamics where the needs for safety and attachment, protection against trauma, and gratification come to depend on the sadistic power to dominate and control others and have them serve one's needs. The United States was built on many positive ideals and the courage of founders, immigrants and pioneers. But there is an equally strong and present historical residue of genocide and enslavement. These "other" people were there to be enslaved, denigrated, seen as inferior. American psychoanalysis has not somehow miraculously avoided this legacy.

Skipping ahead to the present, led by Arlene's reasoning in this paper, we have to acknowledge the sadomasochistic prejudices of the American Psychoanalytic Association. Until the late 1980s they felt justified to exclude and demean the skills and talents of non-medical analysts, especially women. Did these prejudices end with the legal resolution of the lawsuit that opened the doors of training to this "inferior" class of students? No more than societal racial prejudice ended with the election of the first African-American US President! In APsaA prejudice continued in relation to LGBTQ analysts and candidates, subtly perhaps with people of color, and openly against non-TAs and non-certified colleagues. Behind all these prejudices, camouflaged under the rationalizations of pseudo-scientific differences, was a clinging to sadistic power by those few in the ruling circle of BOPS.

Another relevant personal story—we returned to the US in 1977 when Jack was recruited as a tenured professor at the University of Michigan to head up the children's service in the Department of Psychiatry. We both joined the faculty of the Michigan Psychoanalytic Institute. Eventually we were accepted at APsaA, and both became certified in both adult and child psychoanalysis. We were also welcomed to the faculty of the New York Freudian Society, one of the premier independent groups that later joined the IPA, where we became training analysts. The lawsuit against APsaA to admit non-medical people for training was ongoing in the middle 1980s. Perhaps not realizing that Jack was not a physician, the new Head of the MPI Education Committee at the party celebrating his appointment, hugged Jack and exclaimed, "We'll get those psychologists!"

At the same time, Jack was going through the process to become a training analyst at the Michigan Institute. During the final stage of the process, after passing through all the various hurdles, he received a phone call from a senior analyst at MPI seeking to prohibit him from teaching seminars to another local psychoanalytic group unaffiliated with APsaA, a group training psychologists and social workers. The prejudiced idea that non-medical people could not manage clinical responsibility was invoked and Jack was told there would be consequences if he persisted. Jack refused to accept this irrational authoritarian demand. There then ensued a mysterious silence and stall in the TA process, broken only when Jack was informed that they were not proceeding with his appointment. But they refused to offer an explanation. When the lawyers handling the lawsuit against APsaA, based primarily on the issue of restraint of trade, told their APsaA legal counterparts about Jack's situation, it became the tipping point. As the lawyers said, "They threw in the towel," and the case was settled.

Most insidiously the prejudice continues in the form of childism, a term coined by Elisabeth Young-Bruehl to describe societal and institutional prejudices against children that ultimately allow for widespread physical, emotional and sexual abuse. Childism is an apt arena in which to learn more about the operating dynamics of prejudice in general, since the phenomena are often so vivid. It becomes very clear when parents display an irrational but rationalized compulsion to beat, control, own and dominate the child to serve their own needs. At the institutional level, the presence of childism is betrayed often by omissions, slights, and lack of prioritization of issues related to children and parents. We can also see how abused children deny and identify with the aggressor (Anna Freud's term). The abused often become abusers. We now have more female candidates and faculty in our institutes, yet abusive boundary crossing seems as prevalent as ever, and female candidates rarely complain!

The conversation continues and both deepens and expands. We work with many college students and we are disheartened to see that bright, accomplished young women nevertheless still feel that they have to submit to whatever desires their boyfriends articulate. What do the young men want their girlfriends to be? They want them to emulate porn stars, to dress and act the way women do in sadistic porn videos, to be at their beck and call sexually. The price of a relationship is compliance and submission, to act as a slave. Arlene describes progress within the field of psychoanalytic theory and practice, and attributes it to the impact of the thought collective of the political wave of feminism. But what we see all over the world of the abusive and murderous treatment of women and children, the persisting inequality in the actuality of concrete markers like pay scales, and ongoing social attitudes and relationships in supposedly 'enlightened' countries gives us pause and raises an uncomfortable question. What has feminism actually accomplished?

We make a distinction between anger and rage. We have characterized rage in our two-systems model of self-regulation as an overwhelming ego state in response to helplessness, in other words, a potentially traumatic experience if sustained. Anger, on the other hand, can function as a signal to fire the higher areas of the brain, to activate the (frontal cortex) ego to enlist its capacities in the service of identifying the issue, thinking, and planning an effective response to the insult. One can't write a book, run a company, plan a campaign of action, be a whistleblower when in a rage. We suggest that the second-wave feminists and their allied women analysts, both contemporary and subsequently, harnessed their anger effectively to access imagination, science, observation, experience, subjectivity, empathy and more to generate theories that are alive, realistic and useful.

Blaming Freud was and is a waste of time and energy, and we appreciate Arlene's effort to correct the record. In that spirit, it seems worth adding to her description some points arising from Freud's last writings, published posthumously in 1940. There he distinctly delineated and modified his concept of Eros. He designated one of the two basic instincts as Eros, whose aim is to bind together, to establish greater unities, and to preserve them. Freud called the energy of Eros libido, stressing that this should not be equated with sexuality alone, as is so often done even today. "The greater part of what we know about Eros," Freud wrote, "...has been gained from a study of the sexual function, which, indeed, in the prevailing view, even if not according to our theory, coincides with Eros" (1940, p.151). We see this as relevant to thinking about prejudice, as dominance and submission, the sadomasochistic closed-system functioning and gratification that enter into prejudice, stand in stark contrast to Freud's overarching characterization of Eros. Prejudice belongs squarely in the realm of sadomasochism. Arlene's thesis of two thought collectives coming together seems to us to express Freud's late conceptualization of the open-system binding together and uniting characteristic of Eros.

We suggest that the model of so-called normal femininity and masculinity described in classical psychoanalytic theory is actually one of pathology, that becomes oddly resonant in some of the difference-feminism thinking. Many women accept this myth that men are innately aggressive and that women are and should be more caring, loving and conciliatory. Female politicians like Hillary Clinton are often pushed in this direction, and even some female psychoanalysts try to paint women as more collaborative, better facilitators, less power-hungry, less personally ambitious than men. It was easy to turn Hillary Clinton's competence, skill, experience, intelligence and assertiveness into some witch-like danger and fear of difference. "Lock her up" was the war cry of the opposition in an effort to control and suppress the real power of her assertive competence. Such a model elucidates closed-system sadomasochistic self and other-representations of men and women built on a foundation of defensive externalizations of feared and despised aspects of the self, defined as such by cultural imperatives. Men repudiate their own nurturing and receptive dimensions and externalize them on to women; women, afraid of being seen as aggressive, externalize on to men. Thus, instead of the representations of gender roles becoming more overlapping, they have polarized further.

Given the conflation of assertion and sadistic aggression, many women don't know what to do with their anger and aggression and they suppress their assertion as well. Here our additional differentiation of assertion and aggression is critical. There is a cultural, male-centric unwillingness to distinguish between assertion, an open-system characteristic, and aggression that can manifest in both open and closed-system functioning. Aggression is what culturally defines masculinity. The gun culture in America relates to a masculine need to feel powerful and fearless, not a scared "pussy," a derogatory name for female genitals.

We advocate using anger as a signal that can activate assertion to push back against and change theories that perpetuate prejudiced stereotypes, to effect legislation and be alert to biases of any kind, since they all operate on the same sadomasochistic principles. We should make sure that our President is not prejudiced, that the men in our lives, our analysts, partners, brothers and sons are not prejudiced, and assert ourselves if they are. The theory may have changed and many women may have changed but most men have not. They will not change until confronted by all people who will not tolerate the sadism of those in power.

Section I: *Essay and Discussions: Rage and Creativity*

Response to Jack Novick and Kerry Kelly Novick

Arlene Kramer Richards

Thank you Kerry and Jack for your thoughtful discussion. You have added something that the discussion clearly needs: a point of view that connects many forms of prejudice and many forms of disrespect of the people seen as other and therefore lesser. I agree that racism, childism, anti-feminism, anti-Semitism, anti-Native Americanism, and anti-immigrant acts and statements are all destructive. I also agree that Anna Freud's career is proof of her father's respect for women. Psychoanalysis was ready for powerful women, and even a first female president of the IPA. And a second. But I think that feminism has had some useful consequences: more women doctors, more women lawyers, more women in Congress, more girls sports teams, more women on the Supreme Court, more women owning our own businesses, more women daring to do math, more women willing to report rapes, more women willing to ask for help with severe superegos. And there are other things those late 20th century viragoes helped change. The point here is that a circle of like-minded people can form a thought collective that can change the ways other thought collectives think.

I really loved your point about rage preventing creative thought. I think one person's rage can translate into another person's thought and create a climate of opinion that can change thinking and behavior. I suppose that idea comes from my experience of the student protests when Vietnam awaited any student whose GPA did not measure up. Their rage changed what their parents, friends and eventually political representatives thought. They forced an end to the senseless war. Even if the enraged person does not directly change her environment, her passion can inspire others. Those others can state her position in perhaps less passionate but more persuasive terms. They can negotiate.

It has become fashionable among young women to disavow feminism, especially the feminism of their mothers and grandmothers. My paper was an attempt to show the positive effects of the feminist movement on psychoanalytic theory about female development.

CHAPTER 15

When Prejudice Comes Up Against Ambition: Response to Arlene Kramer Richards' "Rage and Creativity"

Lucille Spira

The ideas set forth by Arlene Kramer Richards in "Rage and Creativity: How Second-Generation Feminist Thought Collective Influenced Psychoanalysis," and the rich contributions of her discussants, led me to think about the links between longing, ambition, and prejudice. In her paper, Richards identifies herself as an "equal opportunity feminist." To me, that implies both a philosophy and a modus operandi based on inclusiveness and fairness. As an advocate of "equal opportunity," I want to focus my discussion on how an interplay of institutional policies, prejudicial behavior, and patriarchal structure can thwart ambition. This is a continuation of my desire to understand what some people confront when they overcome, or attempt to overcome, arbitrary barriers steeped in racism, sexism or social snobbery (A. K. Richards and L. Spira, 2012; see Appendix). Here, also, I will mention particular points from the discussions of Richards' work in this volume that address my interest and illuminate the role of thought collectives as potentially empowering forces.

Ambition

How many women have been told they are being too ambitious when they set their sights on something a person in power thinks should be beyond their reach? In part, it is these institutionalized, restrictive voices that gave rise to the resurgence of feminism in the 1960's and 1970's. As Arlene Kramer Richards explains, during this wave of second generation feminism, many women set about taking charge of their destinies, claiming the power to decide who they w/ could become. Some gathered in groups to share their thinking, feelings, and experiences and to gain support for their aspirations. With that encouragement, many women began speaking up for themselves and, in the process, experienced an important source of power.

The psychological benefit of having one's voice heard, even when the tone is angry, is beautifully described in this volume in two contributions, one written by Sandra Cohen and the other by Paula Ellman. In another essay, Merle Molofsky, who identifies as a mother, wife, humanist and feminist, uses her independent voice as a writer and psychoanalyst. It was not always that way, she says. As a young woman, she asked her boyfriend's permission to attend a consciousness raising group. He angrily said, "No," adding that such groups were only for lesbians, to him, a devalued group. At that time, it was not unusual for young and even older women to ask for permission to do things outside their roles as mother, wife or girlfriend. Molofsky did not attend that consciousness raising group but she did regain her voice and eventually found a very different kind of person with whom to establish a marriage based on equal collaboration. She says, "The value we most need is to create balance, by adding connectivity to independence."

186

Some of the voices in the women's movement emphasized equal pay for equal work and quality child care. Some wanted safe spaces to shelter from domestic abuse. Some focused on issues having to do with women's bodies and sexuality. In Dorothy Evans Holmes' scholarly discussion here, she expands on the categories of "equal opportunity" feminists and "difference" feminists as mentioned by Arlene Kramer Richards. One thing many women expressed and share today is the wish to be seen and understood as an individual and not as a category. Looking at contemporary women, it is clear that no woman can speak for all women. Breaking the glass ceiling might be a major priority for some women, but others are still fighting to earn a decent minimum wage that puts food on the table. While some women are calling for women to "lean in" others are calling for men to "lean out" *(The New York Times,* Oct. 2019).

Pioneering women psychoanalyst, whose work is now highly regarded were people who formed and shared their ideas even if doing so meant being ignored by the power structure of the time. Arlene Kramer Richards, Nancy Kulish, and Rosemary Balsam describe the situation for women psychoanalysts during the time of the 2nd generation feminists. Kulish points out that energy coming from psychoanalysts who trained originally in disciplines other than psychoanalysis, e.g., Nancy Chodorow, helped empower women psychoanalysts to formulate their ideas about women's psychology, including a final debunking of penis envy, well-discussed here by Cordelia Schmidt-Hellerau. Why do revisions in theory about women's bodies and psychical impact matter? Nancy Goodman, in her up close and scholarly contribution, here, speaks to this question. She says that she found gender specific theory empowering as it allowed her as a woman psychoanalyst to listen to herself and to her patients in new ways. It expanded our listening and our idea of unconscious fantasy with its metaphors and defenses, as she so artfully points out.

A Vignette: A Convergence of Sexism and Racism

Margaret Morgan Lawrence, M.D., an African American woman, who eventually became a child psychoanalyst, was the first African American graduate of New York Psychiatric Institute and the first African American woman certified in psychoanalysis at the Columbia Psychoanalytic Center.

In the 1930's, Margaret Morgan, later, Dr. Margaret Morgan Lawrence, a well-qualified graduate of Cornell University, applied to Cornell Medical School and was rejected. Race? Gender? After all, being rejected or blocked from fulfilling one's ambition is part of the collective history of many women, particularly members of marginalized minority groups.

The New York Times, in a recent obituary about her, says that the Dean told her she would not be admitted because an African American male whom they had admitted (many years before) did not "work out." Eventually, she learned what the Dean meant by his not "working out." That male medical student died from TB before he could graduate!

Who can ensure they will not die at an inconvenient time? To me this weird explanation for racial profiling captures the irrational aspect of prejudice as discussed by Bird (1957), a psychoanalyst.

Dr. Margaret Morgan Lawrence (then, Margaret Morgan) continued in her pursuit of a medical education and was accepted at Columbia University College of Physicians and Surgeons. There, she found a more benign gatekeeper, one willing to open a door rather than shut out a qualified applicant who did not fit the usual medical school profile. However, her admission was contingent upon her accepting that white patients might not allow her to treat them. One can only imagine how this caveat stung.

At that time, she was one of ten women students and one of a very few African American students at Columbia University College of Physicians and Surgeons. After graduation, she applied for an internship at Babies Hospital and was rejected. Racism and sexism once more joined to keep the door locked; the doctors' residence did not accept women and the nurses' residence would not accept a Black woman. Yet, she found an alternative path that resulted in a long, stellar career. In one of her psychoanalytic papers (1982), she cites Dr. Charles Lawrence, III, who believed that the purpose of segregation is to define as (inferior) not to separate. This seems applicable to sexism as well as racism. Lee Jenkins, in this anthology, speaking from the perspective of a Black male psychoanalyst says that both white women and Black men had had to deal with intrusive and limiting conceptions of their nature and place in life.

If a "thought collective" existed at a time when prejudice and racial separatism was the norm, who would have been in her "thought collective" or her support network? Certainly, the expectation must have been that she model herself after the male medical students and doctors. But as Schmidt-Hellerau cautions us here, where women identify with the macho aspects of their male colleagues, there is a loss to them and to what they might contribute.

Perhaps she was able to rely almost exclusively on an internalized supportive voice developed during her upbringing. We know that such supportive voices can be internalized from interactions with parents, teachers, mentors, friends and religious and social groups. They are also nourished by the satisfaction in personal achievements. These voices fuel us when, without external support, we are made to feel unwelcome. Or, perhaps her ambition was strong enough to empower her, to allow her to put aside the indignities and loneliness she must have experienced. An article about her mentions that she had a mentor, the only African American doctor on the faculty, Dr. Charles Drew, whom her daughter, Dr. Sara Lawrence Lightfoot, says was an encouraging voice (as reported in *Health Matters*). Dr. Benjamin Spock was a person she encountered in her professional training who she came to admire; the admiration was for his manner with his child patients, not because he was a member of the power structure.

Dr. Margaret Morgan Lawrence must have known at the outset that she would be one of a very few, or even a first. Perhaps some people prepare themselves beforehand to weather negative pushback. Perhaps Dr. Lawrence prepared herself to encounter racism and sexism as she approached a border marked, "Reserved for white men." Pioneers like her and like those referred to by Arlene Kramer Richards, including Karen Horney and Melanie Klein, pave the way for others who do not fit the established profile. Sometimes where there is a "closed" mind policy, those with the "different" voice, e.g., Klein and Horney, decide to take their ideas elsewhere and start what Arlene Kramer Richards describes as a "thought collective." As many here have pointed out, through all these efforts, profiles change and many women are freer to express their voices.

As we see from the rationale given for Margaret Morgan's (later, Dr. Margaret Morgan Lawrence) rejection by Cornell medical school, one failure, or, perceived failure, by a minority person who is for all intents and purposes a "first," closes doors for other members. Former First Lady Michelle Obama reports that she understood that fact very early and kept it in mind in her role as First Lady *(On Becoming,* 2018). When a "first" succeeds there is an extraordinary pressure. The "good enough" that might be acceptable for the dominant group is not good enough for a first. She must work a lot harder. This reality can overly strain one's ego, an often ignored negative result of prejudice.

It is not surprising that Dr. Margaret Morgan Lawrence's psychotherapeutic work with African American poverty stricken families was focused on finding and interpreting ego strengths of the family members (Margaret Morgan Lawrence, 1982). The families and children seen in the therapeutic nursery setting were assigned to a multi-disciplinary team making use of principles from psychoanalytic developmental theory. She believed that each of the individuals in the families who were seen in that milieu had unrecognized inner resources and ego strengths that needed to be uncovered and built upon. Her actions and interventions were designed to support the patients' self-esteem. She did not let a young male patient destroy an artwork that he had created in his therapy (Margaret Morgan Lawrence, 1999). The message was that what came from him was not garbage; rather as a creative production it was an expression of self to be valued. Perhaps such interventions on her part were one way of showing "Black lives matter." The therapeutic nursery setting, and family psychotherapy program, during her auspices can be likened to a thought collective. There, ego psychology and "massive-dose" therapy (her term) can be considered a philosophical stance directed to empowering both patient and staff.

Brief View of Prejudice from a Psychoanalytic Perspective

As I understand Bird's (1957) idea, prejudice is a negative, irrational thought that functions as an idée fixe. The prejudiced person, unconsciously identified with the hated object, must separate himself/herself from him/her. In this example, what is projected and condemned is ambition (which Bird suggests may derive from the condemnation of oedipal wishes and sibling rivalry). To paraphrase, 'I am not the audaciously ambitious one deserving of wrath. You are the one deserving of contempt when you want what society deems out of bounds for you and your group.'

While Bird's ideas and treatment helped his patient, Stoute (2017) cautions the psychoanalytic community that explaining prejudice as only rooted in oedipal conflict avoids the reality of the impact of culturally transmitted prejudice on African Americans and others. Her review of the early psychoanalytic literature points out how African Americans were disparaged and stereotyped.

It is easy to understand how the negative thoughts that are part of prejudice spark negative actions, although Bird (1957) focused on thoughts not actions. I remind myself that negative actions are fueled by thoughts, affects, poorly resolved conflicts and negative experiences.

In their discussion here, Novick and Novick point out the presence of institutional sadomasochism that drives prejudice.

Interestingly, Kerry Kelly Novick, here with Jack Novick, reports that she had to go to England and the Anna Freud Center to find training as a child psychoanalyst. She did not let circumstances quash her ambition. I wondered whether the unavailability of a program suitable for her was because the establishment considered work with children less important than work with adults. In my professional experience, most of the work with children and their parents was assigned to social workers, my professional group, one heavily composed of women, and excluded from training at APsaA membership Institutes for many years.

Jack Novick, encountering a different issue that also threatened to interfere with his professional development, describes how he turned to the legal system to prevent the Institute where he was a member from disallowing him to teach others who were not members of an APsaA Institute training program. The message, among other things, was that outsiders are not worthy of being taught what Jack Novick had learned. Perhaps, they were seen as too ambitious.

The Future

Future thought collectives within psychoanalysis might put ideas like those discussed by Harris (2005), and mentioned here by Kulish, in the forefront. Harris does not hold to the idea of fixed and inborn feminine and masculine characteristics. She (2011) points out that even in a cohort group—a young women's sports team—she observed difference and what she describes as "emerging and unpredictable desire for bodies, power and intimacy."

Hart (2019) whose discussion of diversity in a recent volume of TAP, where he focuses on the importance of understanding the multiple ways in which diversity might be considered, reminds us that we might have to come out of our comfort zone as we widen our scope. As we think about our binary view of gender, he suggests that those steeped in this traditional idea of gender become more accustomed to accepting that the pronoun *"they"* might refer to one individual. He cautions that focusing on the issues, experiences, and dynamics of a particular aspect of diversity loses breadth, just as focusing on the multiplicity of one's diversity, loses depth. As I understand Hart, contemporary psychoanalysis needs to find a balance between breadth and depth as it strives toward inclusion. One hopes that a thought collective considering race and diversity, similar to the one that led to changes in how we understand women and their ambition, holds promise.

Rosemary Balsam, here, speaks to how she benefited from psychoanalytic journal issues that addressed single topics, such as gender. She points to former JAPA editors, Harold Blum and Arnold Richards, who published single issues devoted to one subject, often topics formerly underrepresented in the literature. Such collections allow a reader to consider different perspectives, deepen knowledge about a particular subject and potentially generate further explorations.

I also recognize that thought collectives are not always forces for growth; ideologies can imprison. The particular ideology of a thought collective and the character of its members determines whether it is a force for growth or imprisonment. William Fried, in this volume, comes at this another way when he says that, "one might justifiably conclude that there are now not one, but two psychoanalyses, the earlier male, and the later female; the earlier derived from the experiences, biases, and conceptualizations of men; the later from those of women." The implied question there is: How do the formerly ignored not identify with the aggressor?

As psychoanalysis widens its scope, we might think about how a concept like primary femininity may shift when we consider the impact on a girl's development when she is raised by two fathers. Will our ideas about what is primary to boys and girls shift with the growing changes in our definition of family or will such concepts not even be part of the discussion? This question came to me as I read about a gay father raising two daughters with his male partner who is also a parent to the girls. One father expressed the thought that girls' doll play might be different when raised by two dads. But he found himself surprised when his daughters play mommy and daddy rather than daddy and daddy or mommy and mommy (*Gays with Kids;* online site). When he told them it was fine for them to play mommy and mommy or daddy and daddy they responded that what they wanted to play was mommy and daddy. This father is learning to recognize and consider his girls' voices and agency. Kimberly Kleinman, here, suggests that thinking of caring for a child as a gendered activity is not beneficial and perhaps harmful.

Alison Feit, in her very creative discussion in this volume, highlights the factors in her development that led her to raise her sons to embrace both humanist and feminist values. Her hope is that they will continue to be the compassionate, nurturing, and active young men that she now witnesses through the lens of fulfilled motherhood. She reminds us that feminists are not born that way but that they internalize feminist values in a relational system; the overall environment counts too.

The world is changing. Institutional psychoanalysis is opening up, but what role psychoanalysis will play in the direction the world moves, particularly around attitudes steeped in prejudice and thwarted ambition, is a question. Will our collective voice turn to others previously excluded and welcome not only their presence but also their unique voices? Our world has a long way to go toward respecting all of its citizens, particularly less privileged women, children and many members of marginalized minority groups. Perhaps thought collectives that address diversity can refine theory, define issues and empower people toward a better understanding of how the psychological and social interact. Sometimes a clinical setting, like the one Margaret Morgan Lawrence oversaw, one with a philosophical stance that flows from theory grounded in clinical research, can be a force to better understand the perceptions, feelings and behavior of cohort groups previously ignored. Where we confront prejudice, with its gatekeepers who attempt to stifle ambitions, fail to recognize strengths and silence opposing voices, we might all benefit from a team or "thought collective," as Arlene Kramer Richards sees it, as a catalyzing force. But an interplay with the political and legal system seems essential in moving our society toward a feminist ideal of equality and opportunity.

Addendum

As I read about Dr. Margaret Morgan Lawrence, and wrote my discussion, I wondered what it was like today for women physicians of color. Soon after, I got an answer. A recent New York Times article, "For Doctors of Color, Microaggressions Are All Too Familiar", by Emma Goldberg, 8/11/2020, reported on the experiences of a number of women of color, all physicians in major hospitals or health care settings. One doctor, discussing what she experienced as a Black woman physician, said that even after she introduced herself as a doctor, she was mistaken for a food service worker or a janitor, and was asked by a patient if she was there to pick up the trash. Further, she pointed out that she does not believe that a patient would say that to a white male physician. This sounds familiar and resonates with the treatment of Dr. Margaret Morgan Lawrence discussed above. A question becomes: Racism, sexism, or a convergence of both?

Goldberg's article found that these microaggressions toward women doctors of color, routinely occur in medicine. According to the experts cited, such behaviors can have a negative impact on self-esteem, as I suggested in my discussion. What makes it even more challenging for the Black woman physician is that she might be the only one of her race in her medical setting and consequently is alone with her discomfort. One such physician says that she felt validated when she learned that others like her had similar negative experiences. To me, this supports Richards' idea of the importance of a "thought collective" to empower. One interviewee suggests that the first step is to hear and validate the personal experience of the one who reports inappropriate and destructive behaviors steeped in racism; I add, rooted in sexism as well.

References

Bird, B. (1957). A Consideration of the Etiology of Prejudice. *Journal of the American Psychoanalytic Association,* 5:490-513.

Harris, A. E. (2011). Gender as a Strange Attractor: Discussion of the Transgender Symposium. *Psychoanal. Dial.,* 21(2), 230-238.

Hart, A. H. (2019). Why Diversities? *The American Psychoanalyst.* Vol. 53, No. 3, 8-10.

Lawrence, M. M. (1982). Psychoanalytic Psychotherapy Among Poverty Populations and the Therapist's Use of the Self. *J. Amer. Acam. of Psychoanalysis and Dynamic Psychotherapy.* 10 (2). 241-255.

_____. (1999). Creativity and the Family. Gender and Psychoanalysis, *An Interdisciplinary Journal.* 4 (4).399-411.

Obama, M. *On Becoming Michelle Obama.* New York: Crown Publishing Group. (2018).

Richards, A.K. and L. Spira (2012). What We Learned from Proust: Psychological and Social Determinants of Snobbery and Prejudice. *International Journal Of Applied Psychoanalytic Studies.* Vol. 10, 1, 75-86.

Seelye, K.Q. Margaret Lawrence, 105, Dies; Pioneering Black Female Psychoanalyst. *The New York Times.* (Dec., 2019).

Stoute B. J. (2017). Race and Racism in Psychoanalytic thought: The Ghost in Our Nursery. Special Section Conversations on Psychoanalysis and Race. *TAP,* Vol. 51, (1).

*It Happened Here: Dr. Margaret Morgan Lawrence, A Pioneer in Children's Mental Health Research. *New York Presbyterian Health Matters.*

Whippman, R. Enough Leaning In. Let's Tell Men to Lean Out. *The New York Times.* (Oct., 2019).

*No author attribution.

Response to Lucille Spira

Arlene Kramer Richards

Thank you Lucille for your expansive view of what women experienced before second wave feminism and how that relates to what other groups have faced in trying to achieve respect for our humanity. Your vignette of the career of a black woman who became a physician and then a psychiatrist and psychoanalyst encapsulates the struggles she faced as so many others of her generation and generations before hers faced in the United States. By being classified as black she was treated as a member of a devalued group. It was seen as legitimate to exclude, exploit, beat, maim and even kill members of that group just for being black. The same was true for women.

In earlier times in the United States when black people were enslaved, they and their labor were valuable to their enslavers (I cannot bring myself to call those people their "masters"), it was not permissible to kill them because they were property. Ironically, becoming free made them prey to being murdered. Ironically also black women were and are less likely to be murdered by whites than black men were and are. They were still seen as valuable property, not dangerous, but useful.

In the United States the racial laws were more draconian than in any other country. Even a person with a single black ancestor, a single great-grandparent, was and is legally defined

199

as black. Marked as black, like being defined as female, meant and means accepting deference to white males.

The achievements of a black woman who became able to use her talents as an instrument to help children overcome similar difficulties are important especially because they can inspire others to identify with her and develop their own talents to help others.

By including homosexuals in the groups excluded and devalued Lucille has widened the scope of our discussion again. There is a history of changing values in this sphere. While the Greeks of Plato's time valued man to man love above heterosexual love, and in other times it was considered part of love, neither more or less valued than heterosexual love, homosexuality has been considered criminal or shameful or both in the past two centuries in the West. The argument was that it was their choice so they should be held responsible for it. The homosexual community argued that it was not a choice but an inborn impulse for some people and was therefore just as legitimate as was heterosexuality for most people.

What Lucille did not bring up here is the more recent trans-gender and genderless identity groups that have become the latest group in American society to object to being marginalized and devalued. Here the argument has been that socially imposed gender denies the individual freedom of choice of self-expression.

I think that for all of these groups the agenda is two-fold, just as it is for women. Equality of opportunity and respect for difference are on all of these groups' agendas. At the moment in our country I am proud of what we have achieved and aware that we all still have a far way to go to achieve these simple goals.

Narrative Voices:
Feminism and Psychoanalysis

Section II: *Narrative Voices: Feminism and Psychoanalysis*

My Story:
Growing Up With The Women's Movement

Judith L. Alpert, Ph.D.

New York University Postdoctoral Program
in Psychotherapy and Psychoanalysis

New York University Department of
Applied Psychology

I was born in 1944. My mother wanted me to be a dental hygienist. Maybe I might meet a nice dentist and have a good life, she thought. As I was growing up, I did not see women working outside the home. My path was clear: find *someone,* marry *someone,* and have children.

When I graduated from Tufts University in 1966, I was not engaged. While I got my B.A., I did not get the "MRS." that "the girls" talked about. That was unusual at the time, at least among my college friends. But I had fallen in love. I had fallen in love with Psychology. A gift from an uncle resulted in enough money for me to get a master's degree at Teachers College, Columbia University. I wasn't straying too much as it was *only* a master's degree. Once there, Dr. White offered me a full NIMH stipend and my path to a Columbia University Ph.D. was clear. I was going to become a psychologist.

I married in 1967, after my first year in graduate school,

and was thankful to my husband, who was studying in New Haven, for letting me commute to and live in New York for three days a week and return to New Haven and to my wife responsibilities for four days a week. I had to wash the dirty dishes that had amassed while I was studying in New York, entertain his friends, do the laundry, clean the apartment, and squeeze in my studies. I was thankful for the 6:19 a.m. New Haven Railroad train ride to New York, which enabled me to complete my readings for my 9:00 a.m. Tuesday class.

Sometime during 1967, both my husband and I were introduced to the women's movement. It made a lot of sense to both of us. He encouraged me to get involved, although I didn't need much encouragement. I don't think he realized how much it would change our lives. I don't think I did either. While he intellectually agreed with the movement, he did not want to wash dishes, do laundry, etc., and for me, there was no turning back. He finally got on board.

My husband, at the time, was at the law school at Yale University where Anna Freud taught a course with Al Solnit and Joseph Goldstein. I attended the course and made a few female law school friends. There were very few women at the law school at that time. I learned that women were only called on once a semester, on "women's day", when divorce and custody issues were discussed. At the time, there were no groups for women law students. I joined the Yale University Law Wives Association and we discussed the growing women's movement. We discussed the sexual harassment I had experienced at Columbia as a graduate student. The law wives were smitten with the very issues that Betty Friedan wrote about in 1963.

My involvement in the women's movement escalated in 1968 when I moved to New York City. I joined the New York

Radical Feminists, marched in numerous marches in NYC and in Washington, D.C., was a marshal at several of the marches, appeared in photos in the New York Times, one time because I was assigned to Bella Abzug for the march and we were holding onto each other, and the other when I was already a mother and carrying my one year old as I marched, started a consciousness raising group which met for 20 years, weekly at first and then less frequently … . You get it . I was involved. I was hooked. I was changing and I was going to change the world.

I wanted to get others involved too. I wanted to save other women as well as future generations of men and women. I started a nonsexist child rearing group in the mid-1970's as I continued to engage in other feminist activities.

Fearing that I would go inward and lose my social consciousness, I was initially reluctant to enter psychoanalysis. As life was so stressful and advancement in my career demanded my entering treatment, I entered treatment with an older female analyst. She began her career late in her life, and supported my career. *Analysis did not interfere with my feminism.*

How did I combine my feminism with my professional activity? In 1971, ten days after my daughter was born, I began to teach an undergraduate Psychology of Women course at Marymount Manhattan College. While there may have been other Psychology of Women courses taught that year, to my knowledge, it was the first year that any Psychology of Women courses were offered. I have taught graduate students in my NYU Psychology of Women course every year (except when on sabbatical) since then. My guess: I have taught the course about 40 times and probably for more years than some of you readers have been a woman! What is striking to me is how "we have come a long way, baby" and how we have not. One issue that women continue to struggle with is how to combine career and family. How different the challenges might have been if Nixon had signed the Child Care Bill and if we had had universal child care, a need addressed by many of the contributors to this volume.

When I first began to teach, I remember worrying about whether there was enough material to teach. There were only two textbooks on the topic at the time. One or two years later, there was a flood of textbooks, several journals in the field, and a division of Psychology of Women within the American Psychological Association and, later, a women's group within the Division of Psychoanalysis of the American Psychological Association.

The field of Psychology of Women has changed. Pre 1970's the field focused on sex differences and inferiority. In the 1970s we set out to prove there was no difference between men and women and, if there was a difference, it was due to sex-role socialization. In the 1980's, we were reading Chodorow and Gilligan and Belenky and these readings affirmed that difference did not equal inferiority. In the 1990s, the focus was on deconstruction, multiculturalism, and the acknowledgment of diversity. Men's studies also became a focus at this time. Over the last 20 years, there has been attention to women and violence, oppression of girls and women in the developing worlds, challenges to the gender binary and intersectionality.

The field of Psychoanalysis and Women has changed. For example, we no longer ask:

Is psychoanalytic theory relevant to the psychology of women?

Are women masochistic?

Would psychoanalysis be different if it were developed and nurtured by a woman?

Can psychoanalysis and feminism co-exist?

As the groups and field developed, so did I. My professional identity focused on women's issues. Also, for example, early on I did research on women and multiple roles. Later (1986), I edited *Psychoanalysis and Women: Contemporary Reappraisals*, which was published by The Analytic Press. More recently I have been involved in writing about women and trauma (e.g. child sexual abuse, women and violence, transgenerational transmission of trauma, sexual boundary violations in therapy).

While this is written for *Rage and Creativity: How Feminism Sparked Psychoanalysis*, (IPBooks), I think this piece could probably be best thought of as the growth of a field; and of a woman who grew with it.

Section II: *Narrative Voices: Feminism and Psychoanalysis*

Two Feminist Males in My Life: Psychoanalyst and Husband

by Selma Duckler

Former Actress, Advocate for the Arts; Former President of American Psychoanalytic Association Foundation and Former Committee Chair on Foundations; Distinguished Service Award, APsaA; published film reviewer.

My parents were Jewish immigrants from Poland who arrived in the United States in 1921. My father was 13 and my mother 15. When they got here, my father went to high school and my mother went to work. They had met at a party and were married in March 1930. I was born in January of the following year; my mother, who always said she wanted a girl, wound up crying. Why? Because, as she put it, a "woman is born to suffer". Later in life, my mother would tell me that it is "a man's world and the sooner you know that, the better", and when I announced that I wanted to go to college, my mother would say, "College? You will spend your college education at the kitchen sink. Men don't want a college woman. Men don't like women smarter than they are. Women in college are there because they can't get a man."

College talk also made my father violent. There was always something that made him violent, and I lived in fear of his outbursts. I would think, "Maybe tonight it won't happen. Maybe tonight". I was almost always wrong. It didn't take long for me to realize that I was not going to be allowed to go to college or ever leave home. My father was impulsive, crazy, and infantile, and my mother did not protect me. Her main idea about me was that I should grow up in order to some day write her story so that the world would know all about her suffering. Between my father's temper and my mother's need for me to be her scribe, I tried my best just to survive. My friends would say, "Selma, you are adopted, because parents don't treat their kids like they treat you". My mother never had a kind thing to say to me and when my father blew up, she would retaliate or descend into a world of self-pity. So I lived in the fantasy that I was adopted.

Since I wasn't going to college, I stopped going to school and set up a tent in the living room where I lived. Inside the tent, I had all my books, some crackers and jam. One night my parents wanted to talk with me. They said they thought my problem was that I was "oversexed" and that my father would "do nice things" with me so that I wouldn't be so "oversexed." It was insane, what they were saying. I took this jar of jam and threw it against the wall where it broke and spattered. That was when my mother took me to the family doctor while my father told me I'm crazy and that I should be sent to the mental institution. This doctor said there was nothing wrong with me, and I should see a psychoanalyst. He knew of one in Milwaukee, the other side of the state. We drove to Milwaukee and I met Dr. Black. In the first meeting, he said I was precocious. That night when I looked up the meaning, I was shocked to discover it wasn't an insult. It was possibly the first positive comment someone ever had given to me.

Dr. Black wanted to see me twice a week. I wasn't going

to school anyhow, so I took the train every Tuesday and Thursday to Milwaukee for the remainder of the school year. I was 17 and acting out in every self-destructive way possible. But Dr. Black was incredibly patient. When he discovered how ignorant I was about anatomy (my parents didn't want me to learn the word for "penis", menstruation was considered to be a "curse"), he sat on the couch with me with an anatomy book and we looked at it together. It was fascinating. I had no idea. When I told him I wanted to be an actress, he frowned and suggested I become a pre-med. I thought he was out of his mind. No one had ever wanted me to go to school, let alone medical school. I went back to school and graduated, started the University of Wisconsin, and got a job. When my father's checks bounced and I couldn't pay tuition, I called an uncle in Phoenix to ask about what to do about my life. He sent me a ticket to come to see him. He and my aunt thought I should go to LA but I wanted to go back to Dr. Black. He meant so much to me, and I loved him. But I had no money. I decided to call just to tell him, and to my surprise Dr. Black said he would help me get a job and I could pay him when I could. I was shocked. Not only that, he said that if I could not pay him, not to worry about it. He would still see me. I was beside myself. So I went back into therapy, and I got a job myself.

Dr. Black was the first feminist I had ever met. I came to him injured, vulnerable and desperate. He treated me with respect and kindness. He took on a parental role outside analytic boundaries. He had taken chances with his practice—real risks—to help me. He was more to me than my parents. During that time, I also started to see a man ten years older than me, whom I married a year later, Lawrence Duckler. He was the second feminist I ever met. These two men treated me with care and kindness. In their eyes, I was not "just" a woman, but also a person. It always had been one or the other but never both. But to these men, I was accepted as someone with a mind who was equal in stature and respect. I was to be taken seriously. I didn't have to play the role of a mindless, cute joke.

Long after this experience in therapy, in a long term analysis in Oregon, I decided I was going to devote my life to the development of psychoanalysis in the community, to pay him back for his kindness and love to me. He had saved my life. Dr. Black had such esteem for me, and I had never known that was something that existed before. He helped me begin to have some semblance of my own sense of self-respect.

I have had a myriad of varied experiences in my life—jumpstarting Portland to have an analytic institute, becoming the first lay person to chair a committee for the APsaA, having five children, being an actress, conducting programs for the Portland ACLU, teaching creative dramatics, writing movie reviews and a chapter of a book. Life has been full and rich, none of which would ever have happened without analysis, Dr. Black, and my husband, who I sadly lost eight years ago after sixty-two years of a happy marriage.

When my daughter, Merridawn, was filing out her enrollment form for college, next to the box asking about religion affiliation, she wrote, "Freud". I always think about that. She was raised in a family so different from my own. I came from a poverty-stricken family, with shame about being a woman, and she came from a family that owed a lot to psychoanalytic treatment—the ideas, the respect for inner life, and the value placed on the expression of self and especially on the importance of childhood and adolescence.

My three daughters are ardent feminists, as are my two sons. I realize my story takes place about a decade before the rich essays in this volume. But these archaic views still exist. Our culture is still deeply patriarchal. These views of women may be hidden behind excuses, different kinds of language, but dehumanizing attitudes towards women still exist in so many places, and they continue to threaten to poison our soul.

Section II: *Narrative Voices: Feminism and Psychoanalysis*

In the Wake of the Second Wave

by Les Von Losberg , M.A.,
MFA

Poet, conceptual artist, singer-songwriter, and Japanese taiko drummer. Co-founder, with Merle Molofsky, of Poets Union, a Brooklyn-based grassroots literary arts organization (1976–1985) and Poets Union Press, and of Kizuna Daiko with Chika Croteau and Yoko Ibanez in 2016. His poetry has appeared in newspapers and small press

Les Von Losberg and his grand-daughter Leah

journals; his art in the Katonah Museum, the Hammond Museum, the Westchester Museum of Contemporary Art, the Blue Door Gallery and other venues. He is a writer for the insurance industry and an estate, business and retirement planner.

Arlene Kramer Richards' article, "Rage and Creativity: How Second Generation Feminist Thought Collective Influenced Psychoanalysis", gave me pause to think about how feminism, embraced by so many young people I knew then, had influenced me during my early adulthood.

I once told a therapist I had been in treatment with for many years that all my personal and political values were rooted in my pathology. In some ways I was wrong, in others quite right. As I look back, many of my values are linked to a struggle with gender expectation norms that for me lasted well into my 20s. It was a struggle that led me to read feminist authors, to attend seminars on sexuality, to create an improvisation theater group called the Park Slope Sexual Theater (PSST!) to explore notions of masculinity and femininity, to create with Merle Molofsky a grassroots literary arts organization called Poets Union in which egalitarianism was a primary value, and to spend nearly eight years studying martial arts.

For me, it was the time of men's groups and of attempting to confront the gender stereotypes that oppressed us. It was a time of long hair, macramé necklaces and tie-dyed shirts, bright patches on your naturally worn-through jeans, embroidered Indian mirrored shirts, and of friendships with women that as often as not led to sex that was neither casual nor committed but uncommittedly friendly. These examples may seem at this remove trite, trivial or even inconsequential, but they were grist for the mill of change.

For much of my life, and especially during those times, the struggle was not with determining what kind of man I would be—long-haired and necklaced as I was at the time —but with whether I was "man enough". My struggle was not with biology, but with the social and cultural influences and demands that defined masculinity and femininity. In this intimate struggle, the gender politics that had so infused our culture was an unexpected aid in altering my focus to determining what kind of man I could be.

The way to engagement in this struggle was fraught. If I

were to characterize my parents, each with a single word, for my father I would choose "reserved"; for my mother, "bitter". And, as I knew myself as their only son, "wrong". Until I left for college, to return only two summers to work seven days a week to pay my own way through school, I thought of myself as ill-formed, broken, not good enough, and not quite human. I felt through my teen years at home that I was an inconvenience, a disappointment, unwanted and essentially unloved.

My parents' relationship seemed tumultuous and angry. They would argue, my mother vituperative, denigrating and bitter; my father furious and, as I thought then, impotent in the face of my mother's assaults. Their anger frightened me and early stifled my own. The only "fight" I ever had was with a boy who lived on my block in Brownsville-East New York, Brooklyn. I was five or six. I remember being surrounded by older boys egging us on. My next memory is of hiding behind my grandmother as the boy's mother stood in our apartment doorway yelling about me hitting her son in the stomach and making him throw up. I have no memory of hitting him or coming back to our apartment.

I was bullied as a child. My mother often cursed me profanely, occasionally slapped my face, tried at least once to kick me in anger, and would humiliate me in front of friends. I was bullied on my block in Brooklyn multiple times, once in grade school, and in Junior High by boys who—for reasons I did not understand—wanted to fight with me. I was timid, withdrawn, and was not the first pick as a playmate or a partner, not invited to the parties kids my own age gave, unable to relate. I felt an outsider, the beggar at the table, in many cases simply unworthy.

On entering high school, I decided to change my life. I

become outgoing, played sports, joined clubs and activities. In college, more of the same. In 1969, my birthday fell early in the draft lottery. I temporized to allay my muddled feelings and joined the local Naval Reserve Unit that summer, staying on at college for graduate school. I did not do this principally for patriotism, but because I felt that if I did not enlist in some branch of the service, I would think myself a coward for the rest of my life. It was a "manly" thing to do, if not the most dangerous option.

During my two years on active duty, my master's degree got me a billet teaching high school equivalency to prisoners in the Third Naval District Correctional Center in Brooklyn. At the end of my active duty, I stayed in Brooklyn, doing part-time work, writing poetry and engaging in Brooklyn's grassroots art life. More important than what I did was who I met. I met men and women, some younger than me, some older, who were thoughtful and intelligent, complex in their response to the fluidity of a world that was tumultuously changing around us.

Of the people who changed my life, the majority were independent women. They were gay, straight, or bi-sexual women who knew who they were or who were engaged in the struggle to find out, just as I was. The difference between us was not a biological issue, but one of the courage to face the tumult, to see it as useful rather than obstructive, to embrace ambivalence and confusion. In addition, the community I lived in was young, and, if not counter-culture, then attempting to develop a local culture embracing a broader spectrum of experience than commitment to a cookie-cutter just-for-the-money nine-to-five job implied.

There was art, there was music, there was theater, there were weekends of volleyball, softball, running in Prospect

Park; and there were parties where the door was always open. In the years I lived there, I never witnessed a fight or an argument at a party or neighborhood event. I felt the same feeling I had for the first time in high school, that I was accepted in the community, which felt both empowering and safe. I should not be misconstrued as remembering this in the roseate glow of youth. Not everyone liked me or liked me equally; and I did not like everyone or everyone equally either. Life was real, as now, and, thankfully, not withheld.

I have had many teachers in my life, men and women in high school who related to me as the human being I didn't think I truly was, friends who sought me out as much as I sought them. I had good friends in college and respect for and from my peers; I was trusted and given responsibility that I was both willing and able to fulfill. After college and a short-lived disastrously masochistic marriage, I met some men and more women who were independent, socially and culturally and politically aware, and patient and tolerant and trusting of the damaged person I was and the person I could become. They taught me to think, not to search my mind for what to regurgitate, but what to ask to move beyond what I already had stored away. They taught me to open my mind to individuality and possibility. They opened my mind to the fact that life is not a textbook, but a blank book to be filled. They taught me this, not formally but by example.

All this sounds too literary, I know, as well as exaggerated and over-blown. Yet, when I think back on those early relationships, most often with women, and look at the trajectory of my life: as a husband, a parent and a grandparent; as a poet, visual artist, singer song-writer, martial artist, taiko drummer, teacher, and while still incomplete, a yet more complete human being, it was the zeitgeist that women created that gave men like me space to breathe a different life into being than the one to which men, like women in their artificially prescribed roles, were bound.

Women Whose Writings Inspired Me

by Margery Quackenbush, PhD, LP

Psychoanalyst and Former Executive
Director of the NAAP; Recipient:
Miriam Berkman Spotnitz Award for
Scholarly Excellence, Advisor on the NYS
Psychoanalyst Case Narrative Exam.

Arlene Kramer Richards' thoughtful, well-researched article on the effects of feminism on psychoanalysis inspired me to consider how psychoanalysis has empowered women. Sigmund Freud empowered his own daughter, Anna Freud, to become a leading and influential psychoanalyst—one who, I agree with the Novicks' in their discussion here, that it is of concern Ms. Freud is currently ignored by APsaA.

As a licensed psychoanalyst, I work with candidates who want to become New York State licensed psychoanalysts. My work empowers them. Holding a license to practice a profession is empowering. In order to obtain a license one must pass an examination. The exam consists of writing two cases. The candidate is asked questions to determine the course of treatment. When the two cases are accepted, the candidate obtains a license.

In order to work with candidates who want to take the exam, I have been inspired by many psychoanalytic writings by women. It is clear from my readings that Freud encouraged the women who worked with him to write down and present their cases. His daughter, Anna, was the one of his six children who became a psychoanalyst. Helene Deutsch was his first assistant.

Anna Freud wrote *The Ego and the Mechanisms of Defense.* Her book deals with the ways and means by which the ego wards off unpleasure and anxiety, and exercises control over impulsive behavior, affects, and instinctive urges. She writes of the nine methods of defense: regression, repression, reaction formation, isolation, undoing, projection, introspection, turning against the self, reversal, and sublimation. In the exam the candidate is asked to explain the defenses that the patient exhibits.

Helene Deutsch wrote *The Psychology of Women* about the development of women and girls. The purpose of her book is to explain the normal psychic life of women and their normal conflicts. Deutsch said, "we know that the degree of psychic health is not determined by the absence of conflicts but by the adequacy of the methods used to solve and master them". Also in her book she said, "pathology reveals the normal conflicts and helps us to understand normal processes in the light of morbid ones." Intrapsychic functions are those that come from ego development and its handling of conflict. Candidates are asked to explain the autonomous functioning of the patient they are writing about when taking the exam.

Lucy Freeman is not a psychoanalyst but she wrote about her psychoanalysis in her books, *Fight against Fears* and *Farewell to Fear.* She gives a view of psychoanalysis from the couch. She writes of the types of interventions that during her six years of analysis freed her from her fears and dependencies. Freeman also co-authored *Freud and Women,* with Herbert Strean, a psychoanalyst, that highlights the importance of women in Freud's life and work. In the exam, interventions are asked for to show how the analyst's comments, questions, and other interventions moved the treatment forward.

Dr. Ruth Lax is a psychoanalyst who wrote *Becoming and Being a Woman*. Joyce McDougall, a prominent French psychoanalyst, said of Lax that "her years of experience and reflection on female psychosexual identity lead her beyond Freudian and feminist stereotypes to a passionate plea for recognition of the fact that girls, like boys, are born with zest, aggression, curiosity, and the impetus for self-fulfillment." About retirement, Dr. Lax wrote, "women who have led active gratifying lives, especially if they combined marriage and motherhood with a satisfying work experience, have the ability to cope with retirement in an adaptive way". In the exam the candidate is asked to demonstrate the reality testing ability of the patient they are writing about.

Joyce McDougall wrote many books in English and French. France was her home but she came to the United States to speak and conduct supervision. In her book, *The Many Faces of Eros*, she wrote, "To the extent that the masculine and the feminine parts of every individual are well integrated and accepted, we all have the potential to be creative - to sublimate the impossible wish to be both sexes and to create children with both parents". She also says "at one and the same time, the creator wishes to caress his or her medium of expression and to attack it in an effort to master it". Candidates are asked to gauge the patient's reality testing in a similar manner when taking the exam.

Phyllis Meadow, the founder of two psychoanalytic institutes, wrote in her book, *The New Psychoanalysis*, that "the analyst takes it as her task to elaborate the mental and emotional causes behind an individual's conscious ways of thinking and perceiving the world". She also says that "when Freud recognized the strength of a counterforce to 'knowing' one's impulses, the emphasis shifted from making the unconscious conscious to the study of resistances that prevent an individual from knowing his own thoughts and feelings". On the examination it is extremely important for candidates to understand and explain the nature of the resistance(s) in the case they are presenting.

Ethel Person is a psychoanalyst and psychiatrist, who wrote *The Sexual Century*, and *Dreams of Love and Fateful Encounters: the Power of Romantic Love*. She says that "aside from brief moments in infancy and childhood, we hardly ever come first. Being the most important person in someone else's life is one of the defining premises of passionate love". In analysis transference enables the patient to feel they come first in the session with the analyst. This can be demonstrated by the deepening of the transference. Understanding transference is what differentiates psychoanalysts from other mental health professionals. It is an important subject to understand when taking the exam.

Rosemary Balsam, a contributor here, who writes on feminine and gender theory, says that psychoanalysis remains almost silent on the body's procreative potential in everyday life, while primitive cultures were very aware of the procreative and nourishing potential of the female body. Balsam has many provocative ideas. She writes that being sexually supportive to men is treated as a function of and measure of health for those possessing a female body. In the exam the candidate has an opportunity to show how the healthy narcissism of the patient can be used so that the patient may develop their own activities and goals.

Just this summer, during the pandemic, I found an inspiring female analyst, child psychiatrist, and writer Dr. Anna Ornstein. She is the author of *My Mother's Eyes: Holocaust Memories of a Young Girl*, and many psychoanalytic papers. She lived in Hungary with her family as a young woman when Hungary was taken over by the Nazis. Anna and her mother were sent to Auschwitz. When they were finally freed, their emancipators sent them on their way and they had to figure out how to get home, which fortunately they managed to do. In her article, "The Relativity of Morality in the Contemporary World", she "explores the similarities and differences between the rise of fascism in the 1930's and our current political climate with special attention to the role of morality both on an individual and a collective basis". Her story of trauma, psychoanalysis, and training enables us to see the importance of psychoanalysis, encouraging candidates to enter psychoanalysis, train as psychoanalysts, and become licensed to practice as psychoanalysts. In the exam it is important to tell how patients process trauma and find their own way while in psychoanalytic treatment.

References

Balsam, R.H. (2019) "On the Natal Body and it's Confusing Place in Mental Life," J. Amer. Psychoan. Assn. , 67(1): 15-36.

Deutsch, H. *The Psychology of Women: Volume II—Motherhood*, Bantam Books, New York, NY, 1973.

Eigen, M. *Rage*, Wesleyan University Press, Middletown, CT, 2002.

Freeman, L. *Farewell to Fear*, G.P. Putnam's Sons, New York, NY. 1969.

Freud, A. *The Ego and the Mechanism of Defense*, International Universities Press, New York, 1982.

Freud, S. *Collected Works* (24 volumes), *Standard Edition*: The Hogarth Press, London, 1953-1968.

Lax, R. *Becoming and Being a Woman*, Jason Aronson, Northvale, NJ, 1997.

McDougall, J. *The Many Faces of Eros*, W.W.Norton & Co.,1995.

Meadow, P. *The New Psychoanalysis*, Rowman and Littlefield, New York, 2003.

Ornstein, A. "*My Mother's Eyes, Holocaust Memories of a Young Girl*, Emmis Books, Cincinnati, Ohio, 2004.

Ornstein, A. (2020) "The Relativity of Morality in the Contemporary World", *Psychoanalytic Inquiry*, 40:4, 223-233,

Person, E. *Dreams of Love and Fateful Encounters: The Power of* Romantic Love, Penguin Books, New York, NY, 1989.

James Joyce's Independent Molly

by Paul Schwaber, Ph.D.

Professor of Letters Emeritus at Wesleyan
University; Psychoanalyst; Numerous
presentations and publications, most
notably: *The Cast of Characters: A Reading
of Ulysses* (Yale University Press, 1999.)

It is appropriate that the last chapter of *Ulysses* be Molly
Bloom's. It affords readers a chance to know Molly closely, as
she lies head to toe with her sleeping husband at the end of
the extraordinary day the book presents, June 16, 1904. She
doesn't speak but thinks busily, indeed passionately, about
women and men, both specifically and generally, as well as
about Leopold surprisingly asking her to make breakfast for
him, which reverses their usual pattern. She also ponders her
fulfilling sexual experience a few hours earlier with Blazes
Boylan, and what it could portend for her and for her marriage. Through the day we readers have followed the odys-
sean travels of Leopold and several other male Dubliners,
grown especially aware too, in time, of his painful expectation
that Boylan and Molly, who is a singer and with Boylan, her
agent, planning a tour of Belfast soon, will become intimate.
We've learned also that since the Blooms' baby boy, Rudy,
died eleven days after birth, they have not had complete intercourse—perhaps because of fear they might lose another.
But neither, apparently, has insisted. Meanwhile, their oldest

child, Milly, has reached adolescence, angering her mother by growing separate, flirtatious, and aware of her own attractiveness. She now works as a photographer's assistant in a town outside of Dublin. Silently, but reflecting busily and intensely, Molly reveals a great deal about her feelings and by the end delights recalling how she got "Poldy" to propose. Joyce had told his friend Frank Budgen that Molly would have the last word in *Ulysses*. Famously, it is "yes," repeated three times, reaffirming her love for her husband: "yes I said yes I will Yes." And thus this astounding modern epic ends.

Molly is memorable, wonderfully depicted, an artistic triumph, clearly as believable a person as Leopold, Stephen Dedalus and others in the book. She is the key woman. Yet her intriguing thoughts and feelings were presented, after all, by James Joyce. Though no woman, he had through his art given birth to her. Before long too, he had a dream about her—and kept a record of it:

> I saw Molly Bloom on a hillock under a sky full of moonlit clouds rushing overhead. She had just picked up from the grass a child's black coffin and flung it after the figure of a man passing down a side road by the field she was in. It struck his shoulders, and she said 'I've done with you.' The man was Bloom seen from behind. There was a shout of laughter from some American journalists in the road opposite, led by Ezra Pound. I was very indignant and vaulted over the gate into the field and strode up to her and I delivered the one speech of my life. It was very long, eloquent and full of passion, explaining all the last episode of *Ulysses* to her. She wore a black opera cloak, or *sortie de bal,* had become slightly grey and looked like la Duse. She smiled when I ended on an astronomical climax, and then, bending, picked

up a tiny snuff box, in the form of a little black coffin, and tossed it toward me, saying, 'And I have done with you, too. Mr. Joyce.' (Ellmann, R., p. 549).

Surely a fascinating dream, inviting and suggestive, no doubt deserving interpretation from Joyce himself—if only we had his associations, thoughts and confirmations. But one thing is undeniable, at least to me. Molly here is signing off, angrily and potentially creatively—supporting Arlene Richards' thesis in this book—and announcing her independence and implicitly her freedom to interact connectively with any reader. She's "done with" not only her husband but her creator too. On the evidence of his own dream, James Joyce, however powerful or brilliant, no longer can control her. She is free, independent—available henceforth for any adventurous reader.

References

Ellmann, R. (1959, 1982). *James Joyce: New and Revised Edition*. New York: Oxford University Press.

Section II: *Narrative Voices: Feminism and Psychoanalysis*

Changing Views of Masculinity

Herbert H. Stein, M.D.

Psychoanalytic Association of New York, Member APsaA, Published extensively including: *Moving Images Films Through a Psychoanalytic Lens* (IPBooks).

Something that I think worthy of mention in Part I of this volume is the changes in our understanding of the role of men that must accompany the changes in our understanding in the role of women. Alison Feit's "A Letter to My Sons" brought this question to my mind.

It is my impression that this accompanying shift in our understanding of masculinity (and by "our" I am referring to the world of psychology and psychoanalysis as well as the culture in which we live) is most important for those most vulnerable males going through "adolescence", that sometimes tumultuous period of transition from a child to an adult.

As illustrated in this volume, the changing view of femininity has been stated and proclaimed widely at times, and for good reason. Women have been and to a lesser but not insignificant extent still are disadvantaged in our society. The changes in our view of masculinity, however, is occurring with less fanfare and less notice.

This presents difficulties for adolescent males in particular because in "growing up" they are trying to see what it is they are supposed to become. I remember how difficult that could be at times in my own adolescence so many years ago; but, that was in an era when we thought the roles of men and women were clearly defined. During that formative period, somewhere between 13 and 30, the questions of identity for females and males are composed of not just who I am but also who I will be, or perhaps who I should be.

I write this not to provide a treatise on the complicated issue of masculine identity in this ever-changing landscape, but merely to point up the issue of a changing "target" for masculinity that must inevitably accompany the changes in our view of femininity described here, and will leave the work of defining those changes and the problems they bring to others, particularly those who work regularly with adolescents.

APPENDIX

Appendix

Bracha L. Ettinger

[An Israeli-born French painter, visual artist, training psychoanalyst (TAICP, WAP, NLS), feminist theorist, philosopher, and writer. Author of The Matrixial Borderspace (Univ. Of Minnesota Press, 2006) and Matrixial Subjectivity, Aesthetics, Ethics, Vol.I: 1990-2000), Vol.II: 2000-2012 (Palgrave Macmillan 2020)].

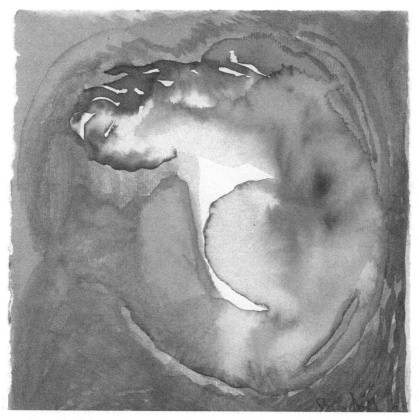

© Courtesy of the artist.

Bracha's Statement:

"I DECIDED I WAS AN ARTIST IN 1981, at a moment when many feminist artists and art historians rejected painting because of its phallocentrism. I knew excellent women artists who refrained from painting in the '80s, but I couldn't. I've painted all my life; it's like breathing. It's painful that we'll never know what women painters of the seventeenth and fifteenth centuries, and even the nineteenth century, could have given the world, and this requires lamentation, which implies intimate matrixial—a term I've employed throughout my work—alliances with the unknown that resist the idea of "purity."

I understand that many women artists turned their backs on painting, believing it's impossible to bring major transformation in this realm, oversaturated with maleness. But the project of painting has a long road to go, still, to discover the uncanny compassion beyond figuration and empathy and beyond abstraction too, to feminize the subject. The artistic has a potential for humanizing because only there aesthetics breeds ethics.

Working on compassion and the spirit, the psyche within the cosmos, is a proposal to go beyond modernity with its "empathy versus abstraction" perspective. In Western historical abstraction, such a feminine-matrixial dimension was unimaginable; this abstraction rejected it a priori as it worked toward the flat surface, the nonhuman, the crystalline inanimate. Surrealism, working with the unconscious, missed what I call "subreality"—it was blind not only to the female as subject, but also to the affective strings that link our kernels. And that's why the almost failed geometries of Hilma af Klint—who was working before and then alongside the modernists but was omitted from art history for so

236

long—are so important; a spiritual aspiration drove her beyond "pure" forms.

In my paintings, a kind of holographic depth and shadowy figures emanate, and the process reflects on the unconscious as a virtual diffraction of elements, transconnecting with the resonance that transcends them. Memory with oblivion in pentimento. To paint is to self-fragilize myself, to make myself vulnerable in accessing the other and the cosmos, to join as I differ, to withness what I give witness to. In my process, the abstract universe encounters the one we live in—a world absorbed by pain and violence—and offers itself up to it in a kind of trust after the end of trust. In the past ten years, my methods of abstraction have engaged the quivering moves of the butterfly and the jellyfish, its hovering tendrils in the water—ocean, spring, and womb.

I don't start oil paintings with blankness. The first brush touch is already an encounter with traces. I work with tiny color lines toward light and translucency, to give witness—in the feminine—to the spectral ashen traces of catastrophe, imprinted, transmitted, transformed, and cross-inscribed. During the day, I work with oils on my "Pieta," "Eurydice," and "Medusa" series—layer upon layer, painting over a long period of time in various transparencies. I continue working at night on my "Chrysalis" series and in notebooks, where I draw with ink and write down ideas.

The question of how to keep humanizing the subject remains. My process, pregnant with affects, brings about a crisis of the flat surface and suggests non-perspective depth. By weaving a space of passage, its symbolic domain opens, and its "phallic" appropriation becomes impossible. As we re-own the potential and specificities of the body, its joy and its pain, its differences in jointness, painting as materialized consciousness gives new definitions of subject matter and of subjectivity. Painting becomes a wound space and a healing space where I carry, where I miscarry.

For me it was crucial to work the abstract with certain found images that testify to the killing of Jewish women, mothers, and children in Mizocz, Rovno, Ukraine, on October 14, 1942—which echoes the massacre (including of members of my family) in the Ponary forest in 1941—in the "Eurydice" series. The "Medusa," "Chrysalis," and "Pieta" series refer also to the massacre of women in the Baltic Sea in 1945 by fire in the water, in resonance with my own shell shock. I was wounded during a long night when I led an operation to save drowning young people (the Eilat shipwreck in 1967). Forty years later, I found myself trying to find the meaning of the gasping mouth and the burnt smell. I didn't expect this nightmare to reemerge; I had to struggle with images that came forth in my paintings. As my matrixial abstraction meets the residuals of trauma in its search for light, it also offers the sublimation of/from the specificity of the feminine, and it offers the shocks of the archaic maternal a relief. The subject-depth space is symbolic, but also corporeal. And the name of the truth it carries for me, as it transpires and inspires, is beauty.

I once wrote that I hoped neurobiologists would discover resonance neurons, but artists are not going to wait for the science. I believe in the passage from art to science, from art to politics, from painting to the cultural, even if this can't be immediate."

–Bracha L. Ettinger as told to Anne Godfrey Larmon (*ARTFORUM, 7/2018*)

What We Learned from Proust: Psychological and Social Determinants of Snobbery and Prejudice (2013)

Arlene Kramer Richards and Lucille Spira

International Journal of Applied Psychoanalytic Studies, 10(1):75-86.

Proust's original contribution to understanding social exclusion is the focus of this paper. Proust's psycho-logical novel, *In Search of Lost Time* is used to show how social exclusion is related to early feelings of exclusion from the parental couple in the family. Proust's addition shows how a child who wins his mother's attention by acting as a victim suffers from both guilt and humiliation which he may resolve by defending another victim or by excluding others if he identifies with the aggressor. This paper shows how excluding others from events, opportunities, and equality under the law can be an attempt to repair the humiliation of having been excluded. This expands Anna Freud's idea about identification with the aggressor.

Writers of novels give us a window into the passions that drive social exclusion through their imaginative creations. Proust's *In Search of Lost Time* is particularly rich in this regard. In fact Probst-Solomon (2001) pointed out that Proust is the first major twentieth century writer to make prejudice a central theme in his work. His memoir-like novel, conveyed as if it were seen though the eyes of a narrator, stimulated us, among other things, to think about how the social and psychological intertwine. His depiction of the social mores of characters from all walks of life and different developmental stages suggests one root of why a person might find pleasure in excluding others or casting them as dangerous outsiders.

A Scream Goes Through the House is Weinstein's (2004) metaphor for works, like that of Proust, that touch the minds and souls of its readers. Literature exposes readers to the feelings and thoughts of a writer› characters, incidentally or deliberately teaching about life and its vicissitudes. The rich landscape Proust presents to his readers highlights the connection between art and life; the boundaries are permeable. Great books fill readers with excitement and expand the imagination; they allow us to consider what might make the writer' heroes, heroines, and villains behave or feel as they are portrayed. Lesser (1957) a literary scholar influenced by psychoanalytic theory showed that great works engage the whole psyche rather than just gratify the id. Such reflections by the readers can lead to thoughts about what motivates real people to take actions that otherwise seem mysterious. As the reader confronts unfamiliar circumstances described in a novel, what the author has shown him/her might better enable a person to connect with a new a situation, a point implicit in Victor Brombert's (2004) memoir *Trains of Thought.*

When reading a novel, some readers internalize and digest the words and ideas expressed by the author's characters. The capacity to use what we internalize and our associations can serve as a bulwark against loneliness and the sense of alienation. Alternatively, where an author's work might make the reader too uncomfortable, defenses might arise disallowing that person from seeing herself, or others, as like the author's creations. This idea might be represented in the statement: "It's only fiction." Despite the tendency of some to create distance for themselves from novels that spark painful feelings, others have used literature, including myths, to better understand the vicissitudes of life (Mendelson, 2007). For example, Freud used Greek mythology to communicate his theory of neurosis and may even have been inspired to create his theory by what he assimilated from the Greeks.

Proust engaged the interest of many writers, psychoanalysts and readers. The various ways in which he drew in his readers in ways that resonated with their own feelings and experiences is well illustrated by Aciman (2004), who asked a number of prominent authors and literary critics to discuss a favorite scene from Proust's *In Search of Lost Time* (2003). Psychoanalysts found much in Proust to elaborate on and expand their psychological theory. Poland (2003) concentrated on Proust›s view and demonstration of reading and writing as a sublimation that can remake one›s world. Miller (1956) and Halberstadt-Freud (1991) were interested in analyzing the author from the evidence of his imaginative productions. Halberstadt-Freud developed her theory of perversion by way of an analysis of Proust's work. Kohut (1977) saw the hero of *In Search of Lost Time* as suffering from a fragmented self's tragic man, one in search of a self— and different from classical guilty man; one who suffers from within the residue of his Oedipal resolution. More recently, Fried (2008) creatively used Proust's portrayal of the hero's treatment of Albertine to illuminate the impact of the analyst's planned absences on both patient and analyst.

We used Proust's novel to show how, for some people, continuous longing for love, though painful, might be more satisfying than requited love (Richards & Spira, 2012). We saw a connection between how a child and his parents negotiate the challenges of the Oedipal phase—the time when we are longing for the exclusive love of one of our parents while in the throes of ambivalence toward the other parent—not only has psychological impact but wider social ramifications as well. We will elaborate that idea here.

Is excluding other people a social or psychological phenomenon? It depends on how you look at it. For example, one young woman told her therapist that she could never date a man from her father's ethnic background; in her experience men from that cultural group, pride themselves on having more than one woman at a time. She understood his infidelity as socially determined. Focusing on the psychological aspects of such behavior would address the woman's perception of her relationship to her father and to her mother and her own wishes, fears and moral judgments.

That being excluded can be painful is obvious; that the excluder suffers may be less apparent. The pleasure in excluding is the sense of power, but power implies exercising free will and therefore leads to responsibility and its handmaiden: guilt. Social norms play a role in what is shameful and what is a source of pride. Excluding another person serves a defensive purpose as well. Often the impulse to exclude arises from the shame and sense of being degraded by the experience of having been excluded.

Proust's memoir-like novel, *In Search of Lost Time* develops understanding of social and psychological aspects of social exclusion. His psychologically rich character portrayals depict heroes, heroines, and anti-heroes from all spheres of society. He describes in affecting detail how the painful experiences of childhood motivate adult social behavior. His work shows how social snobbery can spring from psychological roots—the adult assures himself that rather than be excluded, he can exclude others. That snobbery is mainly on the basis of class; prejudice excludes others on the basis of race, religion, gender and/or sexual orientation.

Proust himself witnessed social snobbery and experienced prejudice. Though baptized as a Catholic, the religion of his father, he was Jewish by virtue of being the son of a Jewish woman; as a gay man he was a member of another excluded and devalued group. He himself, comparing being Jewish with being homosexual, believed that the rationalization for excluding both kinds of people is to accuse them of criminality:

> ... like those judges for whom to be a Jew is to be a traitor-that homosexuality can easily lead to murder; .... (Proust, 1997, p. 219)

He believed neither Jews nor homosexuals were treated fairly in society and under the law. His Catholic father reinforced his belief that he would have been better off not associating with Jews or going to a hotel that had too many of them as guests (White, 2009).

Proust and His Novel

Proust's hero-narrator, sometimes referred to as M or Marcel, eagerly sought his mother's love in a way that appeared successful. The narrator shares many characteristics with the author Proust though there are major differences—unlike the historical Proust, his character is heterosexual and an only child. Proust's hero is not explicitly a member of any excluded group. The novel introduces the theme of exclusion when we are told about a young boy suffering in his bedroom because he is exiled from his parents's dinner table. The boy's parents are entertaining their rich neighbor Swann; Swann's wife, Odette, has not been invited because of rumors about her sexual past. She is excluded from their social circle because she had been kept by rich lovers. Her sexual choices give the bourgeois family the right to exclude her from society. But what did the young boy do to be excluded? This night the young boy does not get his good night kiss; his sexual wish gets him into trouble just as Odette's sexual behavior earned her social obloquy.

Unhappy about not getting the kiss he desires, he sets out on a campaign to get it. He solicits the maid to give his mother a note asking her to come to his room. Before handing over the note he realizes that this maid is too protective of his parents to casually interrupt them. To counteract what he sees as her servility, he tells her that his mother is expecting to hear from him. He hopes to make her feel as if she is acting on his mother's request rather than his own. The boy's plan works in that the maid sees to it that his mother gets his note. Believing that the note will bring his mother to him, he calms down. But when he gets word that his mother has said that she has no reply, he sees that his ploy did not work and once again feels painful longing. He provokes exclusion by trying too hard to get included in his mother's attention.

Proust's boy longs for his mother's kiss. He believes that he can avoid the pain of being excluded by pursuing her until she gives in. He knows that dinner will eventually end and his mother will have to ascend the staircase to get to her room. He chooses to wait on the staircase to catch her. When she sees him there, she attempts to encourage him to go back to bed. He experiences her as being annoyed with him. His father enters the scene and seeing the boy's suffering becomes alarmed that his son will become sick if he does not get his mother's attention. He urges his wife to stay with their son. She does so reluctantly and spends the time lying beside him reading him stories.

One story she reads is about a young orphan boy befriended by a woman named Madeleine who acts like a surrogate mother. When the child in the story grows up, he falls in love with Madeleine, and eventually persuades her to marry him. The boy wins his "mother" and lives happily ever after. Is Proust implying that a child who hears such a story and gets his mother to sleep with him can take it to mean that he can also get to marry his mother when he grows up? Does the boy in Proust's story feel content or powerful? Not as he tells it.

The Aftermath of That Night

Proust's hero sees beyond the moment when his wish was gratified. What little Marcel's persistence has gained humiliates him. He recognizes that his mother did not want to stay but did so only because the father asked her to. The father feared the boy would make himself sick; the reader surmises that he felt pity for Marcel. Marcel realizes that he has caused his mother pain; he sees that she looks sad and deduces that it is because she perceives him not to be strong enough to manage growing up. He feels guilt about causing his mother pain and shame about eliciting his father's pity. The next morning he feels regretful. The narrator writes of the young Marcel's regret: "And if I had dared now, I should have said to Mamma: 'No I don't want you to, you mustn't sleep here'" (Proust, 1913/2003, vol. 1, p. 51). It is from this time that the boy thinks of himself as a sickly child.

As an older man Marcel happens to see a copy of Francois

le Champi and recalls that crucial night of his childhood. He says:

> ... during the night that was perhaps the sweetest and saddest of my life when I had alas! ... won from my parents that first abdication of their authority from which, later, I was to date the decline of my health and my will, and my renunciation, each day disastrously confirmed, of a task that daily became more difficult.... (Proust, 1927/2003, vol. 6, p. 287)

Taking Proust's work as a novel in the style of memoir, the narrator's description of the bedtime scene can be seen as a screen memory for other experiences where he was both over-stimulated by his need for closeness with his mother and humiliated by his father's condescending indulgence.

Recaptured memories may be understood as involuntary memory and memory screens. The latter condensed memories cover over ones that our psyche cannot as easily tolerate: they are attempts to hide us from pain.

As we recall memories, often, what we remember is not what we actually experienced (Lehrer, 2008). Freud's archeological metaphor seems to apply here; what we excavate, and bring to light, becomes transformed by the process of the excavation. A memoir writer has the liberty of weaving those now transformed involuntary recollections and screen memories into his narrative. As we know, when we mine our unconscious, or even tap into our preconscious thoughts, distortions occur. In short, it is useful to think of what is reported in a memoir as the author's remembered version or vision of his experience (Birkerts, 2007); our memories are not without defense. This process might have contributed to Proust's work. This recalled moment comes after the reader has already witnessed the growing adolescent and the adult man only achieving pleasure at the cost of great pain. His Oedipal victory left him full of guilt and shame for the rest of his life.

Proust's Lesbian Lovers

Proust also shows a woman who suffers from Oedipal victory. Mlle. Vinteuil, brought up by her adoring father after her mother dies when the daughter was still a young child. Clearly an Oedipal victor, she becomes an adult who loves women and feels spiteful hatred for her father, which she acts out with her lover. The young narrator looks through an unshaded window to see Mlle. Vinteuil dare her lover to threaten to spit on a picture of her father in a sado-masochistic love ritual. Love and aggression are linked as is the typically the case in life. Could it be that the aggression allowed Mlle. Vinteuil to withstand the village ostracism that she suffered for being a gay woman? Or, as Halberstadt-Freud (1991) suggests, the inclusion of the sado-masochism love ritual may be Proust's way of having his character dis-identify from her masochistic father. Her open sexual play with her lover makes them a topic of gossip; members of the community pity her father. The narrator describes himself as a child passing the home of M. Vinteuil while on a walk with his parents. The little boy was aware that:

> People said: "That poor M. Vinteuil must be blinded by fatherly love not to see what everyone is talking about-a man who is shocked by the slightest loose word letting his daughter bring a woman like that to live under his roof! … He may be sure it isn't music that she's teaching his daughter. (Proust, 1913/2003, vol. 1, p. 207)

Mlle. Vinteuil and her lover are excluded from the society of the narrator, his family and their friends. They are excluded from the social life of their little town. Prejudice against lesbians forces them to find another context for their lives. Mlle. Vinteuil and her lover become part of a group of lesbian artistic women who share camaraderie, creativity, and love not unlike the situation of a number of lesbian women during Proust's time (Souhami, 2005). They exclude the heterosexual world that excluded them. This is an example of how one gains power by excluding others. We see with the situation of Mlle. Vinteuil one of Proust's contributions to understanding social exclusion—how the psychological and the social are intertwined.

Proust and Social Determinants of Love

The social definition of a character's status determines personal choices as well. Proust's haughty intellectual character Baron Charlus is homosexual. He takes an uneducated and unscrupulous tailor as his lover and closest companion. Does knowing that he would be rejected if society knew that he was homosexual cause him to choose a lover who is degraded? Even though Swann has a Jewish mother, he has entrée into aristocratic circles where ladies of the nobility are interested in him. Rather than choose one of them, he falls in love with the degraded Odette with whom he had a tumultuous courtship. Does he choose a beloved who is as socially unacceptable as his mother would have been to many in society portrayed in the novel? These characterizations tempt us to twist Lord Acton's famous statement about politics to: Prejudice tends to make strange bedfellows.

Social Snobbery and Class

Proust exquisitely depicts social snobbery based on class as well as sexual orientation. He shows snobbery within and among all levels of society. Proust's Duchess de Guermantes, behaves contemptuously towards anyone whom she considers less sophisticated, aristocratic, or cultured than herself. That includes almost everyone. A matron at a public toilet excludes an indigent woman while toadying up to bourgeois patrons. The narrator likens the matron's condescending behavior to that of a duchess: the society dinner is the duchess-es's social realm; the matron's toilet is hers. Housekeepers are also snobs: one bullies an inexperienced kitchen helper.

But the social snobbery is not simple disdain for those lower on the social scale. The bourgeoisie exclude the aristocrats: the hero's grandmother initially resists overtures made to her by an aristocratic acquaintance whom she knew from childhood. The grandmother believes that nice people associate only within their own social class.

Her grandson, M, is determined to break down barriers. He is the same character who got his mother to sleep the night in his room. As a young man he uses that same persistence to ingratiate himself with the aristocratic Guermantes set. Proust himself crossed the barrier from a bourgeois family into the society of aristocrats and great artists when he was a young man. He used his wit and entertaining skills to make himself a desirable companion for people of greater achievement and social status than he himself had at that time. Kristeva (1993) sees this blending of fact and fiction as an overarching theme in Proust's work and as an example of the fluidity of barriers. Under certain circumstances, social barriers expand and contract as time compresses.

Social Snobbery and Prejudice

As Proust mixes fiction with fact, he provides insights into the nature of prejudice. He uses the Dreyfus case as part of his narrative. Dreyfus was a French military officer convicted of treason. This became a cause célèbre in France. One faction claimed that he was framed because he was a Jew while the other side believed he was guilty of spying against France for Germany. Proust's characters clash: Dreyfusards versus anti-Dreyfusards. The Dreyfusards are M, Swann and the young noble St Loup. In the real world the Dreyfus affair separated those of the Jewish "race" from the old aristocracy of the army officers. Even those like Proust who had been baptized and others who had converted to Christianity were seen as of the Jewish "race." French artists like Zola and middle-class people who shared the values of hard work, learning and the philosophy of liberty, equality and brotherhood sided with the Dreyfusards. The French old guard aristocrats and peasants wanted the conviction to stand because they believed that reversal would upset the social order. Proust has an anti-Dreyfus character assert that you cannot be both a Jew and a Frenchman. Proust uses the Dreyfus affair in his novel as a metaphor. The viciousness of ethnocentrism and religious bigotry is on a continuum with the viciousness of the small town attack on the lesbian lovers.

Most interestingly, Proust alerts us to the ironic capriciousness of prejudice. Odette Swann had not been welcome at either aristocratic or bourgeois homes even after marrying the wealthy Swann. When she allies herself with the anti-Dreyfusards she suddenly finds herself welcome in aristocratic circles. Just as Odette becomes acceptable to St Loup's aristocratic relatives, St Loup, Swann and the narrator fall out of favor with those aristocrats who had formerly welcomed them. Having similar prejudices serves to draw otherwise disparate people together. He shows how social barriers can give way when they conflict with racial prejudice.

Discussion

If Freud taught us that the Oedipus myth is a story of exclusion from the loving couple, Proust shows us that exclusion from the social group is the heir of Oedipal conflict in the social sphere. Social exclusion can be seen as a way to mitigate the pain of Oedipal humiliation. By turning passive exclusion into active exclusiveness, the social snob does to others what she felt had been done to her. Proust shows little Marcel longing for his mother while she is at dinner with adults. The dinner guest Swann becomes the barrier between little Marcel and his mother with the Oedipal rivalry displaced from his father to the visitor who represents the intrusion of society into the family. Thus Proust links the social scene with the Oedipal rivalry and longing. In this way he establishes the link between the Oedipal exclusion and the social exclusion that later gets played out when the adult M wants to keep his lover for himself and away from her social circle.

Freud showed how the child who was not the Oedipal winner suffered from revenge fantasies. Proust shows the child who wins by suffering, spending much of his life having fantasies of winning by losing. The side effect of Marcel getting his father's permission to have his mother stay the night with him is accepting as his identity the sufferer from illness, the child who is no threat to the father or any other man, the mama's boy who can only suffer at the hands of women whom he loves. As an adult he becomes a torturer of his beloved, Albertine, because he cannot allow himself to be excluded from her presence. He keeps her prisoner so that she would have to cheat on him in order to have any life of her own. He repeats the triangle of himself with his mother and father but transforms it into the triangle of his love, himself and other women. Here again Proust transforms the personal into the social when he describes M's jealous fantasy that his beloved is actually having sex not with a single other person, but with a whole group of lesbians. He is jealous of the group of women, not simply of another woman.

A second way in which Proust develops a Freudian idea is the extension of identification with the aggressor into the social realm. Proust shows how the excluded Mlle. Vinteuil and her lover create a social circle of lesbians and exclude the villagers who excluded them. Once again the sexual and the social are linked in the psychological realm and use the same adaptive strategy. For M identifying with the aggressor was not adaptive. He tried to become the excluder with his lover, but it only brought pain on himself. It worked for him when he found his way into the Guermantes set where others were excluded. It also worked for Odette when she joined the anti-Dreyfusards who had excluded her and were now excluding Dreyfusards.

✳ In the novel, Proust shows how common ideas and ideals fuse a social group, thus extending Freud's (1921) idea. For Freud the group is formed around love for a leader and a sense of equality among the members. Proust shows how the group can be protected by having a boundary which consists of a differentiation between the members of the group who love each other and non-members who are hated. Hating the Jews made the French anti-Dreyfusards feel closer to each other in proportion as they felt hatred for him and the other Jews.

Another original idea in Proust is the power of identification with the victim. While Anna Freud (1936/1966) later described the defensive use of identification with the aggressor,

Proust used his own understanding of human nature to show the defensive use of identification with the victim. M enters a social realm by identifying with Dreyfus. Since Dreyfus was disempowered and humiliated, M could see him as a fellow sufferer who was also weak, fragile and unable to cope. By supporting Dreyfus M attempts to undo being a victim, but at the same time becomes a member of a group that identifies itself with the victim. Being a member of a group gave him power; being a member of the group enables him to transform weakness into power. In the novel, such groups are comprised of homosexuals, lesbians, Jews, and intellectuals.

For Proust group membership is more than sharing values, or ethnicity or religion. Social bonding and perceived sameness are important. As Begley (2009) adds, Dreyfus never shared in the gambling, drinking, and whoring that was the after hours routine of many in the military establishment. Begley implies that because Dreyfus did not share their pleasures, he did not enter their circle of mutual trust; he did not become part of their group. Thus he became vulnerable to scapegoating. Proust shows in his depiction of military life that sharing after-hours comradeship increases social bonding. In Proust's lesbian scenes forbidden behavior fosters bonding even more than sharing activities that are not forbidden.

In Proust's own life his alliance with the Dreyfusards created new bonds and strengthened others. Looking at the Dreyfus affair from the point of view of Proust's mother, Bloch-Dano (2007) shows how Mme. Proust's sons aligned with their mother. This alliance in support of Dreyfus, formed between mother and sons, excluded Monsieur Proust, who could not accept that the military establishment would have found Dreyfus guilty if he were not so. If the Oedipal wish was alive in the sons, it played out as a forbidden wish that allied them as Jews (Probst-Solomon, 2001) just as the lesbians allied with each other and as the officers bonded. Tadie (1996/2000) differs here and suggests Proust's support of Dreyfus was spurred by social bonding with his school chums and literary friends rather than a result of any allegiance to the Jewish religion.

An example of the bond between Proust (1957) and his mother forged on the Dreyfus affair is the following letter written by Proust to his mother in September 1899:

> ... Don't be too sad about the verdict. It's bad for the army, for France, for the judges who had the cruelty to expect poor exhausted Dreyfus to repeat yet again the effort of summoning up his
>
> courage ... And nothing can go less than well for him now, morally in the world's esteem, physically in the liberty which I suppose is restored to him at this very moment. As for the verdict itself it will be judicially repealed. Morally it's repealed already.... (Proust, 1957, p. 73)

In this letter the adult Proust is soothing his mother rather than needing her to soothe him. Like Marcel and M, Proust feels empathy for his mother, wants her to suffer less and tries to make that happen.

Proust's hero regains his self-esteem and thus his own power when, as an adult, he sees an antique edition of the novel his mother read to him the evening of that fateful night of his childhood: Francois le Champi (George Sand 1850/1977). He recaptures the feelings and eventually masters them. Poland (2003) believes that what started out as M's longing for his mother developed into longing for love and acceptance. That longing was restructured in a new compromise formation that allowed M to see people in an unidealized way that, at the same time, allowed him to see himself as older, stronger and able to be a writer. Having written that letter, Proust realizes that he has a story worth telling. The adult M realizes that he has a story worth telling when he goes to a party and sees the society people from his past with the children grown, the young now old and power transferred to a younger generation.

In current life humiliation and exclusion pervade schools and other institutions. Understanding that such behaviors come at least in part from the experience of having felt excluded oneself and from the inevitable experience of having felt powerless and in need of protection while growing up is beautifully exemplified in Proust's work. Being an Oedipal "victor" comes at a great price to self esteem and adult development (Gil, 1987; Halberstadt-Freud, 1991; Lasky, 1984). It can exacerbate not only feelings of guilt but also ones of humiliation. Oedipal victory can also propel one to exclude others and/or to fight on behalf of the excluded as Proust showed.

Social Snobbery and Prejudice in Contemporary Life

Do officially sanctioned humiliation and exclusion still pervade schools and other institutions? Corbett (2009) reported that a school in the south holds a senior prom for the African American students and another one for its white students. The students say that they want one prom with all students invited. Some say it is harmless tradition to hold two proms. We believe it was prejudice. By dividing the students according to race, the white parents were humiliating the black students in an act of prejudice. If the parents claimed that the black students could not afford the expensive white prom, they would be humiliating them by social snobbery. By claiming that each group would prefer to be separate they were ignoring the students's feelings. Not having one's feelings understood about not being included can sting; not having ones feelings understood about wanting to be inclusive can sting also. However we categorize this exclusionary behavior, early experience and the intertwining of the psychological and social play a role. Understanding that such behaviors come from the experience of having felt excluded oneself and from the inevitable childhood experience of having felt powerless is beautifully exemplified in Proust's work. Being excluded from the parental couple's love-making humiliates the child, but replacing the parent as the best beloved makes the child an Oedipal victor. Being an Oedipal "victor" comes at a great price to adult development (Gil, 1987; Halberstadt-Freud, 1991; Lasky, 1984). It inhibits growth by provoking guilt. When it is gained by exhibiting helplessness and evoking pity such victory produces humiliation as well.

Humiliation can also propel a person to humiliate others by excluding them or to oppose the humiliation of others. Proust himself opposed the humiliation of Dreyfus as his hero M did in the novel by becoming Dreyfusards. Becoming an adult requires accepting responsibility for participation in society. It also requires that each person finds a way to satisfy her/his loving and aggressive impulses without hurting him/her self or others. That some of us lose this struggle is unfortunate. Recently (Garelick, 2011) a celebrated fashion designer was drinking in a bar when he allegedly excoriated a female patron; the woman was unknown to him. He was reported to have been overheard saying: "Dirty Jewish face, you should be dead. Your boots are of the lowest quality, your thighs are of the lowest quality. You are so ugly I don't want to see you. I am John Galliano." Proust's work suggests that such outbursts derive from the person reacting to childhood experiences where he felt humiliated. The perpetrator discharges his pain by causing his victim to feel it. By announcing his own name he asserts his identity; he asserts that he is not the victim; he exults in being the perpetrator.

It seems that Proust found a way to undo his humiliation by embracing his creativity and contributing to society by standing up for justice in the Dreyfus affair. Poland (2003) concluded that he undid his humiliation finally by writing his books.

The point of this paper is that including the social along with psychological understanding (Hamer, 2002) better enables us to understand our tendencies to exclude others and our responses to being excluded. Becoming an adult requires accepting responsibility for participation in society. Including the social along with psychological understanding also makes our interpretations to our patients more applicable to real life.

References

Aciman, A. (Ed.). (2004). *The Proust project*. New York: Farrar, Straus & Giroux.

Begley, L. (2009). *Why the Dreyfus affair matters*. New Haven, CT: Yale University Press.

Birkerts, S. (2007). *The art of time in memoir*. Minneapolis, MN: Graywolf Press.

Bloch-Dano, E. (2007). *Madame Proust: a biography* (translated by Alice Kaplan). Chicago, IL: The University of Chicago Press.

Brombert, V. (2004). *Trains of thought: from Paris to Omaha Beach, memories of a wartime youth*. New York: Anchor Books.

Corbett, S. (2009). A prom divided. *New York Times*, March 24.

Fried, W. (2008). The sweet cheat gone: here and there—elation, absence, and reparation. *Canadian Journal of Psychoanalysis*, 16, 3-22. [→]

Freud, A. (1966). *The ego and the mechanisms of defense*. New York: International Universities Press Inc. (Original work published 1936.)

Freud, S. (1921). Group psychology and the analysis of the ego. *Standard Edition*, 18, 65-144. [→]

Garelick, R. (2011). High Fascism. *New York Times*, March 7.

Gil, H. (1987). Effects of Oedipal triumph caused by collapse or death of the parent. *The International Journal of Psychoanalysis*, 68, 251-260. [→]

Halberstadt-Freud, H. C. (1991). *Freud, Proust, perversion and love*. Berwyn, PA: Swets and Zeitlinger. [→]

Hamer, F.M. (2002). Guards at the gate: race, resistance, and psychic reality. *Journal of the American Psychoanalytic Association*, 50, 1219-1237. [→]

Kohut, H. (1977). *The restoration of the self*. New York: International Universities Press.

Kristeva, J. (1993). *Proust and the sense of time*. New York: Columbia University Press.

Lasky, R. (1984). Dynamics and problems in the treatment of the "Oedipal Winner". *Psychoanalytic Review*, 71, 351-374. [→]

Lehrer, J. (2008). *Proust was a neuroscientist*. New York: First Mariner Books.

Lesser, S.O. (1957). *Fiction and the unconscious*. Boston, MA: Beacon Press.

Mendelson, E. (2007). *The things that matter: what seven classic novels have to say about the stages of life*. New York: Anchor Books.

Miller, M. (1956). *Nostalgia*. New York: Houghton Mifflin.

Poland, W.S. (2003). Reading fiction and the psychoanalytic experience: Proust on reading and on reading Proust. *Journal of the American Psychoanalytic Association*, 51, 1262-1282. [→]

Probst-Solomon, B. (2001). Citizen Proust: on politics and race. *Reading Room Journal*, 1, 97-111.

Proust, M. (2003). *In search of lost time (6 volumes)* (translated by C.K. Scott Moncrieff and Terence Kilmartin, revised by D. J. Enright, introduction by Richard Howard). New York: Modern Library Edition. (Original work published: vol. 1, 1913; vol. 6, 1927.)

Proust, M. (1997). A race accursed. In *On art and literature 1896-1919* (translated by Sylvia Townsend Warner, introduction by Terence Kilmartin, pp. 210-229). New York: Carroll & Graf Publishers (Original work published 1954.).

Proust, M. (1957). *Letters to his mother* (translated and edited by George D. Painter with an essay by Pamela Hansford Johnson). New York: The Citadel Press.

Richards, A.K., & Spira, L. (2012). Proust and the lonely pleasure of longing. In B. Willock et al. (Eds), *Loneliness and longing: psychoanalytic reflections on a crucial aspect of the human condition*. London: Routledge.

Sand, G. (1977). *The country waif* (Francois le Champi, translated by Eirene Collis, introduction by Dorothy Wynne Zimmerman). Lincoln, NB: University of Nebraska Press. (Original work published 1850.)

Souhami, D. (2005). *Wild girls: Paris, sappho, and art: the lives and loves of Natalie Barney and Romaine Brooks*. New York: St Martin's Press.

Tadie, J.-Y. (2000). *Marcel Proust: a life* (translated by Euan Cameron). New York: Penguin Books. (Original work published 1996.)

Weinstein, A. (2004). *A scream goes through the house: what literature teaches us about life*. New York: Random House.

White, E. (2009). *Proust*. New York: Penguin.

Appendix

Women's Liberation Movement

From Wikipedia, the free encyclopedia

en.wikipedia.org/wiki/Women's_liberation_movement

The women's liberation movement (WLM) was a political alignment of women and feminist intellectualism that emerged in the late 1960s and continued into the 1980s primarily in the industrialized nations of the Western world, which effected great change (political, intellectual, cultural) throughout the world. The WLM branch of radical feminism, based in contemporary philosophy, comprised women of racially- and culturally-diverse backgrounds who proposed that economic, psychological, and social freedom were necessary for women to progress from being second-class citizens in their societies.[1]

Towards achieving the equality of women, the WLM questioned the cultural and legal validity of patriarchy and the practical validity of the social and sexual hierarchies used to control and limit the legal and physical independence of women in society. Women's liberationists proposed that sexism—legalized formal and informal sex-based discrimination predicated on the existence of the social construction of gender—was the principal political problem with the power dynamics of their societies. In general, the WLM proposed socio-economic change from the political left, rejected the idea that piecemeal equality, within and according to social class, would eliminate sexual discrimination against women, and fostered the tenets of humanism, especially the respect for human rights of all people. In the decades during which the women's liberation movement flourished, liberationists successfully changed how women were perceived in their cultures, redefined the socio-economic and the political roles of women in society, and transformed mainstream society.[2]

Background

The wave theory of social development holds that intense periods of social activity are followed by periods of remission, in which the activists involved intensely in mobilization are systematically marginalized and isolated.[3] After the intense period fighting for women's suffrage, the common interest which had united international feminists left the women's movement without a single focus upon which all could agree. Ideological differences between radicals and moderates, led to a split and a period of deradicalization, with the largest group of women's activists spearheading movements to educate women on their new responsibilities as voters. Organizations like the African National Congress Women's League,[4] the Irish Housewives Association,[5] the League of Women Voters, the Townswomen's Guilds and the Women's Institutes supported women and tried to educate them on how to use their new rights to incorporate themselves into the established political system.[6][7] Still other organizations, involved in the mass movement of women into the workforce during World War I and World War II and their subsequent exit at the end of the war with concerted official efforts to return to family life, turned their efforts to labor issues. [8] The World YWCA and Zonta International, were leaders in these efforts, mobilizing women to gather information on the situation of working women and organize assistance programs.[9][10] Increasingly, radical organizations, like the American National Women's Party, were marginalized by media which denounced feminism and its proponents as "severe neurotics responsible for the problems of" society. Those who were still attached to the radical themes of equality were typically unmarried, employed, socially and economically advantaged and seemed to the larger society to be deviant.[11]

In countries throughout Africa, Asia, the Caribbean, the Middle East and South America efforts to decolonize and replace authoritarian regimes, which largely began in the 1950s and stretched through the 1980s, initially saw the state overtaking the role of radical feminists. For example, in Egypt, the 1956 Constitution eliminated gender barriers to labor, political access, and education through provisions for gender equality.[12] Women in Argentina, Brazil, Chile, Cuba, Nicaragua and other Latin American countries had worked for an end to dictatorships in their countries. As those governments turned to socialist policies, the state aimed to eliminate gender inequality through state action.[13] As ideology in Asia, Africa and the Caribbean shifted left, women in newly independent and still colonized countries saw a common goal in fighting imperialism. They focused their efforts to address gendered power imbalances in their quest for respect of human rights and nationalist goals.[14][15][16] This worldwide movement towards decolonization and the realignment of international politics into Cold War camps after the end of World War II, usurped the drive for women's enfranchisement, as universal suffrage and nationhood became the goal for activists[17]. A Pan-African awareness and global recognition of blackness as a unifying point for struggle, led to a recognition by numerous marginalized groups that there was potential to politicize their oppression.[18]

In their attempt to influence these newly independent

countries to align with the United States, in the polarized Cold War climate, racism in U.S. policy became a stumbling block to the foreign policy objective to become the dominant superpower. Black leaders were aware of the favorable climate for securing change and pushed forward the Civil Rights Movement to address racial inequalities. [19] They sought to eliminate the damage of oppression, using liberation theory and a movement which sought to create societal transformation in the way people thought about others by infusing the disenfranchised with political power to change the power structures.[20] The Black Power movement and global student movements protested the apparent double standards of the age and the authoritarian nature of social institutions[21]. From Czechoslovakia to Mexico, in diverse locations like Germany, France, Italy, and Japan, among others, students protested the civil, economic and political inequalities, as well as involvement in the Vietnam War. [22] Many of the activists participating in these causes would go on to participate in the feminist movement.[23]

Socially, the baby boom experienced after World War II, the relative worldwide economic growth in the post-war years, the expansion of the television industry sparking improved communications, as well as access to higher education for both women and men led to an awareness of the social problems women faced and the need for a cultural change.[24] At the time, women were economically dependent on men and neither the concept of patriar-chy nor a coherent theory about the power relationships between men and women in society existed.[25] If they worked, positions available to women were typically in light manufacturing or agricultural work and a limited segment of positions in the service industries, such as bookkeeping, domestic labor, nursing, secretarial and clerical work, retail sales, or school teaching.[26][27] They were expected to work for lower wages than men and upon marriage, terminate their employment.[28][26][27] Women were unable to obtain bank accounts or credit, making renting housing impossible, without a man›s consent. In many countries they were not allowed to go into public spaces without a male chaperone.[29]

Married women from countries founded the British colonial system and thus with a legal code based on English law were legally bound to have sex with their husbands upon demand. Marital rape was not a concept, as under law women had given consent to regular intercourse upon marrying.[30] The state and church, placed enormous pressure on young women to retain their virginity. Introduction of the birth control pill, gave many men a sense that as women could not get pregnant, they could not say no to intercourse[31]. Though by the 1960s the pill was widely available, prescription was tightly controlled and in many countries, dissemination of information about birth control was illegal[32]. Even after the pill was legalized, contraception remained banned in numerous countries, like Ireland where condoms were banned and the pill could only be prescribed to control menstrual cycles[33]. The Catholic Church issued the encyclical Humanae vitae in 1968, reiterating the ban on artificial contraception.[34] Abortion often required the consent of a spouse,[35] or approval by a board, like in Canada, wherein the decisions often revolved around whether pregnancy posed a threat to the woman's health or life.[36]

As women became more educated and joined the work-force, their home responsibilities remained largely unchanged. Though families increasingly depended on dual incomes, women carried most of the responsibility for domestic work and care of children.[37] There had long been recognized by society in general of the inequalities in civil, socio-economic, and political agency between women and men. However, the women's liberation movement was the first time that the idea of challenging sexism gained wide acceptance[38]. Literature on sex, such as the Kinsey Reports, and the development and distribution of the birth control pill, created a climate wherein women began to question the authority others wielded over their decisions regarding their bodies and their morality. [39] Many of the women who participated in the movement, were aligned with leftist politics and after 1960, with the development of Cold War polarization, took their inspiration from Maoist theory. Slogans such as "workers of the world unite" turned into "women of the world unite" and key features like consciousness-raising and egalitarian consensus-based policies "were inspired by similar techniques used in China".[40][41]

Into this backdrop of world events, Simone de Beauvoir published The Second Sex in 1949, which was translated into English in 1952. In the book, de Beauvoir put forward the idea that equality did not require women be masculine to become empowered.[42] With her famous statement, "One is not born, but rather becomes, a woman", she laid the groundwork for the concept of gender as a social construct, as opposed to a biological trait.[43] The same year, Margaret Mead published Male and Female, which though it analyzed primitive societies of New Guinea, showed that gendered activities varied between cultures and that biology had no role in defining which tasks were performed by men or women. By 1965, de Beauvoir and Mead's works had been translated into Danish and became widely influential with feminists[44],[45]. Kurahashi Yumiko published her debut *Partei* in 1960, which critically examined the student movement.[46] The work started a trend in Japan of feminist works which challenged the opportunities available to women and mocked conventional power dynamics in Japanese society.[47] In 1963, Betty Friedan published The Feminine Mystique, voicing the discontent felt by American women.[48]

Aims

As the women's suffrage movement emerged from the abolition movement, the women's liberation movement grew out of the struggle for civil rights.[49][50] Though challenging patriarchy and the anti-patriarchal message of the women's liberation movement was considered radical, it was not the only, nor the first, radical movement in the early period of second-wave feminism[51]. Rather than simply desiring legal equality, those participating in the movement believed that the moral and social climate which perceived women as second-class citizens needed to change. Though most groups operated independently—there were no national umbrella organizations—there were unifying philosophies of women participating in the movement. Challenging patriarchy and the hierarchical organization of society which defined women as subordinate in both public and private spheres, liberationists believed that women should be free to define their own individual identity as part of human society.[49][50][52]

One of the reasons that women who supported the movement chose not to create a single approach to addressing the problem of women being treated as second-class citizens was that they did not want to foster an idea that anyone was an expert or that any one group or idea could address all of the societal problems women faced[53]. They also wanted women, whose voices had been silenced to be able to express their own views on solutions[54]. Rejecting authority and espousing participatory democracy as well as direct action, they promoted a wide agenda including civil rights, eliminating objectification of women, ethnic empowerment, granting women reproductive rights, increasing opportunities for women in the workplace, peace, and redefining familial roles, as well as gay and lesbian liberation.[49] A dilemma faced by movement members was how they could challenge the definition of femininity without compromising the principles of feminism.[49][55]

Women's historical participation in the world was virtually unknown, even to trained historians.[56][57] Women's roles in historic events were not covered in academic texts and not taught in schools. Even the fact that women had been denied the vote was something few university students were aware of in the era.[58][59] To understand the wider implications of women's experiences, WLM groups launched women's studies programs introducing feminist history, sociology and psychology to higher education and adult education curricula to counter gender biases in teaching these subjects. [60] Writing women back into history became extremely important in the period with attention to the differences of experiences based on class, ethnic background, race and sexual orientation.[59] The courses became widespread by the end of the decade in Britain, Canada, and the United States, and were also introduced in such places as Italy and Norway.[60]

Thousands of adherents joined the movement which began in the United States[61] and spread to Canada and Mexico.[55][62]. In Europe, movements developed in Austria[63] Belgium,[64] Denmark,[65] England,[66] France,[67] Germany,[68] Greece,[69] Iceland,[70] Ireland,[71] Italy[72], The Netherlands,[53]

Northern Ireland,[73] Norway,[74] Portugal,[75] Scotland,[76] Spain,[77] Sweden,[74] Switzerland[78] and Wales[79] The liberationist movement also was active in Australia,[80] Fiji,[81] Guam,[82] India,[83] Israel,[84] Japan,[85] New Zealand,[86] Singapore,[87] South Korea,[88] and Taiwan.[89]

Key components of the movement were conscious-ness-raising sessions aimed at politicizing personal issues,[90] [91] small group and limited organizational structure[92] and a focus on changing societal perception rather than reforming legislation.[10] For example, liberationists did not support reforming family codes to allow abortion, instead, they believed that neither medical professionals nor the state should have the power to limit women's complete control of their own bodies.[93] They favored abolishing laws which limited womens rights over their reproduction, believing such control was an individual right, not subject to moralistic majority views.[94] Most liberationists banned the participation of men in their organizations.[95][96] Though often depicted in media as a sign of "man-hating", the separation was a focused attempt to eliminate defining women via their relationship to men. Since women's inequality within their employment, family and society were commonly experienced by all women, separation meant unity of purpose to evaluate their second-class status.[97]

Development

North America

In Canada and the United States, the movement devel-oped out of the Civil Rights Movement, Anti-War senti-ment toward the Vietnam War, the Native Rights Movement and the New Left student movement of the 1960s. [55][98][99] Between 1965 and 1966, papers presented at meetings of the Students for a Democratic Society and articles published in journals, such as the Canadian *Random* began advocating for women to embark on a path of self-discovery free from male scrutiny.[100] In 1967, the first Women's Liberation organizations formed in major cities like Berkeley, Boston, Chicago, New York City and Toronto.[101] Quickly organizations spread across both countries.[102][103] In Mexico, the first group of liberationists formed in 1970, inspired by the student movement and US women›s liberationists.[62][104]

Organizations were loosely organized, without a hierarchical power structure and favored all-women participation to eliminate defining women or their autonomy by their association with men.[97] Groups featured consciousness-raising discussions on a wide variety of issues, the importance of having freedom to make choices, and the importance of changing societal attitudes and perceptions of women's roles.[105][106] Canadian women's lib groups typically incorporated a class-based component into their theory of oppression which was mostly missing from US liberation theory,[91][107] which focused almost exclusively on sexism and a belief that women's oppression stemmed from their gender and not as a result of their economic or social class.[108] In Quebec, women›s and Quebec's autonomy were entwined issues with women struggling for the right to serve as jurors.[109]

Advocating public self-expression by participating in pro-tests and sit-ins, liberationists demonstrated against discrim-inatory hiring and wage practices in Canada,[110] while in the US liberationists protested the Miss America Beauty Pageant for objectifying women.[111] In both countries women's liberation groups were involved protesting their legislators for abortion rights for women[112][113]. In Mexico liberationists protested at the Monument to the Mother on Mother's

Day to challenge the idea that all women were destined to be mothers.[104][114] Challenging gender definitions and the sexual relationship to power drew lesbians into the movement in both the United States and Canada.[115] Because liberationists believed that sisterhood was a uniting component to women's oppression, lesbians were not seen as a threat to other women.[116] Another important aspect for North American women was developing spaces for women to meet with other women, offer counseling and referral services, provide access to feminist materials, and establish women's shelters for women who were in abusive relationships.[90][117][118]

Increasingly mainstream media portrayed liberationists as man-haters or deranged outcasts.[119][116] To gain legitimacy for the recognition of sexual discrimination, the media discourse on women›s issues was increasingly shaped by the liberal feminist's reformist aims.[120] As liberationists were marginalized, they increasingly became involved in single focus issues, such as violence against women. By the mid-1970s, the women's liberation movement had been effective in changing the worldwide perception of women, bringing sexism to light and moving reformists far to the left in their policy aims for women,[121] but in the haste to distance themselves from the more radical elements, liberal feminists attempted to erase their success and rebrand the movement as the Women's Movement.[122]

Asia

By the 1970s, the movement had spread to Asia with women's liberation organizations forming in Japan in 1970.[123] The Yom Kippur War raised awareness of the subordinate status of Israeli women, fostering the growth of the WLM.[124] In India, 1974 was a pivotal year when activists from the Navnirman Movement against corruption and the economic crisis, encouraged women to organize direct actions to challenge traditional leadership.[125] In 1975, liberationist ideas in South Korea were introduced by Yi Hyo-jae a professor at Ewha Woman's University after she had read western texts on the movement which were first translated into Korean in 1973.[88] Similarly, Hsiu-lien Annette Lu, who had completed her graduate courses in the United States, brought liberationist ideas to Taiwan,[89] when she returned and began publishing in the mid-1970s.[126]

In Singapore and other Asian countries, conscious effort was made to distinguish their movement from decadent, "free sex" Western feminist ideals,[127][128][129] while simultaneously addressing issues that were experienced worldwide by women. In India, the struggle for women's autonomy was rarely separated from the struggle against the caste system[130] and in Israel, though their movement more closely resembled the WLM in the US and Europe, the oppression of Palestinian women was a focal area.[131] In Japan, the movement focused on freeing women from societal perceptions of limitations because of their sex, rather than on a stand for equality.[132][133] In South Korea, women workers' concerns merged with liberationist ideas within the broader fight against dictatorship,[134] whereas in Taiwan, theories of respect for women and eliminating double standards were promoted by weaving in Confucianist philosophy.[135]

Europe

In Europe, the women's liberation movement started in the late 1960s and continued through the 1980s. Inspired by events in North America and triggered by the growing presence of women in the labor market, the movement soon gained momentum in Britain and the Scandinavian countries.[65] Though influenced by leftist politics, liberationists in general were resistant to any political order which ignored women entirely or relegated their issues to the sidelines.[136] Women›s liberation groups in Europe were distinguished from other feminist activists by their focus on women›s rights to control their own bodies and sexuality, as well as their direct actions aimed at provoking the public and making society aware of the issues faced by women.[137]

There were robust women's liberation movements in Western European countries, including developments in Greece, Portugal and Spain, which in the period were emerging from dictatorships.[138] Many different types of actions were held throughout Europe.[139] To increase public awareness of the problems of equal pay, liberationists in Denmark staged a bus sit-in, where they demanded lower fares than male passengers to demonstrate their wage gap.[140] Swedish members of Grupp 8 heckled politicians at campaign rallies, demanding to know why women were only allowed part-time jobs and thus were ineligible for pensions[141]. To address the objectification of women, Belgian liberationists protested at beauty pageants,[142] Dolle Minas in the Netherlands and *Nyfeministene* of Norway invaded male-only bars,[53] [143] Irish Women United demonstrated against male-only bathing at Forty Foot promontory[144] and Portuguese women dressed as a bride, a housewife and a sex symbol, marching in Eduardo VII Park.[145]

Reacting on two killings of women in the streets, on the 1st of March 1977 women in West Berlin started demonstrating at night—later to be repeated as Walpurgis Night every year on May Day eve.[1] Women in England, Scotland and Wales took up the idea of Reclaim the Night marches to challenge the notion that women's behavior caused the violence perpetrated against them.[146] Spanish liberationists from the *Colectivo*

Feminista Pelvis (Pelvis Feminist Collective), *Grup per l'Alliberament de la Dona* (Group for Women›s Liberation) and *Mujeres Independientes* (Independent Women) carried funeral wreaths through the streets of Mallorca calling for an end to sexual abuse and a judicial system which allowed men to use alcohol or passion as mitigating factors for sexual violence.[147] In Iceland, women virtually shut down the country; when spurred by liberationists, 90% of them took Women's Day Off and refused to participate in household duties or work, instead of attending a protest rally.[148]

In almost all Western European countries liberationists fought for elimination of barriers to free and unrestricted access to contraception and abortion.[149][150] In Austria, to advocate for the abolition of section 144 of their criminal code, activists used street theater performance.[151] Prominent French activists declared their criminal actions signing the Manifesto of the 343, admitting to having had abortions,[67] as did German activists who signed the *Manifesto of the 374.*[152] Irish activists took the train and crossed into Northern Ireland to secure prohibited contraception devices and upon their return flouted authorities bypassing the contraband to the public[153]. In the UK, an uneasy alliance formed between liberationists, the National Abortion Campaign and trade unionists to fight a series of bills designed to restrict abortion rights.[154] In Italy, 50,000 women marched through the streets of Rome demanding their right to control their own bodies,[155] but as was typically the result throughout Europe, compromise reform to existing law was passed by the government, limiting the decision by gestation or requiring preliminary medical authorization.[156][155][157]

Throughout the period, publishing was crucial for disseminating the theory and ideas of liberation and other feminist schools of thought.[158] Initially many activists relied on translations of material from the US,[159][160][161] but increasingly the focus was on producing country-specific editions, or local journals to allow activists to adapt the movement slogan the "personal is political" to reflect their own experiences.[162][163] Journals and newspapers founded by liberationists included Belgium's *Le Petit livre rouge des femmes* (The Little Red Book of Women),[158] France's Le torchon brûle [fr] (Waging the Battle),[67] Greece's *Gia tin Apeleftherosi ton Gynaikon* (For the Liberation of Women),[164] Italy's *Sottosopra* (Upside Down),[165] the Scottish *The Tayside Women's Liberation Newsletter* or the British Spare Rib, among many others.[166] In the UK, a news service called the Women's Information and Referral Service (WIRES) distributed news of WLM groups throughout the nation.[167]

In West Germany a book distribution run by lesbians snowballed feminist knowledge from 1974 on. Two feminist monthlies—Courage and EMMA—spread the new ideas. The women's camp on Femø organized by the Red Stocking Movement (Denmark) facilitated international exchange too. 1974 this gathering in the sun gave birth to the first International Tribunal on Crimes against Women held in Bruxelles 1976.

Books like *Die Klosterschule* (The Convent School, 1968) by Barbara Frischmuth, which evaluated patriarchy in the parochial schools of Austria,[168] The Female Eunuch (Paladin, 1970) by Germaine Greer and *The Descent of Woman* (1972) by Welsh author and feminist Elaine Morgan, brought women into the movement who thought that their lives differed from those of women in large urban settings where the movement originated.[169] Other influential publications included the British edition of *Our Bodies, Ourselves* (1971) edited by Angela Phillips and Jill Rakusen;[170] *Frauenhandbuch Nr. 1: Abtreibung und Verhütungsmittel* (Women's Guide # 1: Abortion and Contraceptives, 1971)[171][2] produced in Germany by Helke Sander and Verena Stefan[172] and *Skylla sig själv* (Self-blame, 1976) by Swede Maria-Pia Boëthius, which evaluated rape culture applied analysis and solutions to local areas.[173] In some cases, books themselves became the focus of liberationists' protests over censorship, as in the case of the Norwegian demonstration at the publishing house Aschehoug, which was forced to publish a translation of the Swedish text Frihet, jämlikhet och systerskap[SV] (Freedom, Equality and Sisterhood, 1970),[143] or the international outcry which resulted from the ban and arrest of Portuguese authors Maria Teresa Horta, Maria Isabel Barreno and Maria Velho da Costa over their book *Novas Cartas Portuguesas* (New Portuguese Letters, 1972).[174][175]

As the idea of women's freedom gained mainstream approval,[176] governments and more reformist minded women's groups adopted liberationists' ideas and began incorporating them into compromise solutions.[177] By the early 1980s, most activists in the Womens Liberation Movements in Europe moved on to other single focus causes or transitioned into organizations which were political.[178][179][180]

Oceania

Spreading from the United States and Britain, the women's liberation movement reached Oceania in 1969. The first organizations were formed in Sydney in 1969,[181] and by 1970 had reached Adelaide and Melbourne,[182] as well as Wellington and Auckland.[86] The following year, organizations were formed at the University of the South Pacific in Fiji[81] and in Guam.[82] As in the US and other places where the movement flourished, small consciousness-raising groups with a limited organizational structure were the norm[92][183] and the focus was on changing societal perception rather than legislation.[10][183]

Involved in public protests, liberationists demonstrated at beauty pageants to protest women's objectification,[184][185] and invaded male-only pubs.[185] In Australia they ran petition drives and protests in favor of legalizing abortion[186] and in Auckland led a funeral procession through Albert Park to demonstrate lack of progress on issues which were of concern to women.[187] Liberationists developed multiple publications such as Broadsheet,[188] *Liberaction*,[189] *MeJane*,[190] The Circle[191] and *Women's Liberation Newsletter*[192] to address issues and concerns;.[189] They founded women's shelters[193][86] and women's centers for meetings and child care services,[194][195] which were open to all women,[95] be they socialists, lesbians, indigenous women, students, workers or homemakers[187]. The diversity of adherents fractured the movement by the early 1980s, as groups began focusing on specific interests rather than solely on sexism.[10][196]

Surveillance

The FBI kept records on numerous participants in the WLM as well as spying on them and infiltrating their organizations.[197] Roberta Sapler, a participant in the movement between 1968 and 1973 in Pittsburgh, wrote an article regarding her attempts to obtain the FBI file kept on her during the period.[198] The Royal Canadian Mounted Police spied upon liberationists in Canada,[199] as did the Australian Security Intelligence Organisation surveil WLM groups and participants in Australia.[200] In Germany, the Federal Office for the Protection of the Constitution (German: *Bundesamt für Verfassungsschutz*) kept tabs on activists participating in women's center activities. Having lived in a communal housing project or been affiliated with youth movements made liberationists targets and their meeting places were searched and materials were confiscated.[201]

Legacy

The women's liberation movement created a global awareness of patriarchy and sexism.[121][202][15][203] By bringing matters that had long been considered private issues into the public view and linking those issues to deepen understanding about how systemic suppression of women's rights in society are interrelated, liberationists made innovative contributions to feminist theory.[204] Desiring to know about women's historic contributions but often being thwarted in their search due to centuries of censoring and blocking of women's intellectual work, liberationists brought the study of power relationships, including those of sex and diversity, into the social sciences. They launched women's studies programs and publishing houses to ensure that a more culturally comprehensive history of the complex nature of society was developed.[59][58]

In an effort to distance themselves from the politics and ideas of women in the liberation movement, as well as the personal politics which emerged, many second-wave feminists distanced themselves from the early movement. Meaghan Morris, an Australian scholar of popular culture stated that later feminists could not associate themselves with the ideas and politics of the period and maintain their respect.[122] And yet, liberationists succeeded in pushing the dominant liberal feminists far to the left of their original aims and forced them to include goals that address sexual discrimination[121]. Jean Curthoys argued that in the rush to distance themselves from liberationists, unconscious amnesia rewrote the history of their movement,[205] and failed to grasp the achievement that, without a religious connotation, the movement created an "ethic of the irreducible value of human beings."[206] Phrases that were used in the movement, like "consciousness-raising" and "male chauvinism," became keywords associated with the movement[207][53].

Influential publications

✳ Barreno, Maria Isabel; Horta, Maria Teresa; Velho da Costa, Maria *(1975). Land, Helen R. (translator) (ed.). The Three Marias: New Portuguese Letters (1st English ed.). Garden City, New York: Doubleday. p. 4. ISBN 978-0-385-01853-1. Original publication (1972) Novas Cartas Portuguesas (in Portuguese) Lisbon, Portugal Estudios Cor.*

✳ Benston, Margaret *(September 1969).* "The Political Economy of Women's Liberation" *(PDF). Monthly Review. 21 (4): 13. doi:10.14452/MR-021-04-1969-08_2. ISSN 0027-0520.*

✳ Boëthius, Maria-Pia (1976). Skylla sig sjalv: en bok om våldtäkt [Self-blame: A book of rape] (in Swedish). Stockholm, Sweden: Liber Förlag. OCLC 480560113.

✳ Brownmiller, Susan (1975). Against Our Will: Men, Women and Rape. New York, New York: Simon & Schuster. ISBN 978-0-671-22062-4.

✳ Ehrenreich, Barbara; English, Deirdre (1973). Witches, Midwives & Nurses: A History of Women Healers. Old Westbury, New York: Feminist Press.

✳ Firestone, Shulamith (1972). The Dialectic of Sex (PDF) (revised ed.). New York, New York: Bantam Books. Archived from the original (PDF) on 1 February 2018.

✳ Firestone, Shulamith; Koedt, Anne, eds. (1968). Notes From the First Year. New York, New York: New York Radical Women. OCLC 28655057. Retrieved 27 May 2018.

Appendix

❋ Greer, Germaine (1970). *The Female Eunuch. London, England:* MacGibbon & Kee. ISBN 978-0-261-63208-0.

❋ Hägg, Maud; Werkmäster, Barbro (1972). *Frihet, jämlikhet, syster-skap: en handbok för kvinnor [Freedom, Equality and Sisterhood: A handbook for women] (in Swedish). Stockholm, Sweden:* Författarförlaget. ISBN 978-9-170-54075-2.

❋ Johnston, Jill (1973). *Lesbian Nation: The Feminist Solution. New York, New York: Simon and Schuster.* ISBN 978-0-671-21433-3.

❋ Koedt, Anne (1968). *The Myth of the Vaginal Orgasm. Adelaide, South Australia: Women›s Liberation Movement of Adelaide.* OCLC 741539766. *In 1970 editions were released in London and Boston*

❋ Kool-Smit, J. E. (1967). *"Het onbehagen bij de vrouw" [The Discontent of Women] (PDF). De Gids (in Dutch) (9–10): 267–281.* ISSN 0016-9730. *Archived from the original (PDF) on 12 April 2018.*

❋ Mainardi, Pat (1970). *The Politics of Housework. Boston, Massachusetts: New England Free Press.* OCLC 41038147.

❋ Millett, Kate (1970). *Sexual politics. New York, New York: Ballantine Books.* ISBN 978-0-345-29270-4.

❋ Mitchell, Juliet (1971). *Woman's Estate. Harmondsworth, Middlesex, England: Penguin.* ISBN 978-0-14-021425-3.

❋ Morgan, Elaine (1972). *The Descent of Woman. London, England: Souvenir Press.* ISBN 978-0-285-62063-6.

❋ Morgan, Robin (1970). *Sisterhood Is Powerful : An Anthology of Writings from Women's Liberation Movement. New York, New York: Random House.* OCLC 606144056.

❋ Rich, Adrienne (1976). *Of Woman Born: Motherhood as experience and institution. New York, New York: Bantam Books.* ISBN 978-0-553-11365-5.

❋ Sarachild, Kathie (1970). *"A Program for Feminist 'Consciousness Raising' ". Notes from the Second Year: Women's Liberation. New York, New York: Radical Feminism: 78–80.* OCLC 70702435. *Retrieved 27 May 2018.*

✳ Sarachild, Kathie (1973). *"Consciousness Raising: A Radical Weapon"* (PDF). *Feminist Revolution*. New York, New York: Redstockings: 144–150. Archived from the original (PDF) on 27 May 2017. Retrieved 27 May 2018.

✳ Vinder, K. (pseud.) (1975). *Kvinde kend din krop: En hånd-bog [Woman know your body: A handbook]* (in Danish). Copenhagen, Denmark: Tiderne Skifter. ISBN 978-8-779-736-252.

Criticism

The philosophy practiced by liberationists assumed a global sisterhood of support working to eliminate inequality without acknowledging that women were not united; other factors, such as age, class, ethnicity, and opportunity (or lack thereof) created spheres wherein women's interests diverged, and some women felt underrepresented by the WLM.[208] While many women gained an awareness of how sexism permeated their lives, they did not become radicalized and were uninterested in overthrowing society. They made changes in their lives to address their individual needs and social arrangements, but were unwilling to take action on issues that might threaten their socio-economic status.[209] Liberationist theory also failed to recognize a fundamental difference in fighting oppression. Combating sexism had an internal component, whereby one could change the basic power structures within family units and personal spheres to eliminate the inequality. Class struggle and the fight against racism are solely external challenges, requiring public action to eradicate inequality.[210]

There was criticism of the movement not only from factions within the movement itself,[53][54] but from outsiders, like Hugh Hefner, Playboy founder, who launched a campaign to expose all the "highly irrational, emotional, kookie trends" of feminism in an effort to tear apart feminist ideas that were "unalterably opposed to the romantic boy-girl society" promoted by his magazine.[211] "Women's libbers" were widely characterized as "man-haters" who viewed men as enemies, advocated for all-women societies, and encouraged women to leave their families behind.[54] Semanticist Nat Kolodney argued that while women were oppressed by social structures and rarely served in tyrannical roles over the male population as a whole, men, in general, were not oppressors of women either. Instead, social constructs and the difficulty of removing systems which had long served their purpose exploited both men and women.[212] Women›s liberationists acknowledged that patriarchy affects both men and women, with the former receiving many privileges from it, but focused on the impact of systemic sexism and misogyny on women throughout the world.

To many women activists in the American Indian Movement, black Civil Rights Movement, Chicana Movement, as well as Asians and other minorities, the activities of the primarily white, middle-class women in the women's liberation movement were focused specifically on sex-based violence and the social construction of gender as a tool of sex-based oppression. By evaluating all economic, socio-cultural, and political issues through the lens of sexism without pairing it with racism and classism, liberationists often poorly represented women of color in their analyses.[213][214][215] While women of color recognized that sexism was an issue, some did not see how it could be separated from the issue of race or class, which compounds to impact their access to education, health care, housing, jobs, legal justice, and the poverty and violence which permeates their lives.[214][216][217] For women who did not speak English, or spoke it as a second language, sexism had little to do with the ability to protect herself or utilize existing systems.[218] The focus on personal freedom was another divergence between white women and women of color. Some did not see the intrinsic connection between the liberation of women and the liberation of men that was advocated for by the Women's Liberation Movement and felt that feminists did not care about the inequalities suffered by men; they felt that the liberation of women without the liberation of men from policies that keep men of color from obtaining jobs and limit their civil rights, further preventing them from being able to protect their families, neither improved humanity as a whole nor improved the plight experienced by families.[98][215] Dorothy Height, president of the National Council of Negro Women, expressed that the best way black women could help themselves was to help their men gain equality.[98]

Regarding the "sex-positive" sect that broke away from the women's liberation movement, extending personal freedom to sexual freedom, the meaning of being free to have relations with whoever one wanted, was lost on black women who had been sexually assaulted and raped with impunity for centuries[98] or Native Women who were routinely sterilized.[219] Their issues were not about limiting their families but having the freedom to form families.[220] It had very little meaning in the traditional Chicana culture wherein women were required to be virgins until marriage and remain naïve in her marriage.[221] Though invited to participate within the Women's Liberation Movement, many women of color cautioned against the single focus on sexism, finding it to be an incomplete analysis without the consideration of racism.[214][222] Likewise, though many lesbians saw commonalities with Women's Liberation through the goals of eponymous liberation from sex-based oppression, which included fighting against homophobia, others believed that the focus was too narrow to confront the issues they faced[223] Differences in the understanding of gender and how it relates to and informs sex-based oppression and systemic sexism called attention to differences in issues. For example, many liberationists rejected the performance of femininity as positive behavior, which meant that white lesbians who actively chose to perform femininity had to decide between their desire to be feminine-presenting and their rejection of sexual objectification. Jackie Anderson, an activist, and philosopher observed that in the black lesbian community being able to dress up made them feel confident because, during the workweek, black women had to conform to dress codes imposed upon them.[224] This was and continues to be a sentiment held by most women, who tend to believe that the feeling of confidence derived from performing femininity as dictated by the sexist status quo is the same as empowerment.[225]

See also

* Feminism

* Lesbian feminism

* Radical feminism

* Men's liberation movement

References

See this links for numbered footnotes Internet links: en.wikipedia.org/wiki/Women's_liberation_movement

1. New Fontana 1999, pp. 314.

2. New Fontana 1999, pp. 315.

3. Taylor 1989, p. 762.

4. Walker 1991, p. 83.

5. Connolly 1997, p. 109.

6. Taylor 1989, pp. 763–764.

7. Browne 2017, p. 5.

8. Taylor 1989, p. 764.

9. Hannan 2008, p. 175.

10. Jump up to:[a] [b] [c] [d] Elias 1979, p. 9.

11. Taylor 1989, p. 765.

12. Al-Ali 2002, p. 8.

13. Russell 2012, p. 19.

14. Armstrong 2016, p. 305.

15. Jump up to:[a] [b] Sanatan 2016.

16. Neptune 2011.

17. Rubio-Marín 2014.

18. Bagneris 2011, p. 4.

19. Morris 1999, pp. 522–524.

20. Curthoys 2003, p. 1.

21. Barker 2008, pp. 44–45, 50.

22. Barker 2008, pp. 48–50.

23. Bullock 2010, p. 4.

24. Magarey 2014, p. 16.

25. Bradshaw 2013, pp. 391–392.

26. Jump up to:[a] [b] Cheal 2003, p. 70.

27. Jump up to:[a] [b] Backhouse & Flaherty 1992, pp. 218–219.

28. Mioko 1978, p. 77.

29. Enke 2007, p. 6.

30. Cook 2004, p. 2.

31. Cook 2004, p. 3.

32. Nilsson & Spencer 2015.

33. Franks 2013, p. 46.

34. Rengel 2000, p. 202.

35. Magarey 2014, p. 241.

36. Sethna & Hewitt 2009, pp. 469–470.

37. Adamson, Briskin & McPhail 1988, pp. 37–38.

38. Bucy 2010, p. 306.

39. Magarey 2014, p. 17.

40. Hathaway 2018.

41. Roseneil, et al. 2010, p. 136-137.

42. Bergoffen 2004.

43. Butler 1986, p. 35.

44. Larsen 2014.

45. Tobias 1997.

46. Bullock 2010, p. 13.

47. Bullock 2010, pp. 50–51.

48. Fox 2006.

49. Jump up to:[a][b][c][d] Wiegers 1970, p. 50.

50. Jump up to:[a][b] The Dayton Daily News 1969, p. 11.

51. Thompson 2002, pp. 344–345.

52. Studer 2017, p. 15-16.

53. Jump up to:[a][b][c][d][e] Foley 1971, p. 22.

54. Jump up to:[a][b][c] Bennett 1970, p. 40.

55. Jump up to:[a][b][c] Sethna & Hewitt 2009, p. 466.

56. Myrbråten 2013, p. 20-21.

57. DuBois 1998, p. 10.

58. Jump up to:[a] [b] Lee 2014.

59. Jump up to:[a] [b] [c] Hannam 2008.

60. Jump up to:[a] [b] Browne 2017, pp. 76-77.

61. Enke 2007, p. 2.

62. Jump up to:[a] [b] González Alvarado 2002, p. 56.

63. Der Funke 2003.

64. Jacques 2013.

65. Jump up to:[a] [b] Dahlerup 2017.

66. Barber, et al. 2013.

67. Jump up to:[a] [b] [c] Picq 2008.

68. Perincioli & Selwyn 2015.

69. Greek News Agenda 2017.

70. Haavio-Mannila & Skard 2013, p. 27.

71. Cosgrove 2008, p. 882.

72. Radical Party Archive 1972.

73. Aughey & Morrow 2014, p. 173.

74. Jump up to:[a] [b] Haavio-Mannila & Skard 2013, p. 28.

75. Pena 2008.

76. Browne 2017, p. 4.

77. Morgan 1984, p. 626.

78. Joris 2008.

79. Rolph 2002.

80. Magarey 2014, pp. 25–26.

81. Jump up to:[a] [b] Griffen & Yee 1987, p. 1.

82. Jump up to:[a] [b] The Ladder 1972, p. 47.

83. Omvedt 1975, p. 40.

84. Ram 2012, p. 150.

85. Shigematsu 2012, p. ix.

86. Jump up to:[a][b][c] Cook 2011.

87. Lyons 2000.

88. Jump up to:[a][b] Kim 2000, pp. 220-221.

89. Jump up to:[a][b] Chiang & Liu 2011, p. 559.

90. Jump up to:[a][b] Spain 2016, p. 51.

91. Jump up to:[a][b] Sethna & Hewitt 2009, pp. 468–469.

92. Jump up to:[a][b] Magarey 2014, pp. 29–30.

93. Bracke 2014, p. 85.

94. Pena 2008, p. 108.

95. Jump up to:[a][b] Magarey 2014, pp. 27–28.

96. Sethna & Hewitt 2009, p. 467.

97. Jump up to:[a][b] Adamson, Briskin & McPhail 1988, p. 8.

98. Jump up to:[a][b][c][d] Sklar 2015.

99. Adamson, Briskin & McPhail 1988, p. 39.

100. Yates 1975, p. 7.

101. Yates 1975, pp. 7–8.

102. Sethna & Hewitt 2009, pp. 466–469.

103. Freeman 1972.

104. Jump up to:[a][b] El Universal 2012.

105. Magarey 2014, p. 20.

106. Kanes 1969, p. 11.

107. Adamson, Briskin & McPhail 1988, p. 50.

108. Echols 1989, p. 3.

109. Dupuis-Déri 2007.

110. Wasserlein 1990, p. 64.

111. Bucy 2010, p. 307.

112. Sethna & Hewitt 2009, p. 472.

113. Nelson 2003, pp. 33–34.

114. González Alvarado 2002, p. 58.

115. Tremblay, Paternotte & Johnson 2016, p. 75.

116. Jump up to:[a][b] Brownmiller 1970.

117. Adamson, Briskin & McPhail 1988, pp. 45, 56.

118. González Alvarado 2002, p. 60.

119. Adamson, Briskin & McPhail 1988, p. 70.

120. Dow 2014, pp. 121–122.

121. Jump up to:[a][b][c] Willis 1984, pp. 91–92.

122. Jump up to:[a][b] Curthoys 2003, p. 5.

123. Shigematsu 2015, p. 175.

124. Herzog 2009.

125. Patel 1985, pp. 2-3.

126. Lu 2009, p. 48.

127. Shigematsu 2015, p. 176.

128. Lyons 2000, p. 11.

129. Menon 2011, p. 24.

130. Patel 1985, p. 7.

131. Frankfort-Nachmias & Shadmi 2005, p. 43.

132. Shigematsu 2015, p. 174.

133. Ito 2015.

134. Ching & Louie 2000, pp. 123-125.

135. Chang 2009, p. 94.

136. Miller 2013, p. 20.

137. Kiani 2017, p. 19.

138. Allen 2007, p. 116.

139. Allen 2007, p. 120.

140. Fauré 2004, p. 668.

141. Harr 2014.

142. Degavre & Stoffel 2005.

143. Jump up to:[a] [b] Nørve 2007.

144. McCabe 2010.

145. Pena 2008, pp. 101-103.

146. Browne 2017, pp. 164-167.

147. Rodriguez 1979.

148. Brewer 2015.

149. Studer 2017, p. 15.

150. Allen 2007, p. 123.

151. Der Standard 2004.

152. Brown 2013, pp. 300-301.

153. Farren 2006.

154. Browne 2017, pp. 121-122.

155. Jump up to:[a] [b] Bracke 2014, pp. 87.

156. Allen 2007, p. 124.

157. Roseneil, et al. 2010, p. 145.

158. Jump up to:[a] [b] Denis & van Rokeghem 1992, pp. 76-77.

159. Browne 2017, pp. 47-48.

160. Danielsen 2010, p. 38.

161. University of Gothenburg 2011.

162. Browne 2017, pp. 63-67.

163. Rees 2010, p. 178.

164. Greek News Agenda 2017.

165. Melandri 2016.

166. Browne 2017, pp. 85-87.

167. Browne 2017, p. 85.

168. Fiddler 1997, p. 252.

169. Browne 2017, p. 17.

170. Browne 2017, p. 67.

171. Cristina Perincioli, "Berlin wird feministisch" (2015) p.198

172. Broeck 2007, p. 100.

173. Miller 2013, pp. 28-29.

174. Pena 2008, pp. 63-64.

175. Dias Martins 2012, pp. 24-26.

176. Rúdólfsdóttir 1997, p. 87.

177. Sarrimo 2003.

178. Pena 2008, pp. 112-114.

179. Beccalli 1994.

180. van Oven 2005, pp. 13-14.

181. Magarey 2014, p. 25.

182. Magarey 2014, pp. 26–27.

183. Jump up to:[a] [b] Else 1993, p. 65.

184. Magarey 2014, p. 26.

185. Jump up to:[a] [b] Else 1993, p. 63.

186. Genovese 1998, p. 103.

187. Jump up to:[a] [b] Ministry for Culture and Heritage 2018.

188. Aukland Museum n.d.

189. Jump up to:[a] [b] Magarey 2014, p. 44.

190. Henderson & Bartlett 2014, pp. 105–108.

191. Else 1993, p. 559.

192. Henderson & Bartlett 2014, pp. 91–92.

193. Genovese 1998, p. 128.

194. Else 1993, pp. 96–97.

195. Genovese 1998, p. 131.

196. Else 1993, pp. 97, 554.

197. Echols 1989, p. 8.

198. Salper 2008.

199. Sethna & Hewitt 2009, p. 465.

200. Smith 2017.

201. Perincioli & Selwyn 2015, p. 1970-77 Fear and Terror.

202. Walker 1991, pp. xxii–xxiii.

203. The Winnipeg Free Press 1989, p. 35.

204. Browne 2017, pp. 179-180.

205. Curthoys 2003, p. 6.

206. Curthoys 2003, p. 7.

207. Curthoys 2003, p. 4.

208. Willis 1984, p. 100.

209. Willis 1984, p. 107.

210. Willis 1984, p. 110.

211. Dow 2014, p. 120.

212. Kolodney 1978, p. 300.

213. Thompson 2002, p. 337.

214. Jump up to:[a][b][c] Regua 2012, p. 141.

215. Jump up to:[a][b] Longeaux y Vásquez 1997, p. 31.

216. Thompson 2002, pp. 341–342.

217. Longeaux y Vásquez 1997, pp. 30–31.

218. Castillo 1997, p. 46.

219. Thompson 2002, p. 339.

220. Thompson 2002, p. 349.

221. Anonymous 1997, p. 83.

222. Thompson 2002, p. 342.

223. Klemesrud 1970.

224. Enke 2007, p. 55.

225. *Rottenberg, Catherine (2014). "The Rise of Neoliberal Feminism". Cultural Studies. 28 (3): 418–437. doi:10.1080/09502386.2013.857361. ISSN 0950-2386.*

Parenthetical sources

✳ *Adamson, Nancy; Briskin, Linda; McPhail, Margaret (1988). Feminist Organizing for Change: The contemporary women's movement in Canada. Toronto, Canada: Oxford University Press. ISBN 978-0-19-540658-0.*

✳ *Al-Ali, Nadje (2002). Women's Movements in the Middle East: Case Studies of Egypt and Turkey (PDF) (Report). Geneva, Switzerland: United Nations Research Institute for Social Development. Archived from the original (PDF) on 2 August 2017. Retrieved 18 April 2018.*

✳ *Allen, Ann T. (2007). Women in Twentieth-Century Europe. Houndsmills, Basingstoke, England: Palgrave Macmillan. ISBN 978-1-137-06518-6.*

✳ *Anonymous (1997). "El Movimiento and the Chicana" (PDF). In García, Alma M. (ed.). Chicana Feminist Thought: The Basic Historical Writings. New York, New York: Routledge. pp. 81–82. ISBN 978-0-415-91801-5.*

✳ *Armstrong, Elisabeth (2016). "Before Bandung: The Anti-Imperialist Women's Movement in Asia and the Women's International Democratic Federation". Signs: Journal of Women in Culture and Society. 41 (2): 305–331. doi:10.1086/682921. ISSN 0097-9740. Retrieved 18 April 2018.*

Appendix

✳ Aughey, Arthur; Morrow, Duncan (2014). *Northern Ireland Politics. Abingdon-on-Thames, England: Routledge. ISBN 978-1-317-89083-6.*

✳ Backhouse, Constance; Flaherty, David H. (1992). *Challenging Times: The Women's Movement in Canada and the United States. Quebec City, Quebec: McGill-Queen's University Press. ISBN 978-0-7735-6342-1.*

✳ Bagneris, Jennifer (December 2011). *Caribbean Women and the Critique of Empire: Beyond Paternalistic Discourses on Colonialism (PDF) (master›s degree). Nashville, Tennessee: Vanderbilt University. Archived from the original (PDF) on 19 April 2018.*

✳ Barber, Abi; Russell, Polly; Jolly, Margaretta; Cohen, Rachel; Johnson-Ross, Freya; Delap, Lucy (8 March 2013). *"Activism and the Women's Liberation Movement". Sisterhood and After. London, England: British Library. Archived from the original on 27 September 2017. Retrieved 23 April 2018.*

✳ Barker, Colin (June 2008). *"Some Reflections on Student Movements of the 1960s and Early 1970s". Revista Crítica de Ciências Sociais (81): 43–91. doi:10.4000/rccs.646. ISSN 0254-1106. Retrieved 19 April 2018.*

✳ Beccalli, Bianca (March–April 1994). *"The Modern Women's Movement in Italy". New Left Review I. First (204). ISSN 0028-6060. Retrieved 21 May 2018.*

✳ Bennett, Lorraine M. (5 April 1970). *"How Far Yet to Go, Baby?". The Atlanta Constitution. Atlanta, Georgia. p. 40. Retrieved 20 April 2018 – via Newspapers.com.*

✳ Bergoffen, Debra (17 August 2004). *Zalta, Edward N. (ed.). "The Stanford Encyclopedia of Philosophy: Simone de Beauvoir". plato. stanford.edu. Stanford, California: Stanford University. Archived from the original on 11 March 2018. Retrieved 19 April 2018.*

✳ Bracke, Maud Anne (11 July 2014). Women and the Reinvention of the Political: Feminism in Italy, 1968–1983. New York, New York: Routledge. ISBN 978-1-317-67412-2.

✳ Bradshaw, Jan (2013). The Women's Liberation Movement: Europe and North America. Oxford, England: Pergamon Press. ISBN 978-1-4831-6082-5.

✳ Brewer, Kirstie (23 October 2015). "The day Iceland's women went on strike". BBC. London, England. Archived from the original on 17 February 2018. Retrieved 22 May 2018.

✳ Broeck, Sabine (2007). "Blackness and Sexualities in the Interracial Diaspora". In Wright, Michelle M.; Schuhmann, Antje (eds.). Blackness and Sexualities. Berlin, Germany: LIT Verlag. pp. 95–106. ISBN 978-3-8258-9693-5.

✳ Brown, Timothy Scott (2013). West Germany and the Global Sixties: The Anti-Authoritarian Revolt, 1962–1978. Cambridge, England: Cambridge University Press. ISBN 978-1-107-47034-7.

✳ Browne, Sarah (2017). The Women's Liberation Movement in Scotland. Oxford, England: Oxford University Press. ISBN 978-1-5261-1665-9 – via Project MUSE.

✳ Brownmiller, Susan (15 March 1970). "Sisterhood Is Powerful". The New York Times. New York City, New York. Retrieved 21 April 2018.

✳ Bucy, Carole (Summer 2010). "Reviewed Work: Freedom for Women: Forging the Women's Liberation Movement, 1953–1970 by Carol Giardina". The Register of the Kentucky Historical Society. 108 (3): 305–308. ISSN 0023-0243. JSTOR 23387564.

✳ Bullock, Allan; Trombley, Stephen, eds. (1999). The New Fontana Dictionary of Modern Thought (3rd ed.). Harper Collins Publishers. ISBN 978-0-00-255871-6.

✳ Bullock, Julia C. (2010). The Other Women's Lib: Gender and Body in Japanese Women's Fiction. Honolulu, Hawaii: University of Hawaii Press. ISBN 978-0-8248-6075-2 – via Project MUSE.

✳ Butler, Judith (1986). "Sex and Gender in Simone de Beauvoir›s Second Sex". Yale French Studies (72): 35–49. doi:10.2307/2930225. ISSN 0044-0078. JSTOR 2930225.

✳ Castillo, Adelaida R. Del (1997). "La Visión Chicana" (PDF). In García, Alma M. (ed.). Chicana Feminist Thought: The Basic Historical Writings. New York, New York: Routledge. pp. 44–48. ISBN 978-0-415-91801-5.

✳ Chang, Doris (2009). Women's Movements in Twentieth-Century Taiwan. Champaign, Illinois: University of Illinois Press. ISBN 978-0-252-09081-3.

✳ Cheal, David (2003). Family: Critical Concepts in Sociology. IV: Family and Society. London, England: Routledge. ISBN 978-0-415-22633-2.

✳ Chiang, Lan-Hung Nora; Liu, Ying-chun (July 2011). "Feminist geography in Taiwan and Hong Kong". Gender, Place & Culture. 18 (4): 557–569. doi:10.1080/0966369X.2011.583341. ISSN 0966-369X.

✳ Ching, Miriam; Louie, Yoon (2000). "Minjung Feminism: Korean women's movement for gender and class liberation". In Smith, Bonnie G. (ed.). Global Feminisms Since 1945. London, England: Routledge. pp. 119–138. ISBN 978-0-415-18491-5.

✳ Connolly, Linda Mary (September 1997). From Revolution to Devolution: A Social Movements Analysis of the Contemporary Women's Movement in Ireland (PDF)(PhD). Maynooth, County Kildare, Ireland: National University of Ireland Maynooth. Archived from the original (PDF) on 28 April 2018.

✳ Cook, Hera (2004). The Long Sexual Revolution: English Women, Sex, and Contraception 1800–1975. Oxford, England: Oxford University Press. ISBN 978-0-19-925239-8.

✳ Cook, Megan (5 May 2011). "Women's movement—The Women's Liberation Movement". Te Ara Encyclopedia of New Zealand. Wellington, New Zealand: New Zealand Ministry for Culture and Heritage Te Manatu. Archived from the original on 31 January 2017. Retrieved 2018-05-04.

✳ Cosgrove, Art (2008). A New History of Ireland, Volume II : Medieval Ireland 1169–1534: Medieval Ireland 1169–1534. Oxford, England: Oxford University Press. ISBN 978-0-19-156165-8.

✳ Curthoys, Jean (2003). *Feminist Amnesia:* The Wake of Women's Liberation. *London, England:* Routledge. ISBN 978-1-134-75393-2.

✳ Dahlerup, Drude (24 August 2017). "Rødstrømpebevægelsen" [F eminist Movement]. *Den Store Danske (in Danish). Copenhagen, Denmark: Gyldendal. Archived from* the original *on 21 April 2018. Retrieved 21 April 2018.*

✳ Danielsen, Hilde (2010). "The liberated woman and the housewife in the 1970s"(PDF). *Nätverket (16): 36–41.* ISSN 1651-0593. *Archived from* the original *(PDF)on 23 May 2010. Retrieved 23 May 2018.*

✳ Degavre, Florence; Stoffel, Sophie (2005). "Transmission et renouveau. L'Université des Femmes à Bruxelles" *[Transmission and renewal: Women›s University in Brussels]. Les Cahiers du CEDREF (in French) (13).* ISSN 2107-0733. *Retrieved 1 May 2018.*

✳ Denis, Marie-Noëlle; van Rokeghem, Suzanne (1992). Le féminisme est dans la rue: Belgique 1970–1975 (in French). Bruxelles, Belgique: Erreur Perimes Pol-His. *ISBN 978-2-87311-009-3.*

✳ Dias Martins, Ana Margarida (Spring 2012). "Novas Cartas Portuguesas: The Making of a Reputation" *(PDF). Journal of Feminist Scholarship (2): 24–39.* ISSN 2158-6179. *Archived from* the original *(PDF) on 21 April 2018. Retrieved 22 May 2018.*

✳ Dow, Bonnie J. (2014). Watching Women's Liberation, 1970: Feminism's Pivotal Year on the Network News. *Champaign, Illinois:* University of Illinois *Press.* ISBN 978-0-252-09648-8.

✳ DuBois, Ellen Carol (1998). *Woman Suffrage and Women's Rights. New York, New York: NYU Press. ISBN 978-0-8147-2116-2.*

✳ Dupuis-Déri, Francis (10 November 2007). "Retour sur le Front de libération des femmes". Le Devoir *(in French). Montreal, Quebec, Canada. Archived from* the original *on 7 May 2018. Retrieved 7 May 2018. Back to the Women›s Liberation Front*

✳ Echols, Alice (1989). Daring to be Bad: Radical Feminism in America, 1967–1975. *Minneapolis, Minnesota:* University of Minnesota Press. *p. 5.* ISBN 978-0-8166-1787-6.

✳ Elias, David (30 July 1979). "Women at war". *The Age. Melbourne, Australia. p. 9. Retrieved 27 April 2018 – via* Newspapers.com.

✳ Else, Anne (1993). Women Together: A History of Women's Organisations in New Zealand: Ngā Rōpū Wāhine O Te Motu. *Wellington, New Zealand: Daphne Brasell Associates Press and Historical Branch, Department of Internal Affairs.* ISBN 978-0-908896-29-5.

✳ Enke, Anne (2007). Finding the Movement: Sexuality, Contested Space, and Feminist Activism. *Durham, North Carolina:* Duke University Press. ISBN 978-0-8223-9038-1.

✳ Farren, Grainne (21 May 2006). "The essential story of how Irish women cast off their chains". Irish Independent. *Dublin, Ireland. Retrieved 28 April 2018.*

✳ Fauré, Christine (2004). Political and Historical Encyclopedia of Women. *Abingdon-on-Thames, England: Routledge.* ISBN 978-1-135-45691-7.

✳ Fiddler, Allyson (1997). "13: Post-war Austrian Women Writers". *In Weedon, Chris (ed.). Post-war Women's Writing in German: Feminist Critical Approaches. Providence, Rhode Island: Berghahn Books. pp. 243–268.* ISBN 978-1-57181-902-4.

✳ Foley, Eileen (29 January 1971). "The Many Facets of Women's Lib". The Detroit Free Press. *Detroit, Michigan. p. 22. Retrieved 20 April 2018 – via* Newspapers.com.

✳ Fox, Margalit (5 February 2006). "Betty Friedan, Who Ignited Cause in 'Feminine Mystique,' Dies at 85". The New York Times. *New York, New York. Retrieved 19* April 2018.

✳ Frankfort-Nachmias, Chava; Shadmi, Erella (2005). Sappho in the Holy Land: Lesbian Existence and Dilemmas in Contemporary Israel. *Albany, New York: SUNY Press.* ISBN 978-0-7914-6317-8.

✳ Franks, Jill (2013). British and Irish Women Writers and the Women's Movement: Six Literary Voices of Their Time. *Jefferson, North Carolina:* McFarland & Company, *Inc.* ISBN 978-0-7864-7408-0.

Rage and Creativity

* Freeman, Jo (1972). "The Women's Liberation Movement: Its Origins, Structures and Ideas". In Dreitzel, Hans Peter (ed.). Family, Marriage, and the Struggle of the Sexes. Recent Sociology. 4. New York, New York: Macmillan Publishers. OCLC 433026433.

* Genovese, Ann L. (February 1998). The Battered Body: A Feminist Legal History (PhD). Sydney, Australia: University of Technology Sydney. hdl:10453/20131.

* González Alvarado, Rocío (2002). "El espíritu de una época" (PDF). In Millán, Márgara; García, Nora Nínive (eds.). Cartografías del feminismo mexicano 1970–2000. Mexico City, Mexico: Programa Universitario de Estudios de Género, Universidad Nacional Autónoma de México. pp. 56–83. Archived from the original (PDF) on 11 May 2018.

* Griffen, Vanessa; Yee, Joan (1987). "Developing A Feminist Perspective". Women, Development and Empowerment: A Pacific Feminist Perspective. Pacific Women's Workshop, Naboutini, Fiji 23–26 March 1987. Kuala Lumpur, Malaysia: Asian and Pacific Development Centre. OCLC 846984729. Archived from the original on 25 September 2017. Retrieved 14 May 2018.

* Haavio-Mannila, E.; Skard, T. (2013). Unfinished Democracy: Women in Nordic Politics. Elsevier Science. ISBN 978-1-4832-8632-7.

* Hannam, June (2008). "Women's History, Feminist History". Making History. London, England: Institute of Historical Research. Archived from the original on 28 March 2018. Retrieved 2018-05-27.

* Hannan, Caryn (2008). "Dingman, Mary Agnes". New Jersey Biographical Dictionary. Volume 1: A–K. Hamburg, Michigan: State History Publications. pp. 174–176. ISBN 978-1-878592-45-3.

* Harr, Tina (3 March 2014). "Historien om Grupp 8–det gör de i dag" [The story of Group 8–What they are doing today]. Expressen (in Swedish). Stockholm, Sweden. Archived from the original on 22 January 2017. Retrieved 24 May 2018.

✳ Hathaway, Michael J. (2018-01-04). "China's Forgotten Role in Western Second-Wave Feminism". *AsiaGlobal Online*. Archived *from* the original *on 2 May 2018. Retrieved 2018-05-02.*

✳ Henderson, Margaret; Bartlett, Alison (2014). *Things That Liberate: An Australian Feminist Wunderkammer. Newcastle upon Tyne, UK: Cambridge Scholars Publishing.* ISBN 978-1-4438-6740-5.

✳ Herzog, Hanna (1 March 2009). "Feminism in Contemporary Israel". *Jewish Women: A Comprehensive Historical Encyclopedia. Brookline, Massachusetts:* Jewish Women's Archive. *Archived from* the original *on 30 October 2016. Retrieved 23 May 2018.*

✳ Ito, Masami (2015-10-03). "Women of Japan unite: Examining the contemporary state of feminism". *The Japan Times Online.* ISSN 0447-5763. *Archived from* the original_on *23 October 2017. Retrieved 2018-05-03.*

✳ Jacques, Catherine (10 December 2013). "Aperçu du féminisme belge (XIX-XXe s.)" [*Overview of Belgian feminism (XIX-XX century)] (in French). Brussels, Belgium: BePax. Archived from* the original *on 2 May 2018. Retrieved 1 May 2018.*

✳ Joris, Elisabeth (22 May 2008). "Frauenbefreiungsbewegung (FBB)" [*Women's Liberation Movement (FBB)]. hls-dhs-dss.ch (in French, German, and Italian). Bern, Switzerland: Historischen Lexikon der Schweiz. Archived from* the original *on 22 January 2018. Retrieved 10 May 2018.*

✳ Kanes, Candy (26 October 1969). "Women Trying to Break 'Role as Sex Object' ". *The Dayton Daily News. Dayton, Ohio. p. 11. Retrieved 20 April 2018 – via* Newspapers.com.

✳ Kiani, Shara (2017). "Women's Liberation Movement and Professional Equality: The Swiss Case". *In Schulz, Kristina (ed.). The Women's Liberation Movement: Impacts and Outcomes. New York, New York: Berghahn Books. pp. 19–35.* ISBN 978-1-78533-587-7.

✳ Kim, Yeong-hui (Autumn 2000). "Theories for a Progressive Women's Movement in Korea". Korea Journal. *40 (3): 217–236.* ISSN 0023-3900. *Retrieved 16 May 2018.*

✳ Klemesrud, Judy (18 December 1970). "The Lesbian Issue and Women's Lib". *The New York Times. New York City, New York. Retrieved 22 April 2018.*

✳ Kolodney, Nat (September 1978). "The Semantics of the Women's Liberation Movement". ETC: A Review of General Semantics. 35 (3): 298–301. ISSN 0014-164X. JSTOR 42575349.

✳ Larsen, Jytte (2014). "The women's movement in Denmark". kvinfo. org. Copenhagen, Denmark: The Danish Center for Research and Information on Gender, Equality and Diversity. Archived from the original on 3 October 2017. Retrieved 20 April 2018.

✳ Lee, Jennifer (12 June 2014). "Feminism Has a Bra-Burning Myth Problem". Time. New York City, New York: Time Warner. ISSN 0040-781X. Archived from the original on 8 October 2017. Retrieved 29 May 2018.

✳ Longeaux y Vásquez, Enriqueta (1997). "The Women of La Raza". In García, Alma M. (ed.). Chicana Feminist Thought: The Basic Historical Writings. New York, New York: Routledge. pp. 29–31. ISBN 978-0-415-91801-5.

✳ Lu, Annette (2009). "An End to Patriarchy: Democratic Transformation and Women's Liberation in Taiwan". Georgetown Journal of International Affairs. 10 (1): 47–53. ISSN 1526-0054. JSTOR 43134189.

✳ Lyons, Lenore T. (2000). "A State of Ambivalence: Feminism and a Singaporean Women's Organisation". Asian Studies Review. 24 (1): 1–24. CiteSeerX 10.1.1.892.9750. doi:10.1080/103578200087 13257.

✳ Magarey, Susan (2014). Dangerous Ideas: Women's Liberation–Women's Studies–Around the World. Adelaide, Australia: University of Adelaide Press. ISBN 978-1-922064-95-0.

✳ McCabe, Conor (30 September 2010). "Banshee: Journal of Irish Women United – Looking Left, DCTV". Irish Left Review. Ireland. Archived from the original on 13 October 2015. Retrieved 21 May 2018.

Appendix

✳ *Melandri, Lea (19 April 2016).* "Collettivi, pratiche e luoghi di libertà" *[Collectives, practices and places of freedom]. comune-info. net (in Italian). Milan, Italy: di Comune. Archived from the original on 19 April 2016. Retrieved 21 May 2018.*

✳ *Menon, Ritu, ed. (2011).* Making a Difference: Memoirs from the women's movement in India. *New Delhi, India: Women Unlimited in collaboration with Women's WORLD (India). ISBN 978-81-88965-67-0.*

✳ *Miller, Stuart (Spring 2013).* Recognising Men's Violence as Political: An Analysis of the Swedish Feminist Movement and Its Interaction with the State *(master's degree). Lund, Sweden: Lund University. Archived from the original on 16 August 2017.*

✳ *Mioko, Fujieda (Winter 1978).* "Japanese Women Speak Out". *Quest: A Feminist Quarterly. IV (2): 74–86. ISSN 0098-955X.*

✳ *Morgan, Robin (1984).* Sisterhood is Global: The International Women's Movement Anthology. *Feminist Press at CUNY. ISBN 978-1-55861-160-3.*

✳ *Morris, Aldon D. (1999).* "A Retrospective on the Civil Rights Movement: Political and Intellectual Landmarks" *(PDF). Annual Review of Sociology. 25 (25): 517–539. doi:10.1146/annurev. soc.25.1.517. ISSN 0360-0572. Archived from the original (PDF) on 19 April 2018. Retrieved 19 April 2018.*

✳ *Myrbråten, Charlotte (8 October 2013).* "A pioneer of women's history studies" *(PDF). Hubro International. Bergen, Norway: University of Bergen (2013–2014): 20–23. Archived from the original (PDF) on 29 May 2018. Retrieved 29 May 2018.*

✳ *Nelson, Jennifer (2003).* Women of Color and the Reproductive Rights Movement. *New York, New York: NYU Press. ISBN 978-0-8147-5827-4.*

302

❋ Neptune, Harvey (2011). ""The Twilight Years": Caribbean Social Movements, 1940–1960". *Exhibitions.nypl.org*. *Harlem, New York:* Schomburg Center for Research in Black Culture. *Archived from* the original *on 27 June 2017. Retrieved 18 April 2018. Summer Institute project: Africana Age: African & African Diasporan Transformations in the 20th Century.*

❋ Nilsson, Jeff; Spencer, Steven M. (31 December 2015). "1965: The Birth Control Revolution". The Saturday Evening Post. *Indianapolis, Indiana:* Curtis Publishing Company. ISSN 0048-9239. *Archived from the original on 17 April 2018. Retrieved 5 May 2018.*

❋ Nørve, Siri (9 May 2007). "Flat organisering—nyfeministene, les-bisk bevegelse og Kvinnehuset" *[Non-hierarchical organization— New feminists, the lesbian movement and the women›s house] (in Norwegian). Oslo, Norway:* Kilden – Information Centre for Gender Research. *Archived from* the original *on 23 May 2018. Retrieved 23 May2018.*

❋ Omvedt, Gail (1975). *"Rural Origins of Women's Liberation in India"*. Social Scientist. *4(4/5): 40– 54.* doi:10.2307/3516120. JSTOR 3516120.

❋ Patel, Vibhuti (September–October 1985). "Women's Liberation in India". *New Left Review I. First (153): 75–86.* ISSN 0028-6060. *Retrieved 15 May 2018.*

❋ Pena, Cristiana (February 2008). A Revolução das Feministas Portuguesas 1972–1975 *[The Portuguese Feminist Revolution 1972–1975] (PDF) (master's degree) (in Portuguese). Lisbon, Portugal:* Universidade Aberta. *Archived from* the original *(PDF) on 9 August 2017.*

❋ Perincioli, Cristina; Selwyn, Pamela (translator) (April 2015). "Berlin Goes Feminist". *Feminist Berlin 1968. Berlin, Germany: Cristina Perincioli. English translation of Perincioli, Cristina (2015).* Berlin wird feministisch: das Beste, was von der 68er Bewegung blieb *(in German). Berlin, Germany:* Querverlag. ISBN 978-3-89656-232-6.

✳ Picq, Françoise (7 October 2008). "MLF : 1970, année zéro". *Libération (in French). Retrieved 30 April 2018.*

✳ Ram, Uri (2012). Changing Agenda of Israeli Sociology, The: Theory, Ideology, and Identity. *Albany, New York:* SUNY Press. ISBN 978-1-4384-1681-6.

✳ Rees, Jeska (Spring 2010). *"Are you a Lesbian?' Challenges in Recording and Analysing the Women's Liberation Movement in England".* History Workshop Journal. *69(69): 177–187.* doi:10.1093/hwj/dbp033. ISSN 1363-3554. JSTOR 40646100. PMID 20514741.

✳ Regua, Nannette (Fall 2012). "Women in the Chicano Movement: Grassroots Activism in San José" (PDF). *Chicana/Latina Studies. 12 (1): 114–152. ISSN 1550-2546. Archived from the* original (PDF) on 22 April 2018. Retrieved 22 April 2018.

✳ Rengel, Marian (2000). Encyclopedia of Birth Control. *Phoenix, Arizona: Oryx Press. p. 202.* ISBN 978-1-57356-255-3.

✳ Rodriguez, Jose Antonio (6 February 1979). "Manifestación feminista en Mallorca contra las agresiones sexuales" *[Feminist demonstration in Mallorca against sexual aggression]. El País (in Spanish). Madrid, Spain. Archived from the original on 25 May 2018. Retrieved 25 May 2018.*

✳ Rolph, Avril (27 April 2002). "Not just the miners' strike—the Women's Liberation Movement in South Wales". *The feminist eventies. York, England:* University of York. *Archived from the* original on 21 November 2008. Retrieved 26 May 2018.

✳ Roseneil, Sasha; Crowhurst, Isabel; Hellesund, Tone; Santos, Ana Cristina; Stoilova, Mariya (March 2010). Changing cultural discourses about intimate life: The demands and actions of women's movements and other movements for gender and sexual equality and change (PDF) (Report). *Work Package 6–Intimate Citizenship. London, England:* Birkbeck Institute for Social Research. *Working Paper 2: Femcit Project, Bergen, Norway. Archived from the original (PDF) on 23 May 2018. Retrieved 23 May2018.*

✳ Rubio-Marín, Ruth (January 2014). "The achievement of female suffrage in Europe: on women's citizenship". *International Journal of Constitutional Law.* 12 (1): 4–34. doi:10.1093/icon/mot067. ISSN 1474-2659.

✳ Rúdólfsdóttir, Annadís Greta (1997). The construction of femininity in Iceland (PDF)(PhD). *London, England:* The London School of Economics and Political Science. U615407. *Archived from* the original *(PDF) on 23 May 2018.*

✳ Russell, Brianna (14 December 2012). Women's Mobilization in Latin America: A Case Study of Venezuela *(master's degree). San Francisco, California:* University of San Francisco. *paper #34. Archived from* the original *on 18 April 2018.*

✳ Salper, Roberta (Fall 2008). "U.S. Government Surveillance and the Women's Liberation Movement, 1968–1973: A Case Study". Feminist Studies. 34 (3): 431–455. ISSN 0046-3663. JSTOR 20459215.

✳ Sarrimo, Cristine (9 April 2003). "Den ihjälkramade kvinnokampen" [The crushed women's struggle]. Sydsvenskan (in Swedish). Scania, Sweden. Archived from the original on 24 May 2018. Retrieved 24 May 2018.

✳ Sethna, Christabelle; Hewitt, Steve (September 2009). "Clandestine Operations: The Vancouver Women's Caucus, the Abortion Caravan, and the RCMP". The Canadian Historical Review. 90 (3): 463–495. doi:10.1353/can.0.0189. ISSN 0008-3755.

✳ Shigematsu, Setsu (2012). Scream From the Shadows: The Women's Liberation Movement in Japan (PDF). Minneapolis: University of Minnesota Press. ISBN 978-0-8166-6758-1. Archived from the original (PDF) on 27 April 2018.

✳ Shigematsu, Setsu (2015). "The Women's Liberation Movement and Sexuality in Japan". In McLelland, Mark; Mackie, Vera (eds.). Routledge Handbook of Sexuality Studies in East Asia. London, England: Routledge. pp. 174–187. ISBN 978-1-317-68574-6.

❊ Sklar, Kathryn Kish (March 2015). "How and Why Did Women in SNCC (the Student Non-Violent Coordinating Committee) Author a Pathbreaking Feminist Manifesto, 1964–1965?". *Womhist.alexanderstreet.com. Alexandria, Virginia: Women and Social Movements. Archived from* the original *on 11 May 2017. Retrieved 21 April 2018 – via* Alexander Street Press.

❊ Smith, Evan (8 March 2017). "ASIO and surveillance of the women's liberation movement in Australia in the 1970s". Hatfulofhistory. Adelaide, South Australia: Evan Smith. Archived from the original on 8 March 2018. Retrieved 28 April 2018. Self-published blog of a Research Fellow in History of Flinders University with citations to source materials.

❊ Spain, Daphne (2016). Constructive Feminism: Women's Spaces and Women's Rights in the American City. Ithaca, New York: Cornell University Press. ISBN 978-1-5017-0412-3.

❊ Studer, Brigitte (2017). "The Women's Liberation Movement and Institutional Change". In Schulz, Kristina (ed.). The Women's Liberation Movement: Impacts and Outcomes. New York, New York: Berghahn Books. pp. 15–18. ISBN 978-1-78533-587-7.

❊ Taylor, Verta (October 1989). "Social Movement Continuity: The Women's Movement in Abeyance". American Sociological Review. *54 (5): 61–775.* doi:10.2307/2117752. ISSN 0003-1224. JSTOR 2117752.

❊ Thompson, Becky (Summer 2002). "Multiracial Feminism: Recasting the Chronology of Second Wave Feminism" (PDF). Feminist Studies. *28 (2): 337–360.* doi:10.2307/3178747. ISSN 0046-3663. JSTOR 3178747. Archived from the original (PDF) on 21 April 2018. Retrieved 21 April 2018.

❊ Tobias, Sheila (1997). "Faces of Feminism: An Activist's Reflections on the Women's Movement". The New York Times. New York City, New York. Retrieved 20 April 2018.

❊ Tremblay, Manon; Paternotte, David; Johnson, Carol (2016). The Lesbian and Gay Movement and the State: Comparative Insights Into a Transformed Relationship. London, England: Routledge. ISBN 978-1-317-02584-9.

✳ *van Oven, Merel (11 January 2005)*. "Invloed van actiegroepen op de huidige positie van de vrouw" *[Influence of action groups on the current position of the woman] (PDF). Atria (in Dutch). Amsterdam, The Netherlands:* Atria Institute on gender equality and women's history. *Archived from* the original *(PDF) on 4 May 2018. Retrieved 4 May 2018.*

✳ *Walker, Cherryl (1991)*. Women and Resistance in South Africa *(2nd ed.). Claremont, Cape Town, South Africa: David Philip Publishers.* ISBN 978-0-86486-170-2.

✳ *Wasserlein, Frances Jane (July 1990)*. "An Arrow Aimed at the Heart": The Vancouver Women's Caucus and the Abortion Campaign (1969–1971) *(PDF) (master's degree). Burnaby, British Columbia, Canada:* Simon Fraser University. *Archived from* the original *(PDF) on 3 February 2016.*

✳ *Wiegers, Mary (22 March 1970)*. "Women's Liberation—What Is It All About?". The Austin American-Statesman. *Austin, Texas. p. 50. Retrieved 20 April 2018 – via* Newspapers.com.

✳ *Willis, Ellen (Spring–Summer 1984)*. "Radical Feminism and Feminist Radicalism". *The 60's Without Apology (9–10): 91–118.* doi:10.2307/466537. ISSN 0164-2472. JSTOR 466537.

✳ *Yates, Gayle Graham (1975)*. What Women Want: The Ideas of the Movement. *Cambridge, Massachusetts:* Harvard University Press. ISBN 978-0-674-95079-5.

✳ "20 años por todas las mujeres" *[20 years for all women] (PDF).* El Universal *(in Spanish). Mexico City, Mexico. 30 May 2012. Archived from* the original *(PDF) on 11 May 2018. Retrieved 11 May 2018.*

✳ "Broadsheet: New Zealand's feminist magazine". *Aukland Museum. Aukland, New Zealand. n.d. Archived from* the original *on 14 May 2018. Retrieved 14 May 2018.*

Appendix

❋ "Come nasce il Movimento di Liberazione della Donna federato al P.R.—Temi e obiettivi di lotta (ottobre 1970)" *[How the Women's Liberation Movement is born, within in the Radical Party—Themes and objectives of the struggle (October 1970)]. RadioRadicale.it (in Italian). Rome, Italy: Radical Party Archive. 15 January 1972. Archived from* the original *on 6 December 2017. Retrieved 21 April 2018.*

❋ "Cross Currents" *(PDF).* The Ladder. *Reno, Nevada:* Daughters of Bilitis. *16 (5–6): 47. February–March 1972. Archived from* the original *(PDF) on 14 May 2018. Retrieved 14 May 2018.*

❋ "Feminism and Transition to Democracy (1974–1990): Ideas, collectives, claims". *Greek News Agenda. Kallithea, Greece. 25 June 2017. Archived from* the original *on 13 May 2018. Retrieved 13 May 2018.*

❋ "Geschichte der autonomen Frauenbewegung" *[History of the autonomous women›s movement]. Der Funke (in German). Vienna, Austria. 10 November 2003. Archived from* the original *on 13 May 2018. Retrieved 13 May 2018.*

❋ "Involvement Is Key To Pat's Liberation". The Dayton Daily News. *Dayton, Ohio. 26 October 1969. p. 11. Retrieved 20 April 2018 – via* Newspapers.com.

❋ "Ngahuia te Awekotuku". *Ministry for Culture and Heritage. Wellington New Zealand: Government of New Zealand. 16 March 2018. Archived from* the original *on 14 May 2018. Retrieved 14 May 2018.*

❋ "Organisationer och aktioner" *[Organizations and actions]. Göteborgs universitetsbibliotek (in Swedish). Gothenburg, Sweden:* University of Gothenburg. *7 July 2011. Archived from* the original *on 29 August 2017. Retrieved 24 May 2018.*

❋ "Sex bias in China Denounced". The Winnipeg Free Press. *Winnipeg, Manitoba, Canada. 6 March 1989. p. 35. Retrieved 27 April 2018 – via* Newspaperarchive.com.

✳ "Wie es zur Fristenlösung kam" *[How the deadline solution came about]*. Der Standard *(in German)*. Vienna, Austria. *16 November 2004. Archived from* the original *on 13 May 2018. Retrieved 13 May 2018.*

External links

✳ Redstockings of the Women's Liberation Movement

✳ National Women's Liberation

✳ Archives on Women's Liberation

Suffrage

✳ Universal suffrage

✳ Women

✳ Black

✳ Youth

✳ Resident foreigners

✳ Expatriates in country of origin

✳ Voting age

✳ Demeny voting

✳ Suffragette

✳ Compulsory voting

✳ Disfranchisement

Women's liberation movement

By country

✳ Australia

  ✳ 1902 Commonwealth Franchise Act

  ✳ aboriginal

  ✳ women

* Canada

* Hong Kong

* India

* Japan

* Kuwait

* Mexico

* New Zealand

* Spain (Civil War, Francoist)

* Sweden

* Switzerland

* United Kingdom

* women

    * Cayman Islands

    * Scotland

    * Wales

Laws

    * 1832

    * 1918

    * 1928

* United States

    * women

    * Native Americans

    * felons

    * foreigners

* District of Columbia

* Puerto Rico

* states
* amendments
  * 15th
  * 19th
  * 23rd
  * 24th
  * 26th
* 1965 Voting Rights Act

Events

* International Woman Suffrage Alliance conferences
  * 1st
  * 2nd
  * 3rd
  * 4th
  * 5th
  * 6th
  * 7th
  * 8th
* Hong Kong 1 July marches
* 2014 Hong Kong protests
* 2019–20 Hong Kong protests

UK

* WSPU march (1906)
* Mud March (1907)
* Women's Sunday (1908)

✳ Black Friday (1910)

✳ Battle of Downing Street (1910)

✳ Women's Coronation Procession (1911)

✳ Great Pilgrimage (1913)

✳ Open Christmas Letter (1914)

US

✳ Seneca Falls Convention (1848)

✳ Declaration of Sentiments (1848)

✳ Rochester Convention (1848)

✳ Ohio Women's Convention (1850)

✳ National Women's Rights Convention (1850–1869)

✳ Trial of Susan B. Anthony (1872–1873)

✳ Suffrage Hikes (1912–1914)

✳ Woman Suffrage Procession (1913)

✳ Suffrage Special (1916)

✳ Silent Sentinels (1917–1919)

    ✳ Night of Terror

    ✳ Prison Special

✳ 1920 United States presidential election

✳ "Give Us the Ballot" (1957)

✳ Selma to Montgomery marches (1965)

Related

✳ Age of candidacy

✳ National Voting Rights Museum (US)

✳ Umbrella Movement

Women
(memorials)

* Suffragists
* Timeline of women's suffrage
  * US
  * in majority-Muslim countries
* Historiography of the Suffragettes
* Women's suffrage organizations and publications
* Women's rights activists
* Leser v. Garnett
* Belmont–Paul Monument
* Centenary of Women's Suffrage Commemorative Fountain
* Eagle House
* Emmeline Pankhurst statue
* Great Petition (2008 sculpture)
* Hunger Strike Medal
* Justice Bell
* Kate Sheppard National Memorial
* Millicent Fawcett statue
* Pankhurst Centre
* Pankhurst Memorial
* Paulsdale
* Suffragette Handkerchief
* Suffragette Memorial
* Women's Rights National Historical Park
* International Women's Day
* Susan B. Anthony Day

✳ Women's Equality Day

Popular culture

✳ "The Women's Marseillaise"

✳ "The March of the Women" (1910 song)

✳ The Mother of Us All (1947 opera)

✳ "Sister Suffragette" (1964 song)

✳ Suffrage plays

✳ Women's suffrage in film

✳ Votes for Women (1912 film)

✳ Shoulder to Shoulder (1974 series)

✳ Not for Ourselves Alone (1999 documentary)

✳ Iron Jawed Angels (2004 film)

✳ Selma (2014 film)

✳ Suffragette (2015 film)

✳ Susan B. Anthony dollar

✳ New Zealand ten-dollar note

✳ 2020 US ten-dollar bill

Categories:

✳ Feminism

✳ Feminist movements and ideologies

✳ Radical feminism

✳ 1960s establishments

July 23, 2020 Issue: Vol. 166, No. 130— Daily Edition 116th Congress (2019–2020)—2nd Session)

Read the Issue Here: congress.gov/congressional-record/ volume-166/senate-section/page/S4468

Congressional Record

United States
of America

PROCEEDINGS AND DEBATES OF THE 116th CONGRESS, SECOND SESSION

Vol. 166	WASHINGTON, THURSDAY, JULY 23, 2020	No. 130

House of Representatives

The House met at 9 a.m. and was called to order by the Speaker pro tempore (Mr. CUELLAR).

DESIGNATION OF SPEAKER PRO TEMPORE

The SPEAKER pro tempore laid before the House the following communication from the Speaker:

WASHINGTON, DC,
July 23, 2020.

I hereby appoint the Honorable HENRY CUELLAR to act as Speaker pro tempore on this day.

NANCY PELOSI,
Speaker of the House of Representatives.

MORNING-HOUR DEBATE

The SPEAKER pro tempore. Pursuant to the order of the House of January 7, 2020, the Chair will now recognize Members from lists submitted by the majority and minority leaders for morning-hour debate.

The Chair will alternate recognition between the parties, with time equally allocated between the parties and each Member other than the majority and minority leaders and the minority whip limited to 5 minutes, but in no event shall debate continue beyond 9:50 a.m.

REST IN PEACE, JOHN LEWIS

The SPEAKER pro tempore. The Chair recognizes the gentleman from California (Mr. McCARTHY) for 5 minutes.

Mr. McCARTHY. Mr. Speaker, in "The Columbian Orator," a collection of speeches that Frederick Douglass read as a young man, there is a speech that says: "Let it be remembered, there is no luxury so exquisite as the exercise of humanity, and no post so honorable as his, who defends the rights of man."

Now, I don't know if Douglass read those exact words, but I do know a man

who embodied them better than anyone else in my lifetime: John Lewis. John's legacy is his love of country and humanity. He rose above prejudice and responded to force with forgiveness.

In his time, there was a lot that he couldn't love about America, but he never gave up on it or wanted to destroy it. Instead, he used what is right with America to fix what was wrong with it.

Because of his patriotism, our Nation has come a long way, not perfect, but more perfect, as we must always strive to be.

John was unquestionably one of the great champions of freedom in the modern age, and he secured his place as a giant in American history long before his career in Congress even began.

Born on a farm without running water or power, the son of a sharecropper rose to become a founding leader of the civil rights movement by the age of 23. As a young student, he showed courage and patience and dignity beyond his years.

From his lunch counter sit-ins, to the Freedom Riders, to Bloody Sunday in Selma, Alabama, his unflinching example of nonviolence was a powerful call to arms. It was made irresistible by the fact that he, like Dr. King, sought to vindicate the core ideas of our founding documents by applying them to everyone.

Today, our task is to continue to uphold these timeless principles for all people. It will not be easy, but I am confident we will succeed, because we have the memories of leaders like John to guide us and inspire us.

I have several memories of my friendship with John that I will always treasure.

I remember my last time speaking with him, just 2 weeks before he passed away, talking about the latest uprising in America. I asked if John would spend a moment in time and do a conference call with the freshmen. They

had not had the opportunity to walk through Selma with him to give them the example of which he lived.

You see, my family and I have joined John many times in Selma, but the one that I will remember the most is on the 50th anniversary. To think for a moment that 50 years before, John came very close to death, and on that day 50 years later, he was introducing the President of the United States. Not only the idea that John would stand for a student about what it was like before.

I remember at the State of the Union of 2015, there was Amelia Boynton Robinson. You see, she was with John that day in hopes of meeting President Obama. She came by my office. And before, we I told Amelia: Just wait right outside my office, because the President doesn't has an escort party, and in that escort party, I am one of them, but stand there and we will make sure when the President comes out, you will greet.

She had a picture of that day, and only the story of John leading.

When John would tell you the story of the march across the bridge, he would say: I can tell you no more, because I cannot remember.

You see, they beat him unconscious, almost to his death, on that Bloody Sunday.

I remember sitting with TIM SCOTT, watching John speak about what happened that fateful day. I will never forget what he said.

When he would tell the story of the march, he would stop at a moment, as I said before, and say: I cannot remember past this point because I had been beaten. And I was carried back, and I almost died.

Reflecting on the violence he endured, he said with humility that he

☐ This symbol represents the time of day during the House proceedings, e.g., ☐ 1407 is 2:07 p.m.

Matter set in this typeface indicates words inserted or appended, rather than spoken, by a Member of the House on the floor.

Printed on recycled paper.

H3685

315

END NOTE

Rage and Creativity: How Feminism Sparked Psychoanalysis is dedicated to all the feminists—women and men—who fought to create their own path and help others in their fight.

Fragment from Vase of Athena: Athena Promachos with Aegis. Metropolitan Museum of Art, New York City. Photo courtesy of Philip Matyszak.

CPSIA information can be obtained
at www.ICGtesting.com
Printed in the USA
LVHW082203170222
711411LV00003BA/13